A lastair Scott was born in Edinburgh in 1954. After university and training as a photographer, he set off on a five-year hitch-hiking journey round the world, for the most part wearing a kilt.

Visiting and photographing sixty countries on six continents provided the foundations of a trilogy of travel books: *Scot Free*, *A Scot Goes South* and *A Scot Returns*.

Subsequent journeys have included cycling 5000 miles behind the Iron Curtain shortly before it fell, a winter dogsled traverse of Alaska (*Tracks Across Alaska*) and a journey around 'familiar and foreign' Scotland (*Native Stranger*).

As well as the solo circumnavigation of Ireland described in this book Alastair's sea voyages include an Atlantic crossing and a solo circumnavigation of the Faeroes.

He now lives, with his wife Sheena, on Skye, working as a pho-tographer, writer, broadcaster and sailing instructor and plotting further bouts of vagrancy.

Other books by Alastair Scott

Scot Free: A Journey From The Antarctic to New Mexico (1986)

A Scot Goes South: A Journey From Mexico to Ayers Rock (1987)

A Scot Returns: A Journey From Bali to Skye (1989)

Tracks Across Alaska: A Dog Sled Journey (1990)

Native Stranger: A Journey in Familiar and Foreign Scotland (1995)

Top Ten Scotland (2003)

Stuffed Lives (2004)

Salt
and
Emerald

A Hesitant Solo Voyage Round Ireland

Alastair Scott

Scottish Maritime Publishing

Published in Scotland
by
Scottish Maritime Publishing
An imprint of Glen Murray Publishing
The Studio, Gas Lane
Kirkcudbright
Kirkcudbrightshire
DG6 4HX

© 2008 Alastair Scott
Alastair Scott has asserted his rights under the Copyright, Designs
and Patents Act, 1988, to be identified as the author of this work.

ISBN
Paper-bound 978-0-9553183-2-0

A CIP catalogue record for this book is available from the
British Library.

All rights reserved.
No part of this publication may be reproduced in any form or by any
means – graphic, electronic or mechanical, including photocopying,
recording, taping or information storage and retrieval systems –
without the prior permission in writing of the publisher.

Printed in Scotland
by Bell and Bain, Glasgow

For Wallace Clark
Inspirer, mentor and a great man of the sea.

Contents

Author's Note

A journey into print takes time. I made this voyage in the summer of 2003 when the rift in Northern Ireland's politics appeared as wide and unbridgeable as ever. That Sinn Féin and the Ulster Unionists could end The Troubles and reconcile their differences within the next decade or two was at that time still considered unimaginable by the majority of the Irish. The unimaginable happened on 8 May 2007 when the former IRA commander Martin McGuinness (Sinn Féin) and the Reverend Ian Paisley (Democratic Unionist Party) shook hands and entered a power-sharing agreement. Part of this book explores the history of The Troubles but I have not altered the text to reflect the latest (wonderful) developments, preferring to leave my account as it is, a personal record of Ireland and the Irish as I found them that summer.

In some instances I've changed the names of the people I met.

Alastair Scott, 2008

Acknowledgements

Sheena, for holding so much together.
Wallace and June Clark for the friendship that led to this voyage and many places besides.
Dervla Murphy and Dr Desmond and Siobhan Moran for hospitality and companionship which fattened me, my notes and ultimately this book.
Kevin O'Leary, John and Joan Scott, Tricia Mulhall and many others who helped me on the way, enhancing my neon image of the Irish.
David Bedlow and Knud of the Commissioners of Irish Lights gave me their time and expertise and lighthouse keeper Gerry Butler willingly shared his experiences of Fastnet storms.
My agent, Jenny Brown.
Glen Murray who, aside from being a passionate and distinguished sailor, corrected, edited and published this book.
Thank you all.

Sprinkled throughout are quotes from what I call 'The Pilot', in reality the Irish Cruising Club's *Sailing Directions East & North Coasts of Ireland* and the companion volume for the *South & West Coasts*. These excellent pilots were, like some of the charts, very old editions and the ICC would like me to point out that in some cases the wording (but not the spirit) is different in the latest versions!

Every effort has been made to contact the copyright holders of published works quoted in this book. Some I have failed to find, others have not replied. I'd welcome hearing from them so due acknowledgement can be credited if the opportunity arises in future. The following have either given approval or are marked 'permission requested from' (PRF), and are listed by page reference.

p.5 Wallace Clark *Sailing Round Ireland*, North-West Books, 1990.

p.8 Hilaire Belloc *The Cruise of the Nona* - by permission of PFD (www.pfd.co.uk) for Hilaire Belloc.

pp.37, 174-5 John Ardagh *Ireland and the Irish*, Hamish Hamilton, 1994. PRF: adultspermissions@uk.penguingroup.com.

p.37 Sean O'Faolain *Irish Journey*, 1941 - by permission of the author, c/o Rogers, Coleridge & White Ltd., 20 Powis Mews, London W11 1JN.

pp.96, 174 Hugh Brody *Inishkillane*, The Penguin Press, 1973. PRF: adultspermissions@uk.penguingroup.com.

pp.109-114 Dervla Murphy *Wheels Within Wheels*, John Murray, 1979. PRF: www.hodder.co.uk.

p.155 Michael Smith *An Unsung Hero: Tom Crean - Antarctic Survivor*, The Collins Press, 2000. PRF: permissions @harper collins.co.uk.

p.159 Leslie Thomas *Some Lovely Islands*, Arlington Books, 1968. PRF: www.orionbooks.co.uk.

p.160 Maurice O'Sullivan *Twenty Years A-Growing*, Oxford Paperbacks, 1933 - by permission of the author's daughter.

p.167 M H Parry *Aak to Zumbra: A Dictionary of the World's Watercraft,* Mariners' Museum (Newport News, Va.) - by permission of the publisher.

p.181 George Cornwallis-West *Edwardians Go Fishing, or, Many Days on Many Waters*, Putnam, 1932. Recorded by Bernard Heuvelmans' in his classic *In The Wake Of Sea Serpents,* Rupert-Hart Davis, 1968. PRF: adultspermissions@uk.penguingroup.com.

p.187 Lynne Truss *Eats, Shoots & Leaves*, Profile Books, 2003 - by permission of the publisher.

p.198 Andrew Phelan *Ireland From The Sea*, Wolfhound Press, 1998. PRF: publishing@merlin.ie.

p.204 Conor O'Brian *From Three Yachts*, Mariner's Library, 1928. PRF: permissions@harpercollins.co.uk.

p.252 Dervla Murphy *A Place Apart*, John Murray, 1978. PRF: www.hodder.co.uk.

IRELAND

ATLANTIC
OCEAN
An tAigean Atlantach

NORTH CHANNEL
Sruth na Maoile

Malin Hd
Tory Is
Portsalon
Inishtrahull
Giant's
Causeway
Rathlin Is
Bloody Foreland
Moville
Portrush
Carnlough
Larne
The Glebe
Gweedore
L Foyle
Aranmore Is
L Swilly
The City
Ballymena
Antrim
Donaghadee
Killybegs
Rossnowlagh
BELFAST
Donegal Bay
Inishmurray Is
L Neagh
Classiebawn
Castle
Castle Ward
Ardglass
Eagle Is
Broadhaven
Sligo
Mourne
Mtns
Inishkea Is
Black Rk
Kilkeel
Achill Hd

IRISH SEA
Muir Eireann

Newport
Clare Is
Westport
Knock
Croagh Patrick
Inishturk Is
Battle of the Boyne
Killary Hbr
Kells
Inishbofin Is
Lough
Ree
Hill of Tara
Lambay Is
Roundstone
Slyne Hd
Kilkieran
Bay
Spiddle
Galway
Ballinasloe
DUBLIN

Aran Is
Cliffs of Moher
Glendalough
Wicklow

Shillelagh
Arklow
Kilkee
Shannon Estuary
Limerick
Bunclody
SAINT GEORGES
CHANNEL
Muir Bhreatan
Loop Hd
Cashel
Enniscorthy
Carrigaholt
Ballybunnion
New Ross
Tipperary
Wexford
Tralee
Waterford
Rosslare
Blasket
Is
Dingle
Anascaul
Lismore
Tuskar Rock
Valentia Is
Youghal
Hook
Head
Kilmore
Quay
Skellig
Michael
Sneem
Kenmare River
Cork
Glengarriff
Kinsale
Cobh
Dursey Is
Bantry Bay
CELTIC SEA
An Mhuir Cheilteach
Castletownberehaven
Glandore
Old Head
of Kinsale
Mizen Hd
L Hyne
Crookhaven
Baltimore
Fastnet
Cape Clear Is

Kilometres
20 40 60 80
10 20 30 40 50
Miles

Dreams

The sea had turned ugly. What started as the odd squall blackening the sky and passing in a bluster had developed into a persistent onslaught, and now that the tide had turned I found myself in the grip of opposing forces. Steep waves collided on all sides. From dark troughs they rose through gradations of grey and green into foaming heads which detached and flailed the deck. They tossed the boat like an unwanted toy. Most alarming was their malevolence. They seemed out to get me. Each assault sounded fatal. I didn't know how much my boat could take and I looked around for the solace of company. None was there. The known world had retreated behind a suffocation of spindrift 400 yards away. My free hand fingered the hilt of a sheath knife, easing it up and down to ensure there'd be no delay. I'd sharpened its blade that morning. The life raft was lashed to the cockpit by my side.

There comes a moment when many a dream turns nightmare. For me the dream was to make a solo voyage round Ireland. The nightmare began at 4.10 pm, 5 June.

The chink in my oilskins, through which I blinked anxiously into the murk ahead, allowed water to course down my neck. Involuntary shivers traced its progress towards my boots. I yearned for a change of clothes but didn't dare leave my post. At any moment I could expect 20,000 tons of ferry travelling at forty knots to cut across my bows. Already in my brief experience the elements had temptation exquisitely figured and had devised the most fiendish concoctions of discomfort and danger. To alleviate one was to exacerbate the other. Only by visualising myself as a case study in the *Report of the Marine Accident and Inquiry Board*, a biannual publication to which I'd subscribed before departure, did I steel myself to tough it out. Then I thought of James Joyce, whom I preferred only marginally to storms. He wrote something about the snotgreen, scrotum-tightening sea. He got that bit right. For me the tightening had only just begun.

Sounding like brutality to horses, the wind shrieked in the rigging as it bent the mast closer to the horizontal. One particular horse screamed louder than the others. Intrigued and distracted from the maelstrom for a while, I listened as its pitch grew tauter and its volume higher. Still its intensity increased and I tracked its movement

1

until it appeared to be coming from below. Then I realised it was the kettle. I'd put it on a low heat earlier when the going was easier and forgotten about it. Peering through a gap in the boards which acted as a door to the boat's interior, I gazed awestruck at a new development in the self-destruction of dreams. The cabin was full of steam and the kettle was boiling more vigorously than it should have been because the stove was on fire.

I threw aside the boards and leapt down into the galley. The port windows were now showing the underside of the Irish Sea, snot-green and a craziness of bubbles. In a panic I seized the on/off knob of the stove and tried to wrench it round. It was immovable, and almost red hot. The exact sequence of events that happened next has become subsumed in a blur of pain and dread but the result was that within the space of fifteen seconds I had burnt a thumb and three fingers, the tip of one finger was hanging off, the cabin was splattered with blood, the fire refused to go out and sea began to spill into the cockpit.

This defining moment was when the principal advantage of solo sailing first manifested itself as its opposite. I was alone. Utterly alone. Stripped of any pretensions of being a skipper, I was the sole – injured – passenger on an over-canvassed yacht in a storm in a shipping lane five miles off the east coast of Ireland. I was beating into a gale on a tack going nowhere.

* * *

I took to sailing relatively late in life. I would deny all suggestion of a mid-life crisis but, of course, it remains a possibility. Boats seemed a natural progression from the previous worlds I had inhabited where my mode of transport was walking, cycling, hitch-hiking or dog-sledding. The image of escape by yacht came close to perfection: nosing into the planet's remotest and least trammelled bays, exotic exploration with all the comforts of home, free fuel and accommodation, a carefree existence divested of the need to rush, and membership of the prestigious club of the sea.

Selective culling is essential in maintaining an illusion. Soon I had much to cull. A glance in any yachtie magazine showed terminal congestion along the British and Mediterranean coasts. Any village with a harbour boasted a resident fleet worthy of the Boat Show. Any photograph of a single yacht in an idyllic setting had been sold to advertisers. Marinas were the sea's new cash crop. Letters to the Editor complained of exorbitant dues and even – a newly acclaimed horror – 'anchorage charges'. The pre-Noah right to drop your pick on the seabed without let or hindrance had been violated. And hackneyed similes dressed as helpful advice – 'owning a boat is like ripping up ten-pound notes under a cold shower' was the most common one – were proffered *ad nauseam* by killjoys who fail to realise that the root of anything to do with boats is passion, not sense. However, I had yet to learn my defence. I would nod appreciatively and let them return to the sanctity of their sitting room sofas.

Clearly the plan would need to be revised. To satisfy my soul's yearning for bays untarnished by man and devoid of maritime squatters, I would have to go somewhere off-beat. Unfortunately that meant somewhere very far away, dangerous to reach or with a godforsaken climate. I thought longingly of the Northwest Passage round the top of Canada, but it had an appalling survival record and three-year delays were common. I fancied Réunion in the Indian Ocean but suspected it might be choc-a-bloc with round-the-world cruisers as it was the first place to buy a pint after leaving Australia. In the end I settled for Tristan da Cunha, the peak of an active volcano in the Southern Ocean.

Things were maturing nicely. I nurtured my dream through disappointment and doubt, and gradually confronted the colossus of my ignorance. I had no inkling of the hours of study that would be required to learn navigation, VHF radio parlance, diesel engine maintenance, the Rules of The Road and dozens of other disciplines, let alone the art of sailing.

At school I'd been pressed into a few sailing lessons on a man-made pond high in the Yorkshire Dales. Not only was Killington Reservoir unmentioned in the annals of Britain's maritime heritage but its anonymity appeared guaranteed by the school's disinclination to provide instructors. I was always the one appointed to stand up to my chest in freezing water holding the bow while three incompetents attempted to rig the dinghy by shouting conflicting instructions. When at last the miraculous happened and we got underway, I was forced to spend two hours zigzagging on an aimless journey in a state of incomprehension and near-hypothermia.

It took thirty years to re-brand the image. I bought a Topper Byte, a fourteen-foot monosail craft like a surfboard with a slight recess for delaying the process of ejection. Below my house on Skye my wife and neighbours watched my maiden voyage into the Sound of Sleat. On a rare day of unmasked sun and the lightest of breezes, I became a skipper and steered my own yacht, small as it was, into a fjord set below mountains vibrant with colour and pomp. I think I waved once, maybe twice, feeling I'd broached utopia, and the party waved back before watching the wind die and my dingy, helpless in one of the West Coast's strongest currents, being carried round a headland and out of sight in the direction of Mallaig. I returned four hours later, having paddled five miles with an old canoe blade. The mystery of sailing remained intact.

I took lessons. I went on courses. I signed on as crew on a transatlantic yacht delivery. I sailed with Willie Ker and Hugh Clay, leviathans of experience and multiple winners of the Royal Cruising Club's blue-water medals, and felt as useful as flotsam in the bilges. Finally, having read Chichester, Knox-Johnston, Ridgeway, Slocum, Claire Francis, Ellen MacArthur, Steve Callaghan (*Adrift*, an account of eighty-four days in a life raft which, incidentally, informed *The Life of Pi*), Peter Bruce's classic *Heavy Weather Sailing* and the South Georgian Pardys on sea-anchor deployment in the Southern Ocean, I emerged seriously scared. For a time even my Topper seemed the height of recklessness. I inclined more towards sofas.

I wasn't really looking for a proper boat when I saw her. I had some time on my hands and thought I'd visit a list of 'Boats for Sale'. The specifications and names meant nothing to me; I was going on price. The chandler had thrust into my hands a flier for one sufficiently outwith my budget to have been instantly dismissed. Then at the end of the day I happened to be passing South Queensferry's pirate harbour, beneath the towering pink grid of the Forth Rail Bridge, where there was, the leaflet said, 'a rare opportunity to purchase a classic cruising yacht, a Nicholson 26…'

She was balancing on her keel at low water while propped against a sandstone wall, a robust, elegant craft, blue topsides with a white deck.

'Thirty-six years old, she is, built in the early days of fibreglass when its strength was underestimated and enough layers were added to withstand rhinoceros attacks', her owner told me. He was in his early fifties, bearded and his hair was prematurely white. Three fingers were missing from his right hand. My flesh crept as I looked from them to the boat's winches.

'Did you … ?'

'No. Accident at work. She's too hard for me to handle now.'

She was, he said, the serious cruiser's boat. She could go anywhere. Her style had evidently slipped from favour. She was heavy (over three tons), of narrow beam and low profile, meaning a wetter ride in heavy seas. Her keel was long and deep, making her hard to turn in confined areas. Her grandchildren had evolved into much lighter boats, faster and more manoeuvrable with their shark fin keels, more spacious with their interiors of padded luxury. But, he stressed, these advantages had been wrested from the reserve of sea kindliness.

'You put this boat in rough weather with a bunch of modern yachts and they'll react like storm-driven corks, but she'll plough on true to her course.'

She spoke to me at once. A three-week delay followed the submission of my offer, still far short of the asking price, before the phone call came. *Ceana of Clyde* was mine.

I'd found my boat. The dream was back on, but Tristan da Cunha was off. At this callow stage of my development I didn't feel up to sea anchor deployment in the Southern Ocean. By default, it was to be Ireland.

* * *

'The circumnavigation is difficult enough to be interesting and yet the distance – 681 miles point to point, usually about 900 miles on the log – fits well into a cruising holiday', Wallace Clark wrote in *Sailing Round Ireland,* a book brimming with enthusiasm. A cruising holiday! I confess this was a disappointment. While clearly not in Tristan da Cunha's league, in my mind I'd nevertheless elevated a maiden voyage round Ireland considerably higher than a 'cruising holiday'.

Other sources were equally dismissive. On his partial circumnavigation of the country in 563, St Columba is credited with voicing the sentiment 'What joy to sail the crested sea and watch the waves beat white upon the Irish shore', but perhaps the aftermath of having just provoked a battle and slaughtered 3000 men inevitably puts you in picnic mood.

However, the Irish Coast Pilot proved to be a cornucopia of bad news. 'June and July both average two Force 7 gale days apiece… on the west coast particularly, a large swell and awful sea can persist long after the gale which caused it has ceased…tides here can produce a steep and dangerous sea very quickly…these banks demand caution as the tide sets obliquely across them…on this wild and rocky shore the weather can change extremely quickly and you might have to run up to 35 miles for shelter…' There were Rathlin Island's infamous tidal traps, the southeast's prowling sandbars, Wexford's 'Coast of A Thousand Wrecks' and West Ireland which faced the 3000-mile fetch of the Atlantic Ocean. It had all the makings of a fine picnic.

Meanwhile, *Ceana* was slowly passing through my kitchen.

* * *

In 2002 Lloyds' List abandoned tradition in favour of political correctness and stopped referring to boats and ships as 'she'. I don't hold with this. Anyone worth their salt knows that boats are feminine. They are intuitive, sensitive and inclined to change direction every five minutes. They are strong yet flexible, tough yet tender. They're too alive to be an 'it', too comforting and motherly to be a 'he'. The virtues of compassion and good fortune all sailors wish their vessel both to bestow and enjoy are more easily entrusted to the female form.

Ceana's interior was a mixture of teak and pine, and smelt of wine cellars. Into the kitchen warmth I carried her cushions to dry before the stove. These were followed by hatches coated in curing resin, freshly varnished floorboards, locker combings, rusty bits of rigging, ropes in the early stages of rigor mortis, mildewed brassware, corroded lights, mysterious gadgets from a lost era...till, eventually, the engine lay in fragments round the Cuisine de France units.

The more you do on a boat, the more you discover needs doing. And everything is awkward, warped, worn or stuck, you can only reach it by dismantling a passage through a labyrinth of fixtures and tubes, and when, triumphant, you deliver it to a chandler, you're told its replacement is obsolete and the nearest equivalent is now of a different size. The list of chores was never completed, is never completed. One day you just have to stop what you're doing and leave.

* * *

Ceana uttered the odd creak as a breeze flexed her sails, driving her south at five knots, her preferred speed. On my left – and by choosing the East-about tour of Ireland, I'd have precious little to look at on my left for the next four months – a desolate stretch of Argyll's rocks moved in and out of focus under a wrap of drizzle. On my right Scarba rose abruptly to peaks lost in cloud, while lower down puppies of mist sported in corries. Fleming was at the helm. He could hold a better course than I could and I was glad to have him aboard. Besides, he freed me to concentrate on navigation and we'd just negotiated a tricky patch of rocks, dog-legs and vital transits. I was feeling raw. My tally of single-handed voyages to date amounted to a distance of seventy miles. I'd dropped and weighed anchor once. This had served to instil optimism before, now it seemed somewhat light. Ahead was the most feared patch of water in Britain, the Gulf of Corryvreckan. I was anxious to avoid being sucked into it as George Orwell once was. He was living on Jura at the time and writing *1984* in an isolated house called Barnhill. One day he took a rowing boat into what in Gaelic is known as 'Brecain's Cauldron'. Brecain was an Irish nobleman and warrior, also known as 'The Prince of Blood', whose entire convoy of fifty curraghs (leather boats) was swamped in the tidal rip (actually believed to have been off Rathlin Island but the name was later transferred to this more violent strait). Orwell was swept through overfalls and was lucky to escape with his life.

As regards tides my timing seemed perfect and the beast was at its most docile but it still raised an eerie gnashing of waves, twisted us off course, stripped us of wind, silenced the tune of motion and left us in a vacuum of suspense. The gust arrived without warning and hit broadside. Pots and pans and charts and books were flung across the cabin floor and I had no choice but to cling to a winch until *Ceana* sorted it out by turning into the wind. I hove-to and sat it out, then put in a third reef and steered out of Corryvreckan's eternal indigestion. Within an hour Fleming ('Fleming Self-Steering Systems' – a steel contraption like the magnified innards of a clock) was back at the helm, I was reading an oil-stained Joyce over a cup of coffee and we were whistling down the coast of Jura with bursts of ten knots on the log, helped by a spring tide. In two days, with a bit of luck, I'd be in Ireland.

Tides

We hold many misconceptions about the sea. We believe it is level. It is not. 'Sea level' is an average we use for convenience but at any one time that level is not constant across the plane of the sea's surface. Imagine, for example, the Pacific Ocean on a calm day with not a ripple on it from end to end, and freeze it. You'd find plateaux on different levels and valleys with height differences of up to sixty feet. These are caused by regional variations in atmospheric pressure and the sluicing effect of tides.

Tides are another case of over-simplification. They are sublime examples of divine mischief. They have a scientific explanation. They have a predictability which allows their character and movements to be anticipated, under normal conditions, to the nearest centimetre and minute. We've known about them for a long time. The world's first tide tables were produced for London Bridge in 1213. Yet tides have never submitted meekly and continue to break out in irrational behaviour, leading lives of their own which compound complexities within a simple theorem. Thus we have springs, neaps, equinoctials, diurnals, semidiurnals, priming and lagging intervals, amphidromes, and a host of other terms to explain their foibles. Such as: why we in Britain have two (semidiurnal) tidal cycles each day whereas the China Sea and the Gulf of Mexico have one (diurnal); why the Mediterranean has effectively none at all; why we have lagging and priming intervals between high waters whereas at certain places in the Eastern Indian Ocean high water occurs at the same time every day; why, when the north-bound flow of water in the Irish Channel between Ireland and Wales is at its fastest, the water level on the Welsh coast is 5.7 feet *higher* than the level on the Irish side – and, conversely, 5.7 feet *lower* when the tide rushes south; why the highest range of tides (springs) at Port Ellen, Islay, can coincide with the smallest range (neaps) just thirteen miles away at Macrahanish. I wasn't the only one to feel this way about their deviant nature.

> …they are continually playing anomalous tricks; and anyone who tries to work up a theory of the tides makes a fool of himself: still more does any poor sailing-man do so who uses science to discover what the

tide may be doing in a place he has not yet tried. He makes not only a fool of himself, but also, very probably, shipwreck.

Hilaire Beloc *The Cruise of the Nona*

I wasn't the least bit worried about making a fool of myself, but very much about making shipwreck.

It is the gravitational pulls of the moon and sun which cause tides. At regular intervals they combine their efforts to produce larger tides, then move out of alignment and produce smaller tides. Of the two, the moon's influence is much the stronger, more than twice as powerful as the sun's. The effect of the moon's orbit around us is to drag the ocean out into a bulge directly below its path, at the area of the earth closest to it, and this is high water. Such is the strength of this force, however, that it acts on the opposite side of the planet as well and simultaneously pulls in the crust of the earth, causing the seabed and the land to flex inwards. This, combined with other determinants, creates another bulge of high water. At any one time there are two high water bulges on opposite sides of the globe. These two bulges maintain their position relative to the moon while the spin of the earth transports us from one bulge to the next and through the intervening troughs of low water.

If the world rested vertically on its axis and the moon stayed neatly at right angles, the highest tides would be found at points on the equator, but the earth lies askew and the orbit of the moon is tilted so that, over time, varying strengths of tide-producing forces are directed at different faces of the planet. The sun's influence also varies in strength because the earth's orbit around the centre of our universe is a similarly imperfect circle. Twice a year the earth reaches its closest position to the sun, each spring and autumn, when the lengths of day and night are equal and the sun appears directly overhead at the equator. At these times the sun adds its strongest pull to that of the moon and the largest 'equinoctial' tides are produced.

Add to these variables the obstructions formed by the continents and the idiosyncratic shapes of the basins holding the seas, and there is ample scope for tidal mischief to take place. Yet overall there is consistency within these variations. The Bay of Fundy, on Canada's east coast between New Brunswick and Nova Scotia, maintains the world's record for tidal range (the difference between high water and low water) which at its greatest reaches a staggering fifty-three feet, the height of a four-storey building. Conversely Tahiti and the Mediterranean, amongst other places, remain bottom of the league and sailors training in these places get their certificates stamped 'Non-Tidal' – a second-class grade and a caveat to potential employers – even though the Mediterranean does experience changes of a couple of feet. In Britain the average range is fifteen feet but this belies a recorded high of forty feet at Beachley on the Severn.

When the sun, moon and the earth fall into alignment, the gravitational pulls assist each other and their effect in increased. Thus when the sun is pulling on one side and the moon is directly opposite pulling on the other, each bulge is stretched out further into what is known as a spring tide. This also occurs when the sun and moon are on the same side of the earth. Big highs and low lows. But a week later the moon has swung round and is now exerting its pull at right angles to the sun's, so the effect is reduced and the smaller neap tides result.

The height of a tide determines the speed of its currents. Springs produce the strongest flows whereas neaps move more slowly as there is less volume of water to shift within the six-hour schedule. But the speed of these currents depends on many other factors, particularly the funnelling effect of land which accelerates it through a narrow passage, and the wind which can push it back and hold it down, or thrust it forward and pile it up. The strongest regular current recorded in the world is found in the Slingsby Channel, British Columbia, where tidal flows can reach sixteen knots (18.4 mph). In Britain, the Pentland Firth is the nearest contender with a far from sluggish 10.7 knots.

As a further endearing complication, tides do not flow at even rates. After slack water (the moments of high and low water) the tide starts moving languidly for the first hour, speeds up in the second, is at its fastest in the third and fourth, slows in the fifth, and dawdles in the sixth.

The Earth turns one revolution every twenty-four hours. Unfortunately for the perfect world, the moon travels a little faster. At the end of twenty-four hours it is already fifty minutes ahead of the earth, dragging the high water bulges eastwards. Thus each day we in Britain find that our tidal highs and lows occur roughly fifty minutes later than the previous day. (*Roughly*! The intervals shorten as springs approach and are said to be 'priming', and lengthen, or are 'lagging', as neaps approach).

A consequence of being the eternal loser in this race is that each individual tidal bulge is unable to move quickly enough to stay under the moon. Restricted by a tardy earth, the depth of water and the interference of the continents, bulges are consistently being left behind (as new bulges form ahead of them) and the result is a circular system of traffic lanes in which their energy is gradually expended. Although these lanes contain movement, where they intersect – at roundabouts, you could say – a calm centre is created where the effects of tides are cancelled out by influxes of water from different directions. Here all tides are invisible and a constant depth is maintained. These amphidromes, as they are called, are stationary and occupy their individual spots on the globe.

I wished I knew all this when I shared an anchorage with my first amphidrome at Port Ellen, Islay, having spent an hour checking and rechecking my calculations of how far *Ceana* would drop from high water to low, unable to believe a figure of four inches.

Traffic

The channel between Islay and Rathlin Island is twenty-five miles wide. Concentrating on my tidal calculations for the passage – ten vectors which would account for my drift during the voyage – I nervously tracked the passage of three bulk carriers. Technically they had to give way to me in deep water but in practice these leviathans seldom do and are often oblivious of small yachts. I swung my boat onto a divergent course but still one ship bore down with such a towering presence that it seemed to leave me no safe course of flight. I shouted into the VHF: 'Large Red Bulk-Carrier eastbound in Rathlin Channel, this is Yacht *Ceana*, Yacht *Ceana*, over...'

No response.

I checked the dials and tried again. Still no response. Now I could read her name, the *Gulf Enterprise*, and a history of rusting dents. A battering-ram fitted to her bow at water level thrust up a wave and pushed it along while churning the surface into white spikes.

'*Gulf Enterprise, Gulf Enterprise*, this is...' I began again. Her trajectory altered, minimally but enough to assure me that we'd miss. I slumped back in relief and was still in that position ten minutes later when her wake shook the wind out of my sails and a lone dolphin surfaced alongside emitting a rude belch of vapour.

In one typical six-month period in 1886 the coastguard station on Rathlin Island logged 1,188 vessels passing through the Channel. This compared with 1,482 vessels over the same period in 1970, shortly before the station closed, but this modern figure included 109 RAF aircraft. The composition of a single day's traffic measured at an interval of almost a century confirms the increased likelihood of *Ceana* getting mown down today, and in much less romantic circumstances.

August 1885		March 1970	
1	Brigantine	13	Coasters
3	Schooners	1	Tanker
2	Smacks	1	Cargo vessel
1	Lugger	3	Trawlers
1	Steam Yacht	5	Motor Fishing Vessels
1	Smack (driven ashore at anchor)	1	RAF Launch
1	Cutter Yacht		2 Aircraft/ 2 Helicopters

Had the 1970 figures also been recorded in August, it would be safe to add on at least a dozen yachts, cutter or otherwise. The seas are busier now than they've ever been and their traffic is defined by purpose rather than the technicalities of their rigging. For myself, I'd rather be run down under the stateliness of a brigantine – unhelpfully defined in dictionaries as a vessel with the foremast of a brig and the main mast of a schooner – than the blandness of a tanker.

Rathlin Island gradually grew from a dark slug on the horizon into a mass of moor borne on a ring of cliffs and escarpments. Its West Lighthouse winked on Bull Point, a small light below an absurdity of concrete, almost an acre of it, sheathing the cliffs. Contrary to expectations lighthouses are not always placed on the point of highest visibility. The Bull Point light could have been built on top of the cliffs at a fraction of the cost but this would have rendered its light too prominent on clear nights, allowing far-off ships to confuse it with closer beacons, and left it obscured in the mist which frequently hugs the cliff line. Instead it was placed halfway down the crumbling crags at a cost of £400,000 in 1912. It remained unlit until the year after hostilities ended in 1918.

Below the light a blur of motion circled stacks colonised by razorbills and their more successful cousins, guillemots. Through binoculars I could see black streaks practising flying techniques for which their bodies were not designed. Guillemots are water artists, diving to 180 metres, but their wings, more effective as flippers, are too stubby for the subtleties of flight. Slow to start and almost impossible to stop, they fly directly at a cliff, aiming well below their intended destination, sheering up into a vertical trajectory at the last moment and hoping their feet will land on a ledge when their momentum expires. Nesting concentrations of seventy pairs per square metre leave little room for error and each new arrival encounters the added complication of defensive beak-stabbing. Often they misjudge things and they fall away until gravity allows their wings sufficient speed for steerage, and round they swing to repeat the manoeuvre again and again.

Quite how birds manage to locate their mates in vast colonies against the background chorus of calls has been studied in Antarctica. Emperor penguins nest in concentrations of 12-14 pairs per square meter in colonies of up to a million individuals. Tests have shown that each bird's call is a unique combination of pitch and spacing and a penguin's hearing is sufficiently acute to recognize one voice in a million. Guillemots, and all species which nest in colonies, are believed to share identical abilities in voice-recognition.

The thick rusty tang of an Irish accent suddenly broke the boat's silence, 'All shups, all shups, thus uz Bal-fast radio, Bal-fast radio…'

I kept clear of Bull Point and the surf breaking about it, and coasted along limestone hanked into the folds of a skirt, outrageous in its whiteness. On 3 July 1987 Richard Branson dropped out of the sky near here, abruptly ending his 2,820-mile flight across the Atlantic, a new world distance record for hot air balloons. Things had quietened down since then. Little gangs of gannets passed like louts looking for action but, after careful scrutiny, they decided I wasn't it. Then I was entering Church Bay's harbour, yanking the tiller round, revving the engine for reverse thrust and throwing ropes to lasso a bollard. My throws fell short. Momentum carried me too far. The wind drove me sideways. Like the guillemots, I made several clumsy attempts. As arrivals go it was a shameful display, particularly among folk who'd be bound to know the difference between cutters, yawls and luggers, and be able to park them to a T. But it went unnoticed. At last I was tied up to Ireland.

Ships and Rigs

shown in their simplest form with their defining features

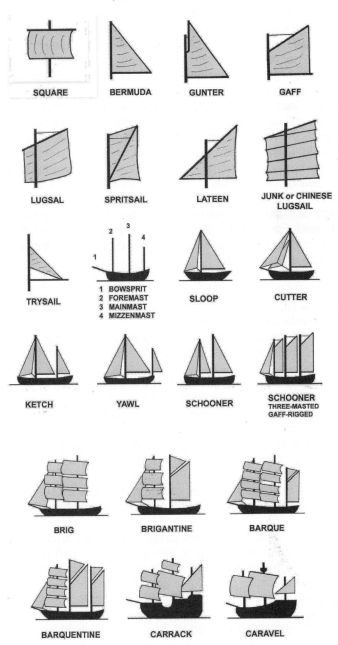

SQUARE   BERMUDA   GUNTER   GAFF

LUGSAL   SPRITSAIL   LATEEN   JUNK or CHINESE LUGSAIL

TRYSAIL

1 BOWSPRIT
2 FOREMAST
3 MAINMAST
4 MIZZENMAST

SLOOP   CUTTER

KETCH   YAWL   SCHOONER   SCHOONER THREE-MASTED GAFF-RIGGED

BRIG   BRIGANTINE   BARQUE

BARQUENTINE   CARRACK   CARAVEL

Ship: formerly a term reserved only for vessels with three or more masts. Everything else was a boat. A full rigged ship or fully rigged ship had all its masts exclusively square-rigged (with square sails).

Fore-and-aft rigged: the opposite of square rigged, where the plane of the sail runs along the line from bow to stern.

Complications: With so many combinations of masts, sails and rigging possible, the potential for creating hybrids is enormous. Thus you get cutter-rigged yawls (a yawl with two headsails), top-sail schooners (a schooner with one or more square sails on its foremast, thus almost a barquentine), hermaphrodite brigs (half brig, half schooner) and a host other knotty technicalities. However, if we think we've got it hard, pity the poor able seaman on a barque. He had to learn the name, location and function of 169 parts of the standing rigging, including fore topgallant lifts, truss-hoop futtock rings, fleads, martingales, horses, crowfoots, parrals and baggy-wrinkles.

Square: actually they were rectangular but this seems to have been overlooked. For centuries the most common sail. Its chief drawback was its inability to be angled into the wind thus restricting a ship to using side and tail winds.

Bermudan: the sail of almost universal choice today. Can drive a boat close to the wind.

Gunter, Gaff, Lug, Sprit, Lateen: different ways of increasing sail size on a relatively short mast.

Junk or Chinese lugsail: never popular in Britain but an efficient sail with parallel stiffeners that make it easier to reef and point into the wind.

Trysail: small triangular sail used as the ultimate canvas in a storm before going 'under bare poles'. (Of course sails are no longer made of canvas. They are made of nylon, polyester, dacron, kevlar, pentex or carbon: either woven or laminated.)

Bowsprit & Masts: 1 Bowsprit, 2 Foremast, 3 Main mast, 4 Mizzen mast (some ships have a fourth, a jiggermast, which is always the smallest).

Sloop: one headsail. The most common rig in use today.

Cutter: two or more headsails, mast set further back than on a sloop.

Ketch: two masts, the mizzen being forward of the steering post. The advantage over a sloop is that sail balance can be improved and with two masts the sails are smaller and more manageable, without any reduction in total sail area. Chichester's *Gypsy Moth IV* was a ketch.

Yawl: easily confused with a ketch. Yawls have two masts, the mizzen being set *behind* the rudder post. This allowed extreme fine-tuning for maintaining a course. With the advent of self-steering gear, yawls have become scarce. Joshua Slocum's classic solo voyage around the world was in the yawl *Spray*.

Schooner: two or more masts (up to seven have been used) with the main mast being the tallest and set furthest aft (towards the stern). Fore-and-aft sails on two or more masts.

Brig: two masts, both wholly or predominantly square-rigged. A variation, the snow or snow brig, had a trysail on a small mizzen mast. From the 16th to the 19th centuries snows were the largest merchant ships in existence, some exceeding 1000 tons.

Brigantine: two masts, one square-rigged (almost always the fore-mast), the other fore-and-aft rigged.

Barque (USA **Bark**): three or more masts, square sails on all but the rearmost mast .

Barquentine: three or more masts, square sails only on the fore-mast.

Carrack or **Nao**: the first ocean-going vessel in Europe. Three masts, seven sails, all square except a lateen at the rear. Forecastle and high rounded stern with an aft castle. Columbus's *Santa Maria* was a carrack.

Caravel: a derivation of the carrack. Smaller, lighter, more manoeuvrable. No forecastle and smaller aft castle. Originally lateen rigged but changed to two square sails and a lateen. Columbus's sister ships, *La Pinta* and *Nina*, were caravels and better suited to exploring the newly discovered coastline.

Others: Galleons, frigates and corvettes utilised the above rigs but were distinguished by their specific roles in war. Clippers tended to be narrow, stream-lined barques.

Rathlin

Deidre Keene answered my knock and we stood on the wheel-chair ramp of her house, a new-build almost lost among fuchsia and birdfeeders. In the background the sea gnawed at the shore and I could hear the muffled snooker shots of rocks being shunted around. She was about sixty, I guessed, with silver hair tied in a pony tail. Her eyes sparkled in a lean sunburnt face. A cold breeze ruffled her frock but she seemed oblivious of it, lighting into a smile as I gave my introduction.

'So you know Wallace Clark, do you?' Her accent was what could be termed mid-Sound, the softness of Ayrshire with the lilt of Antrim. Knowing Wallace Clark, I was to discover, was to prove a repeated fast-track to tea and biscuits in the north.

Out of a winter population of a hundred, Deidre was one of only twelve who had been born on the island and still lived here. 'There's no work', she explained. 'The young all leave. Siobhan's gone to Coventry, Mary's in Southampton, Isobel's in London, David's in Edinburgh, Peter's in Kirkintilloch, Danny was in Ballycastle but he's off to Australia, Rachael's gone to Belfast...' and she named every one and the foreign town that had claimed them.

Rathlin was now populated by 'blow-ins', she added. A friendly term. David, her husband, had blown-in from guttural Ulster thirty-four years earlier and been resident ever since, but he was still a blow-in. Native status was not awarded on any terms other than birth. He sat in the kitchen, a red-bearded figure recently invalided and carrying more weight than he wanted through enforced inactivity. He remained quiet until given space, then he owned it confidently.

'Blow uns, or uncomers', he added. Not a friendly term. 'The wurst are the rich wuns from south-east England. They come for about two months, that's the trend, get themselves on uv-very committee and begin to change thungs.' They bought houses at rates the 'locals' couldn't afford and now an incomer speculator had erected six seafront houses which were on the market for £120,000 apiece.

'£85,000 would be fair, I think', Deidre offered, 'and then maybe we'd get a family living here full time.'

'But there's no wurk', David repeated. 'The last undustry wus the limestone quarry. That closed un the nineteen-twunties. We'd like to start it up again. It could wurk, you know. But we don't get much support here. They did a programme on Rathlun, oh, a long time ago...'

'In the sixties, it was.'

'Yes, about then, and they called it "The Island Betwixt and Between" and it's always been like that. We've always been ignored and forgotten. Not like the Scottish islands. Highlands and Islands Unterprise does much more to support communities. And the Scottish uducation system's better than ours. Particularly the universities and their fees.' He nodded to confirm the truth to himself. 'You know, Rathlun almost became Scottish. It wus only because of snakes that it went to Ireland. Some years back we tried to reverse that decision...', he laughed, '... but it didn't wurk. A pity. We'd be better off under Scotland.'

For centuries Rathlin had been held by the Scots, the MacDonalds in particular, one sept of whom became Ulster Scots and changed their name to McDonnell. In 1617 Sir Randal McDonnell's ownership was contested by a mainland Scot, Crawford of Lismore, who alleged that the island had been granted to his family by James IV in 1500. This broached the wider question of whether Rathlin Island rightfully belonged to Scotland, albeit thirteen miles away, or Ireland, two miles distant. The case was put before James VI (I of England) and a complex legal wrangle ensued.

Sir Randal's lawyers produced as evidence the case of the Isle of Man which had been the subject of a similar dispute. A Norman invader, Giraldus Cambrensis, reported in 1170 that, 'The controversy was at length decided in the following manner: venomous reptiles were brought there on trial; they lived and as a matter of course the island was on this account unanimously adjudged to Britain.' The defence asserted that Rathlin was 'a parcel of Ireland' because of the nature of the soil 'which neither breeds nor nourishes any living thing venomous, but is as clear of them as Ireland, where the isles of the Scottish and of the English in the same sea, breed and nourish the snakes...' Crawford refuted this by pointing out that Iona held no snakes and was Scottish, but this argument was dismissed as proof of the power of missionaries rather than of territorial characteristic. Sir Randal won, and for want of adders Rathlin has been Irish ever since. Yet the mentality of the islanders has never adjusted and to this day Ireland is still referred to as foreign land.

'Talking of poisons', David remarked, 'do you see those ones out there?'

The kitchen window looked onto a steep bank with the same

vegetation that surrounds my home in Skye, so I noticed nothing abnormal, let alone toxic. He smiled at my bemusement, then presented a statistic which verged on the incredible.

'Ninety-six per cent of deaths on Rathlun are cancer related. Mainly cancer of the mouth, nose, throat or lungs. And the kuller, I believe' – he pointed to clusters of green fronds – 'is bracken. Their spores are the carcunogens we breathe in all summer, and I believe the danger they pose is being hushed up.'

David was now a man with a mission. A side-effect from a drug for rheumatoid-arthritis had left him wheelchair-bound. This sudden immobility had persuaded him to do an Open University course in biology and Earth Sciences, and to get to the bottom of Rathlin's secret killer.

Since the decline in agriculture and the abandonment of fields too small for tractor-work, he explained, bracken had grown rife on the island. Whenever Ministry of the Environment employees worked amongst bracken they had to conduct a test beforehand; a frond was shaken for evidence of spore release and, if positive, regulations came into force requiring full protective clothing and face masks to be worn.

"Even just to *cross* a patch of bracken! That's how seriously the MOE regard the threat, but the government keeps the whole thung hushed up.'

'Why?'

'Because they'd be forced to take action and that would cost bullions. The spores are active mainly round July and August. If you cut bracken three times each year, when it's about six unches high un sprung, mid-June and August, and repeat this for three years, you can get rud of it, for a short while. Three years later it's back. Roots extend a long way underground and if you cut a root unto a thousand pieces, you get a thousand new plants. The only way to uradicate bracken is with a specialised weedkuller, but it's expensive. Seventy-five pounds an acre. So naturally the government would prefer to keep this a secret.'

'And you're going to take on the Establishment?'

He smiled, an ace-of-trumps smile. 'You'll be aware of the controversy over Sellafield and the suspicion that its effluence is to blame for the higher uncidence of cancers in Antrum? Well Antrum is also thick with bracken. I thunk the Atomic Energy Commission could become very unterested in my wurk.'

I looked out the window again. The view now appeared heavy with menace, crowding in on us.

'Yes, I know', he added. 'I used to keep them under control but it's not so easy now.'

* * *

The tide and the grand lottery of encounters brought me neighbours. Bert and Linda Surnameless tied up at *Ceana*'s stern and from then on we shared the enforced intimacy of campers, nodding each time one caught the other surfacing to check the weather, engaging in pleasantries over peeling potatoes, and feeling constantly obliged to offer or accept invitations to tea, coffee, beer and G&Ts.   More often than not these exchanges were among the highlights of a cruise, entertaining, informative and revealing glories of human eccentricity, but, unfortunately, not in the Surnamelesses's case.

She'd hung on to a Wensleydale post office career, retiring the moment her pension had been secured. He'd done everything, brilliantly, to the point of boredom. They'd bought a boat. This very summer they'd cruise the west coast of Scotland, Orkney, probably Shetland, and quite possibly pop over to Norway and back. That at least was the plan. I saw through it at once. We were one, they and I, trying to believe we were mariners; desperately doubting we'd cut it.

A knock-down off Anglesey had scuppered their confidence. A plague of gales unnoticed by the Met Office had held them 'stormbound' in every Welsh port. So far they'd taken three weeks to cover 100 miles.

If I ever do the Northwest Passage, if I find myself frozen in for three consecutive years, please promise me, God, that I will not find the Surnamelesses frozen in next to me. While I appreciated the warmth of their cabin, 360° of carpet and the leftovers of someone else's cooking, I couldn't bear to hear one more time Linda's chipmunk giggle as she looked into Bert's eyes – as she'd done since the age of sixteen – thereby bolstering Bert into divulging Indian Customs regulations, Pakistani indigestibles, Bangladeshi longdrops, the chemical deficiencies of Indonesian petrol, puncture repair facilities in a military zone near Abu Simbel and every other detail of their two-year motorcycle trip to Australia.

No, if this is what three weeks' confinement in Welsh ports does to the human condition, I don't want to meet them in Fury and Hecla Strait. I took flight into the hinterland.

* * *

The island proved a turncoat. From the sea it had appeared an innocuous lump, a tableland surrounded by Viking-proof cliffs. Yet within its modest one mile of width and seven of length, bent into a boomerang, Rathlin concealed a washboard of alarming gradients which, on the downward rush, threatened to collapse my folding bike under me. Three gears were insufficient and I ended up taking the bike for a walk. If bracken had taken over fields imprisoned within drystane dykes, brambles were running it a close second. They reached out and raked my legs whenever I deviated to avoid a pothole. I was looking for, in chronological order, axes, Robert the Bruce and Marconi.

Seven thousand years ago Neolithic man discovered here on Raghery, as the island was previously known, a small outcrop of one of the world's hardest rocks. Porcellanite is an extremely fine-grained stone, dark grey to black in colour and frequently speckled. An axe factory was established at the hamlet of Brockley. Such was the importance of Raghery axes, used mainly for felling trees, that trading ships from Tyre and Crete moored in Church Bay and the island appeared in early descriptions and charts when much of Western Europe was unrecorded.

The gorse was in bloom. Dazzled by their conflagrations I missed the turning to Brockley. Besides, I was having difficulty keeping my horizons level. Land sickness had assailed me, and terra firma had gone liquid. I staggered along single-track roads and only just spotted a sign on the wall of East Lighthouse.

> This plaque was unveiled by Princess Elettra Marconi Giovanelli to commemorate the First Commercial Radio Signals by Marconi, Kemp and Glanville for Lloyds of London between Rathlin and Ballycastle, July 1898.

There was little trace of the Signal Station that once commanded a vital observation point on the busy shipping route between Liverpool and America. In the days of sail Lloyds subscribed underwriters to insure ships and their cargoes *only* on the ocean section of their voyages. Once inside UK coastal waters, cover terminated. Transatlantic crossings might vary in length by as much as five weeks, causing anxiety among underwriters keen to secure their profit and reinvest in another venture. In the 1890s Lloyds erected a signal station to record the moment a vessel passed the 'null and void' line. Yet the information was useless until it had been received in London. Semaphore, homing pigeons and the postman in his rowing boat all proved unreliable in relaying messages to the coach depot on the mainland. Thus, in 1898, Lloyds felt they had little to lose by hiring a young Irish-Italian to find a solution with his promising invention, wireless telegraphy.

Guglielmo Marconi (1874-1937), whose mother was Irish, applied for the first patent in wireless telegraphy at the age of twenty-two. Two years later Lloyds commissioned him to set up the communication link between Rathlin and Ballycastle on the Antrim coast. Marconi was too busy to attend to this himself but he sent his assistants, Kemp and Glanville, and after some initial setbacks, transmission was successful.

It's curious how various sites on earth seem to attract history. How strange that Marconi (or rather, young Glanville) and Robert the Bruce should be connected on an unremarkable spot on Rathlin. When Marconi chose the location for his radio station he unwittingly created circumstances in which his twenty-six-year-old assistant, on a short walk from the building, would stumble and fall to his death at the mouth of the cave in which one of Scotland's greatest heroes had hidden six centuries earlier.

Dumfriesshire and Arran also claim to have the cave where the famous spider incident took place; the six-times defeated rebel being inspired by a spider's seventh, and successful, attempt to complete its web, and then leading his army to victory at Bannockburn in 1314. Rathlin's credentials for authenticity are probably the strongest despite the cave being accessible only by boat and providing the most punitive conditions in which to endure a winter.

A man-made shelf still remains set back one hundred yards from the entrance. The Bysset family, who owned Rathlin at the time, supported Bruce's cause. And when, in an often overlooked facet of history, Robert's brother Edward Bruce, Earl of Carrick, was crowned the first King of Ireland in 1316, Hugh Bysset held place of honour at his right hand. I have no idea what business a spider might have in the Bysset's hellhole, but can believe a fugitive might have found it sufferable in an emergency.

I left Rathlin reluctantly. It still seemed a pity to disturb a securely moored boat. The very act of casting off was an invitation to trouble. Yet I had to see Wallace Clark before I fell off the edge of my only Irish chart, and I had to escape the gastro-Australian saga.

Wallace Clark

Among the many unwritten axioms in sailing - which include: *wherever possible the wind will endeavour to come from the direction in which you intend to go, harbour masters will exhibit unpleasantness in proportion to the size of their port, one malfunction on a yacht will simultaneously incite a minimum of four other components to fray, seize, snap or go AWOL* - is the BBC's hallowed principle that *weather forecasts will be broadcast only at times when the least number of people can be expected to hear them.* My alarm went at 0530. 'Winds west to southwest, 4-5, occasionally 6.' I, of course, was heading west.

I released the warps silently and drifted away. The south-bound commuter tide carried me along Rathlin's shore, past crags folded like deckchairs where the odd sheep grazed, ridiculously fluffed and white against the greenery. Their meal flagged into a ribbon of ordinariness. But on the chart it changed character, transformed into a realm of fantasy and brutality. Here even the least noteworthy of features, barely features at all, unfurled names worthy of banners. That unassuming rock was Maddygalla, that jut was Ruenascarrive, that slit was the 'Cave of the Golmens', that lump was Crockascridlin ('hill of screaming') and Sloaknacailly was the 'pit of the hags, the place where women were thrown into the sea'. Behind Rathlin's innocent exterior lay a past that had witnessed no less than five major massacres and half a dozen pitched battles.

The news was hardly better beneath me. Only five metres from the surface lay the wreck of the 14,000-ton cruiser, *Drake*, which sank in 1917. Having escorted a convoy from Gibralter she had just relinquished her duty when the torpedoes of U79 struck her broadside. At the time an anti-submarine net stretched from Fair Head (the mainland promontory nearest to Rathlin) for eleven miles to the Scottish mainland at the Mull of Kintyre. To control this net, a twelve-foot mesh in sections ninety-six feet deep and two thousand yards long, was a formidable task which occupied a fleet of forty drifters in a continuous struggle with the currents. A hydrophone station listened for the enemy's propellers but the Germans grew wise to this and, like U79's daring manoeuvre, learned to silence their engines and drift with the current. No trace of the net remains and the *Drake* too will disappear, soon to be salvaged for the purity of its steel.

Past Rue Point I swung the tiller hard over as *Ceana* crossed a line and entered a river. It cut a clear edge in the chop two hundred yards offshore, a smooth flow of bloody-mindedness which disempowered rudders and swung my hull back the way I'd come. The sails flapped as the wind gave way to this superior force and let me be carried back to land. Every few seconds a miniature whirlpool appeared, a spiralling depression sucking in air and flecks of spume, only to vanish and leave strange creatures of dashing seaweed. Once I could have sworn we were on a downhill rapid but that sensation too evaporated and the wake revealed only a few welts, feeble and innocent. It was eerie, this apparent calm, this gentle simmer on the surface while underneath tremendous forces were in conflict, making a three-ton yacht pirouette across the Irish Sea. But this is what Rathlin is famous for. Almanacs do not squander space on tidal charts. They cover most of Ireland and part of Scotland in two pages. Yet a whole page is dedicated to the tiny island of Rathlin. One billion tons of water travel through the northern narrows of the Irish Sea every six hours, and Rathlin stands in the way. On average one ship is wrecked here every two to three years.

But I felt happier now. I'd been taken up by some counter-current and with my bow locked on Scotland to the north-east, I was moving nicely west to Portrush. Sideways.

* * *

The house lay at the end of a quarter-mile of beech hedge, over-shadowed by ancient trees. Confettied leaves sprinkled to the ground under a gardener's shears but he remained dwarfed by the enormity of his task. A few swans cruised a pond, doubled into a squadron of sails by their reflections. The original Georgian cottage, the birthplace of Charles Thomson whose hand wrote the American Declaration of Independence, still stood as the centrepiece of sprawling additions and trellises heavy with roses. Inside there seemed as many corridors as there were rooms and at the end of one we mounted a spiral staircase and entered the great chamber of a converted barn.

We used to have grand flahoolas in here', Wallace remarked, and pointed to a ship's wheel suspended from the ceiling by chains. 'The party trick was to swing from the chandelier. Lost count of how many times I did it. Pretty schoolboyish, I suppose, but great fun.'

He was seventy-six. The handsome face I'd first known twelve years earlier was now gaunt, the eyes sunken. Waves of white hair stood out in shocks, reassuringly. They had clearly not accepted retirement from a lifetime of sailing. He still talked quickly, through a mouth that moved little but retained a natural bent of smile, still poured out stories from the treasury of a natural raconteur. But I was shocked to find the tall, locomotive-chested man reduced to a frail figure humped over a stick. 'Bad road accident two months ago', he explained. 'Bloody nuisance! Still, I'm on the mend.'

In 1991 Skye's local newspaper, *The West Highland Free Press*, printed a brief report on the first Highland galley to be built for 400 years. Galleys, I was told, were fast, manoeuvrable square-rigged sailing-rowing vessels derived from the Viking longship. Not a single galley had survived and the report mentioned that the replica was based on a few historical descriptions and tombstone carvings. The project was devised and driven by Wallace. I applied to join the crew and sent a CV weak on sailing but strong on dog sledding and enthusiasm. That summer I spent six weeks reviving the voyages of the Lords of the Isles.

The former dance hall now served as a private museum, library and cobwebbery. Robert the Bruce's spider would have been in heaven here. Its contemporaries had rigged their nets all over the place. Tables crowded the floor. Every surface was stacked with files, books, what might have been yellowing manuscripts and boxes, so many boxes, cardboard throwaways, crafted antiques and initialled leather ones you'd expect to contain a foldout shaving kit from the Boer War. And dust. Dust on army decorations, bits of boats, driftwood, an original Jimi Dixon from Tory Island's school of primitive art, ten bookcases, chart cabinets…

'I'm afraid everything's a bit of a mess. But how does that saying go? "Stars are born from chaos within".'

Wallace Clark's name and endeavours were common currency among Ireland's sailing fraternity. When yachting was still something of a novelty he'd joined the few who had 'spliced the mainbrace'[1] on completion of what the old poets called 'the sea-circuit of green Ireland'. In 1963 he sailed a curragh from Derry to Iona, he was an early crew member of Tim Severin's Brendan Voyage and he'd been the first person to stand at the helm of a highland galley for 400 years. Yet sailing was always a sideline. Above all he'd been a businessman, running the family linen factory, William Wallace, which had been an active concern before the demise of galleys in the seventeenth century.

---

[1]The mainbrace was a thick rope controlling a square mainsail. Splicing it, if severed in battle, was vital but dangerous work, earning a reward of rum. The expression was later used for any celebration at sea.

We paused before some army memorabilia. 'Why did you join the B Specials?' I asked. These were hardcore paramilitaries, part of the Ulster Defence Association, which were formed in the 1970s to counteract IRA violence. They manned roadblocks, searched vehicles, and were prime targets for assassination. 'I wasn't going to stand by and watch 400 years of family enterprise – and I like to think we've always been good employers – be driven out of business by terrorist threats.'

'Weren't you worried you'd be taken out?'

He shrugged. 'Of course. But I wasn't one of the mean ones. Some people roughed up those they were suspicious of, and they were more likely to be targeted. You can do an unpleasant job but still be civil about it.'

He stopped opposite a framed cover of *Yachting Monthly*. 'That's the family yacht, *Wild Goose.* Unfortunately I lost her in my home waters. Ran aground at the entrance to Coleraine. A silly mistake. The lifeboat tried to pull me off but we were swamped. And do you know the worst part? The RNLI made a poster of the rescue, so now I relive the trauma every time I see it!' He laughed. 'Always take the greatest care in the waters you think you know the best. Anyway, here are the charts. Take a look and help yourself.'

He was lending all the charts needed to take me round Ireland. I opened drawers at random. Each was congested with stiff slabs of paper, many backed by canvas. They passed on the contagion of excitement which always infects me around maps. Black Sea, the Bosporus, the Greek Islands, the Algarve…I knew I could happily spend half my voyage here and not even reach the recesses occupied by Ireland. North Cape, the Azores, Cape Finisterre…I was already among them, plotting my course to a bounty of unknown islands.

I spent a morning sorting through them and almost got to Tristan da Cunha before returning to my boat, walking lopsidedly. Under one arm was the entire coast of Ireland in fifty-five pieces.

Troubles

I couldn't seem to shake off Scotland. The Mull of Kintyre refused to go away or even diminish but remained a wad of blue like smoke held down on a frosty morning. Antrim was more biddable and revealed progress as it slipped by. Fluted cliffs raised grey faces. They arched inland and formed amphitheatres over lost valleys where a talus of grass and boulders in fantastic patterns sloped down to the sea. I felt a thrill as I failed to spot any sign of man's intervention. Only later did the odd hill farm appear and heather gave way to fields and that startling mosaic of greens which is so idiosyncratically 'the Emerald Isle'. Then despair descended as I jotted notes for my diary. Each field was bordered by a hedge. Each hedge was in blossom. Helpless before the greens, I was a walkover for the whites, pinks and yellows. I flipped shut the notebook and slumped back in the cockpit in a wash of maudlin sentiment.

A jet seared shock waves low overhead and my mind wandered to my nephew who at that moment was fighting his way towards Basra with the Black Watch. I was strongly opposed to the Iraq war and followed events with a growing sense of outrage and foreboding. The previous afternoon in Portrush I'd chanced upon an air show complete with the Red Arrows and the usual ground-based circus of goldfish stalls and PR caravans. It was a dismal affair. Even the Kiddies Safari train had broken down. Two mechanics were working on its engine. Outside the theatres of death there are few sadder sights than that of a plastic chimpanzee still grinning at the wheel of a derailed locomotive. Just beyond it was an Army Field Catering Tent. I went inside to see what my nephew was getting to eat.

An acnied youth had been left in charge and he stood behind a foldout table. There had been no attempt at presentation besides a random scattering of packets. He did his best and launched into an explanation of how what lay between us, a pathetic collection of foil envelopes, was a calorie-counted twenty-four hour ration for an active soldier. It looked very mean to me, barely enough to keep a magpie going.

'OK', I quizzed, 'what would I have for breakfast?'

He contemplated the items before him. I could identify *Oatcakes* as the only likely contender.

'You could have this.' He pointed at *Mince and Dumplings*.

'Fine. What would I have for supper?'

There was now *Treacle Pudding* remaining as the only packet which looked as if it contained anything. This threw him into bewilderment. He pondered the problem but didn't relish the possibilities.

'I think there must be bits missing from this one.'

Poor lad. He may go far but I hope never as far as hostilities. But what was the point? Couldn't the army even come up with one bloody, intact packed ration?

Presumably we were more stretched in Iraq than I had realised.

* * *

Long-keel yachts are notoriously difficult to manoeuvre in cramped harbours, and few come more cramped than Carnlough (*do not enter in SE winds above Force 6*, warned the Pilot). Its narrow entrance was festooned with warps whose victims were dying of algae, and after dodging these I found myself in a basin whose walls were three-deep in boats. I had yet to work out the mysterious effects of 'prop wash' and 'prop walk'; I had no understanding of how *Ceana* preferred to turn under power beyond knowing she never went where I wanted her to go. Neither did she want to stop so I found myself racing to the bow and acting as a fender to protect Carnlough's shipping from my bullish intrusion. It was another undignified arrival which I put down to inexperience, not realising for another week, and another score of near-misses, that a nut had worked loose and reverse gear was failing to engage. Flustered and sweating I tied up against the *Queen Maeve,* a rusting fishing boat whose owner watched me with a porcelain stare.

'Thon's a bit mooch firya', he remarked.

I nodded and tried to conceal the thought-process by which a rabbit going round a tree was fashioning a bowline in my breast rope. 'Can I stay alongside tonight?'

'Ah, ah wont be goin oot soon, mebbe no ferra year.' He belched and lowered a bottle of Guinness.

In spells of sunshine between showers, Carnlough appeared to be made of ivory. The Marchioness of Londonderry had opened a limestone quarry in the nearby hills and plastered the harbour and houses in the stuff. The town was little more than one long street and I walked its length warily, tuned to conflicting political signals. The Londonderry Arms was blatantly Unionist in name, but schoolboys wore the green-and-white strips of Celtic and carried hurling sticks with broad faces as lethal as Polynesian beheading tools. Hurling was synonymous with Gaelic, Catholicism and Republicanism. It took Giles Sweeney to put it all in perspective.

He was using the harbour wall as a sorting table and loading crabs into a pickup whose livery declared 'Sweeney's Seafoods'.

'Scotland, eh?' He nodded at the saltire flapping in my rigging. 'Good catch?'

'Can't complain.' His skin was the same deep tan and looked as hard as the carapaces he was handling. It was his son's business, he explained, lowering his voice and gesturing secrecy ... export! ... a niche market! ... guess where? ... Sweden! ... but the Swedes were very particular about size and quality ... He transferred crabs one by one from creel to fish-box, picking off seaweed, checking the number of legs and folding them neatly under the body before adding it to those already in graded layers, already conveying the same air of resignation as clingfoiled sandwiches. Crabbing was just fun for him in his retirement, and exercise! He rolled his shoulders and pouted his chest, items apparently lost but salvaged from a career, paradoxically, in Health and Safety. In his next breath he broached The Troubles.

'The elections've been postponed to save Trimble' – he tapped the side of his nose – 'no doubt about that. Now the problem began at partition. If both sides had just agreed to let people *warship* as they liked and practised no discrimination, there'd be none of this goings-on today.' He pitched an under-sized specimen into the harbour. 'Are yer not afraid of bein blown up?'

'I'm more afraid of rocks at the moment.'

'Ach, yer safe here. We've never had any trouble here. I've only heard one bomb blast ... Cushendall, it was, five miles away, but we heard it right fine here. We've all sorts mixing here. It all started with the plantations, y'see. We got English protestants who was more yer landowning class and we got Scots Protestants, poor people, not much education, bad lots. And them's the ones that support Paisley, the Paisley Unionists. Paisley!' — he spat the word – 'he's no sky pilot. That's what we call ministers here. He's more hell in him than the devil. But he's old now and when he snuffs it, by Jaysus', he chortled, 'the shit'll hit the fan! He's never done nothing for Northern Ireland but he's got a loyal following among these old, low class people. But young Catholics here don't see any party as having any guts except Sinn Féin. So in the elections this autumn, we could be lookin at a Sinn Féin - Ulster-Unionist coalition, something Paisley vowed he'd never even contemplate!'

I had to understand, he stressed, that Catholics had nothing. No education, no jobs, the worst housing. He'd seen it, twenty-five years ago, houses with no running water, no toilets. So they built new high-rise homes for them with all modcons and the Protestants on Shankill Road looked on and saw *the Catholics now had better homes than they had!*

'Do you hold out any hope for a solution?'

'Solution? We don't need a solution! This is politics here. Let them get on with it. We've a good life here. Look around Northern Ireland and you see good houses, good cars. We've got it better than England or Scotland. I've seen more poor in Scotland than here. And England! They've got it coming. We've got our dissent out in the open. In England it's covered and brimming. One day all the racial tension'll break out, the payback for years of colonial exploitation. I tell you, what we've had's a picnic compared to what they've got coming.'

He laughed. His work was done. In the boxes the crabs had their own troubles. The following evening they'd be in Stockholm.

Potted History No 1

More so than with any other race, I'm told, it's impossible to understand the Irish without understanding their history. Here's my grasp of the facts, phase one.

As the world's sea-level rose following the end of the last Ice Age, Ireland became an island around 6000 BC. It was uninhabited by man but Palaeolithic hunters were on their way, following giant deer which roamed from Denmark to Scotland and England across what would become the 'North Sea' but remained a vast plain of swamps and forest called Doggerland. As the agricultural evolution gradually spread from the Levant, these hunters evolved into Neolithic farmers on the limestone soils of Limerick. By 2000 BC the native people were initiating the Irish cult of celebrating death by building dolmens and megalithic tombs in grand profusion and style. At the same time Rathlin islanders were bartering axe heads for exotica from distant shores: blue faience from Egypt, amber from the Baltic and lapis lazuli from Tyre. Ireland was then the principle source of metal in Europe.

The first major influx of strangers occurred around 1500 BC with the arrival of small, dark-skinned men, the Firbolgs, who carried long-headed battle axes and wore trousers. The Firbolgs probably came from the Biscay coast of Spain but their thousand-year occupation was not to be as permanent as the next immigrants who appeared circa 600 BC. They came in two waves, one arriving in the south from the continent, one invading the north from Scotland, but they were the same race; the iron-wielding Celts (from the Greek *Keltoi*).

The Celts had long dominated western Europe and had even sacked Rome in 390 BC before suffering a reversal. In Ireland they found a safe haven, for the Romans hated the place. 'Hibernia' they called it. *The Land of Winter.* Cold, wet, miserable. Anyone was welcome to it, and the Celts soon consolidated their hold. As a race they were defined primarily by their language which was hived from the great brood of Indo-European tongues and over time split into two major dialects: the P-Celtic, or brythonic Gaelic of Wales, Cornwall and Brittany, and the Q-Celtic, or goidal Gaelic of Ireland, Scotland and the Isle of Man. (As an example, the archaic word for horse was *epos* in P-Celtic, but *equos* in Q-Celtic).

Like any government today the Celts spread across the country, worshiped pagan deities and conducted intertribal feuds. They lacked political unity but the fact that a common language embraced the land allowed a culture to develop that was remarkable for its depth and breadth. The learned *brehons* administered a complex legal system in which every man's status was defined by a credit rating, his *eneclann* or 'honour-price'. Ranked among the highest strata of society were craftsmen and the *aes dana*, men of art, who included bards, harpists, genealogists and historians. The Celts introduced the Latin alphabet and set the groundwork for an education system whose ramifications would last well into the Middle-Ages: Ireland would remain almost unique in Europe as a land where literacy and learning would pervade society and not be held as the esoteric arts of Christian clergy.

Christians had diffused into Ireland before St Patrick's arrival but it was under his thirty-year influence that a radical transformation took place. His dates and origin are obscure but the most colourful account relates how Patrick, a native of Roman Britain, was sixteen when Irish raiders kidnapped him. He turned to God during six years' enslavement as a shepherd before escaping and returning to his family. A discipleship under St Germanus of Auxerre preceded a calling in a dream to return to Ireland and baptize the people. He began in 432 and found the Celts did not submit easily. Until his death in around 461 he lived in constant fear of being murdered but his message spread and within a century monasteries had been established all over Ireland. As fervent as the opposition to Christianity was at times, Ireland remains the only country in western Europe to have produced no martyrs during its conversion.

Ireland's Golden Age of monasticism lasted from the sixth to the eighth century. No less than twelve saints emerged to found centres of devotion and such was their resonance that Irish missionaries carried a revived faith back to the continent and spread its influence wider. They led austere lives, these monks, while creating such masterpieces of calligraphy as the *Book of Kells*. They were not easy on the eye. It was their custom to shave the front and tops of their heads while letting the hair at the back grow long. But eventually their morals declined and not even their appearance or their refuges on the most remote and forlorn sea rocks could save them from the next scourge of Ireland, the Vikings.

They were farmers and piratical entrepreneurs from Norway's western fjords and at their peak their longships penetrated deep into Russia, frequented the coasts of Greenland and Labrador and even reached the palaces of Byzantium. Displaying the wit of butchers, Vikings such as Ivor the Boneless, Haermund Hardaxe and Tryggr Calf-Cleaver plundered Iona and came on to Ireland in 795, returning every few years. Sixty-eight monks were slaughtered in 806. Such was the fear they invoked that one monk, St Gall Priscian, working on a manuscript, blotted his copy with the following marginal note:

> The wind is rough tonight
> tossing the white-combed ocean;
> I need not fear the fierce Vikings
> crossing the Irish Sea

The Vikings carried back the silverware and enamelled reliquaries treasured by each monastery with the result that today the finest examples of Irish craftsmanship from this period are to be found in the museums of Bergen, Stavanger, Oslo and Trondheim. In time the Vikings established colonies and trading posts. Waterford was first, predating even the settlements of Reykjavik, Oslo, Copenhagen and Stockholm. They founded Dublin in the 10th century. They even adopted Christianity and in one of the many ironies that riddle Ireland's history they became more Christian than the Irish themselves, being the first to reform a decadent Church by introducing archbishops.

Although the Vikings defended their bases and travelled with impunity, they never suppressed the Irish tribes and by the time the invaders' power waned, and was broken at the battle of Clontarf in 1014, Ireland was divided into over a hundred kingdoms. Two of these became dominant, Tara in the north versus Cashel in the south, and not until their conflict was resolved by the victory of Brian Boruma (Cashel) did one man effectively rule all of Ireland. Yet he was never crowned 'King' and any stability was short-lived as regional power struggles resumed. Out of these, in 1166, came the events which so momentously altered Ireland's destiny and were to become, for 800 years, 'the Irish Problem'.

Antrim A & E

The day of my departure from Carnlough started well except in one detail. I missed the weather forecast. I read it later on a bulletin board on my way to hospital. *Small Craft Warning issued for Irish Sea. Winds SW, fresh to strong, gusting to Near Gale Force 7 in North Irish Sea later.*

Trapped in a tidal harbour, I had been unable to start my voyage earlier and I squandered the morning sightseeing. By the time the barnacles on my hull had a few more miles under their trapdoors and were back in deep water it was, in meteorological terms, 'later'. The wind was in the early stages of disgruntlement. In no time the visible world shrank to a tableau of white horses surrounded by mist. The Maidens flashed danger somewhere out to my left and ahead a dark escarpment had detached itself from the mainland and was sliding resolutely towards England. P&O's *Voyager* or *Pioneer*, I guessed. *Ceana* was slewed over begging for less sail, bucking in the rising sea, while I tinkered with Fleming's helming and screwed my face against erosion by rain and seawater. And so came about that fateful decision to make a cup of tea.

The stove ran on methylated spirits. A knob operated a flap which either exposed a wad of spirit-soaked wool for lighting, or covered it for extinguishing. It was the simplest and safest system and had never caused a problem before. On this occasion, however, something jammed and flames curled up the sides of the stove. I heard my skin sizzle as a thumb and three fingers wrenched at the knob before the pain registered. I watched the flames rise higher towards the curtains and wood panelling. In desperation I grabbed a dishcloth and released a catch which raised the stove's lid to reveal the blazing spirit wells. I flung the contents of the kettle over the flames and instantaneously the fire was out. But the boat gave a sudden lurch which knocked me off balance and the lid dropped with a finger of my left hand caught between two edges of steel. The tip was guillotined. I knew at once it was serious and was shocked to see how much blood a finger could release in such a short time. Then a rogue wave came pouring down the companionway and forced me back to the task of reducing sail. With a snatch of paper towel and a plastic bag wrapped round my wound, I staggered on deck to try and regain control of this sick adventure.

It took another two hours of motor-sailing in tedious tacks before the opening to Larne Lough appeared. The shelter I hoped to find never materialised. The wind veered and met me on the bow. An adverse tide and ferocious output from Ballylumford power station shunted me about and maintained progress at a crawl. I replaced dressings each time the plastic bags filled and observed miserably how everything I touched left a crimson stain. Soon the cockpit, ropes, sails, instruments and charts resembled the scene of a massacre. The shakes took hold as I reached a vacant mooring buoy opposite East Antrim Boat Club. The buoy was dangerously close to the stern of a P&O freighter and I had no right to use it, but that was the least of my worries. It took four attempts in the face of a twenty-five knot wind to catch it, and then a painful twenty-minute struggle to row ashore.

As luck would have it – and I felt I was due some – East Antrim Boat Club members were just gathering to assess conditions for a race, and one of them (I remain in your debt, Mrs Hall) drove me twenty miles to hospital. Thus I found myself in Antrim Accident & Emergency waiting for two hours among life's other casualties – a drug-sodden woman who alternated between bouts of coma and furniture demolition, a lawnmower accident wrapped in a towel, a couple of DIY mishaps and other unrevealed misfortunes – still wearing my lifejacket and safety harness, still ankle-deep in seawater (a wave swamped my wellies on leaving the dingy). And later, while waiting for a taxi back to the boat, my finger stitched back together ('but I'm afraid you may have permanently lost all sense of feeling in it'), I fell in for a second time with Northern Ireland's hospitality; thank you, Harry and Gwen, for giving me a bed for the night, the loan of the socks and for driving me back to hospital for a review the following morning.

Belfast

Protestants will refer to Britain as 'the mainland', the North as 'the province', Catholics talk about 'the six counties', 'the twenty-six counties', 'the thirty-two counties', implying a common Irishness, anathema to loyalists. Both sides speak of 'Ulster' but inaccurately, for three of the counties of that ancient province are in the Republic (Donegal, Cavan and Monaghan). The Protestant's insulting nickname for a Catholic is a 'Taig' [rhymes with vague], the reverse, a bit less insulting, is 'Prod'. Broadly speaking the terms Protestant/Unionist/loyalist are synonymous, as are Catholic/ nationalist/republican, but with nuances in both cases. Nearly all Protestants are politically Unionist, but many can be very moderate, whereas 'loyalism' (to the Crown) implies something more hard-line and anti-Irish. Likewise, 'Nationalist' means feeling Irish and wanting a United Ireland; 'republican' is a fiercer variant of this, implying support for Sinn Féin, and maybe the IRA.

John Ardagh, *Ireland and The Irish*, 1994

To think that this city rules the Six Counties - the lovely Bann valley, the Glens of Antrim, the lake country of Fermanagh, the plains of Armagh! It is horrible. All the hates that blot the name of Ulster are germinated here. And what else could be germinated here but the revenges of the heart against its own brutalization.

Sean O'Faolain, *Irish Journey*, 1941

I fully expected not to recognise Belfast. My last visit had been almost thirty years earlier, in 1975, as tail-end-charlie in a group posing as Stirling University's athletics team. We performed rather better in the pub than on the track. I remember my surprise at looking up and seeing the city surrounded by fields and hills, people walking the streets as if everyone else in the world had heard of The Troubles except them, and a ship's carcase hauled up close to the city centre, just a few blocks down from Boots, and crawling

with Lilliputian figures. I remember being frisked by security person-
nel at the entrance to *every* shop. But most of all I remember the
fences. Everywhere I looked were posts and grids of wire rising up
to three storeys and enclosing entire buildings. They ringed off gaps
every few hundred yards where premises had been blown up, leaving pockets of emptiness cleared of dust and rubble, their neatness
belying any insinuation of abnormality. Reinforced by sandbags the
fences straddled roads where soldiers, conspicuous in their country
camouflage, fingered automatics and went about their unenviable
business of watching and waiting. And the names – Victoria Street,
Oxford Street, Chichester Street, Shaftsbury Avenue, Wellington
Place – made me think; this *isn't Ireland at all.*

Yet I recognised Belfast at once. Clearly it was still a dynamic
market for the fencing trade. Police stations and council buildings
were still cordoned off behind roof-high barricades. At each of their
corners a tower still stood, its top sheathed in naval grey punctured
with dark rectangles; peepholes or gunports. They remained vacant
but if you stared long enough you'd swear you'd caught movement
in their depths. The army checkpoints and friskers had disappeared
and Belfast was no longer a city under siege, but the hardware remained, just in case. Banks had installed double security doors
which left you momentarily trapped in their entrance halls. There
were noticeably fewer missing buildings in the streets, but the seventies resolve to pour whatever money it took into the city to repair
the physical and political wounds had clearly evaporated, and its
ailing industries had been dealt another blow by the recession.
Courtaulds, DuPont, British Oxygen and Michelin Tyres queued on
Death Row. Belfast was running down. Its centre bustled but within
the space of a few good stone throws – and this country has some
of the best – dereliction and seediness were creeping in.

I took the 'Living History' bus tour. The choice of adjective was
curious. It certainly didn't refer to Harland and Wolfe, our first stop.
Les was our guide. His accent must have irreparably seized in early
childhood. It was easy to imagine we had the Reverend Ian Paisley
with lockjaw on board.

'Onyurluft's Samsun un Goliath…' He pointed out a pair of
cranes shaped like gigantic staples, yellow and bearing the letters
H & W as they stood self-consciously idle over a barren industry-
scape. 'The *Titanic* wuz bult here. Untull recently five thousand mun
were umployed un the yard but now it's down to a hundred un fufty.'

'Could it start up again with a new order?'

Les shook his head. 'Uh doubt it. The skulls have ull moved on.'

A couple of oilrigs had drifted in for a refit but otherwise Harland
and Wolfe's vast estate was being turned into retail parks, offices

and flats. We passed more vacated lots, for sale or lease, and others whose owners had given up hope of even eliciting any interest. Belfast's population, 280,000, was falling as people moved out to satellite communities. I felt sorry for Les. He was finding it hard to come up with any encouraging news as we passed through yet another area of tumbledown houses, grimy walls and litter-infested crannies.

Bravely, he offered: 'Thus uz the lust cobbled street in Bul-fust.'

Suddenly we'd crossed a river divide and were among working-class houses where the road was bordered by kerbstones painted alternately red, blue and white, and union jacks flapped from lamp-posts or blazed immobile behind scores of panes of glass. This was Shankill ('Old Church') Road, an infamous flashpoint in the Troubles and a Protestant enclave in what was predominantly Catholic west Belfast. At its regular spots our bus stopped and we turned out to photograph the murals of Ulster's Defence Association, Volunteer Force, Freedom Fighters and Young Militants. Dark, aggressive murals which covered the gables of houses and featured guns, hooded figures, clenched fists and paramilitary insignia alongside slogans of defiance.

We tensed ourselves for the inevitable gunfire but none came and we were left to wonder at the bravery of a woman pushing a pram to the local shop and returning with a newspaper and a plastic bag dangling below the handlebars as she became silhouetted, and a perfect target, against 'ULSTER WILL ALWAYS REMAIN BRITISH – NO SURRENDER'.

But of course this was what it was all about. She belonged. She was community. Segregated by birth, school, employer, address and whom you talked to, she was on her home ground. Protestant. Unionist. Loyalist. Red, Blue, White.

In twenty years Shankill's population had decreased from 60,000 to 20,000, mainly the result of demolishing highrises and replacing them with monoblock estates of semi-detacheds.

'Who'd want to live here?' I asked.

'There's a tun-year waiting lust fur houses here. It's a but like luving in the Holy Lund. Many loyalists see thus uz sacred soil.'

I tried to gauge his sympathies. Les kept them hidden. I guessed they resided with the other side, which lay just a few hundred yards away, on the Falls Road. The two districts were back to back, the gardens of one formerly abutting the gardens of the other but this untenable situation had been remedied by building between them a stone wall to match the height of the houses, with the addition of a ten-foot fence on top to dissuade the passage of missiles. What stood for Thwarted Aggression had been named the 'Peace Wall'.

Where it crossed a street there were gates which were closed every night, and during the day on Anniversaries when trouble could be expected, forcing anyone shut out into a long detour through less fractious areas.

Along the Falls Road the kerbstones were orange, white and green and republican flags occupied equivalent positions to the Shankill's union jacks. The houses seemed slightly more affluent, better cared for and had neater gardens. The murals too were different; martyrs replaced soldiers, injustice displaced aggression.

It was a depressing tour, as ineptly named as the Peace Wall. The only thing living about it was sectarianism.

* * *

I sought a richer picture in Belfast and found it at a coffee shop overlooking the City Hall in Donegal Square. The thundering permanence of this colossus seemed to make up for the day's worth of defects. It was the antithesis of gap and hole. Against background grime it was white, against plain rectangularity it was all colonnade, arch, cupola and Renaissance dome. I drank in pleasure.

Ten minutes later the sermon started. Six pm Fridays, apparently, was happy hour for evangelists. A battery of preachers had set up amplifiers and speakers by the main gate and were now taking turns to yell into a microphone. *...if ya turn to the wurds of the Uld Tustamunt agun and agun ya'll...und the wrath of the Canaanites wull descend...down, down to Sudom und Gemorrah ya'll be cast...* Volume not content was the key, decibels not love must drive all but the deaf into the arms of Jesus, or whichever particular pen these shepherds had in mind. I couldn't work out where they were going. Eventually they became a shrapnel overlay on rumbling traffic and I was thankful when they stopped, tiring of this city that had turned the ritual abuses of religion into virtues.

I wondered how people born in the nursery of Christianity and thirled to it for 1500 years could resort to the inhuman activities of their civil wars. Is this country, Ireland, named just by chance? I put this ire down to unrequited passion. This fervour and zest for life, so recklessly alive in their reels and jigs, which can spiral at any moment into the depths of despair, into the world's most mournful ballads. The Irish psyche patrols the border of the irreconcilable. On such journeys, and with such momentum, it is no great step to lose the soul and commit the unimaginable. Anger, bitterness, music, religion, history, nationalism, terrorism are just stepping stones to Ireland's convoluted self-righteousness. And this, century upon century, has been elevated to, and confused with, spirituality.

The humbling fact for the rest of us is that we're no different. Within each of our societies exists that same delicate balance, that propensity to sacrifice compassion for pride, tolerance for sabotage, the highest attributes of humanity for the immediate gratification of revenge. The redressing of wrong as right is a terrifyingly easy sleight-of-hand to achieve, and as hard in proportion to resist. In this, the true tragedy, Ireland speaks of us all.

Then the grounds of the City Hall filled up with teenagers. Hundreds of them swarmed in, identically dressed in black. The material for two pairs of trousers was being worn as one, each leg a windsock ballooning at the ankles and liberally ripped. A black army dripping in chains, the more decorated among them also armed with hair raised into multi-tinted spikes. As if to illustrate the preachers' text, a tangle of adolescent male gays lay around the base of a statue giving and receiving French kisses. Above them, Queen Victoria frowned.

As I walked back to catch a train to Larne, the city I had known for a day was disappearing. Belfast's shops were vanishing behind shutters. Soon all the streets' colour and vitality had gone. A ghost town. Odd figures passed but no one lingered among miles of steel slats daubed in graffiti. There'd been a death and shutting yourself off was the only way of coping.

* * *

I let go my mooring before the seagulls were up. Plump black-backed gulls had moved in during the night and now occupied the best perches in Larne – lampposts, P&O hawsers, yachts' rigging, life-ring grottos, a parked soft-top, effluent pipes – with that disregard for human property which is so delightful as long as it's not yours. A couple of escaped bolsters floated by but turned out to be swans on the game for abandoned fish suppers.

'Little bugger - big bugger - little bugger - big bugger...' repeated *Ceana*'s engine to the accompaniment of the exhaust blowing bubbles in the off beats. I stole self-conscious glances at the city as I steamed across Belfast Lough. It felt obscene to be making a racket so early, even allowing for a distance of seven miles and a citizenry time-served in noise. For a while I felt sad that I hadn't persevered and had missed the other side where Belfast laughed and sang and nurtured herself in goodness. It surely had to exist.

We cut into the blue. *Ceana*'s stern ripped a tear across the surface. Ahead of her bow the sun rose and shed an alias which sank on an Irish Sea playing at mill ponds. Gangs of freighters were already jostling for position in the outbound traffic lanes, and I throttled down to time my dash across their paths in the gap that offered the most sporting chance. Cosseting my bandaged finger, daintily picking at all the macho paraphernalia which clutter yachts and delight in finding their operator's weak spots, I was glad there was no wind, no pretext for sails nor the work involved in raising and trimming them. A light hand on the tiller was all the effort required.

'Yacht *Curlew*, yacht *Curlew*...' Liverpool coastguard's voice suddenly announced.

I ignored it, lost in an arithmetical problem that was almost beyond my means. Before me lay the heaviest of Wallace's charts. It was backed in canvas and required two hands and a firm footing to slide it six inches. Whereas the modern charts colour land yellow and depths up to ten metres in shades of blue, the older charts use black for everything. Black lines for shores and rivers, dark thumbprints for mountains, dirty slashings for cliffs. Black dots for beaches, underwater shelving and the extended families of major rocks. Trails of hyphens for the ten-fathom line. Old charts are a celebration of detail and plot twice as many spot soundings as are found in the latest reprints. Such a slap-happiness of marks adds shoals of figures to cluster around imitating rocks. Where islands lie along a ragged coast of skerries and beaches, it takes a practised eye to distinguish what is water and what is the hard stuff.

My eye wasn't practised. My route had just traversed a patch of emptiness and entered the severest intensity of blacks. Off Port Dandy I strained to spot a poser + or * among the crowd of 3, 5, 7, 6, 6, 4, 5. Someone, at some time, had mooched about this area lowering a lead-line every few yards, logging the depth, adjusting the figure according to the state of the tide, and plotting its position through a triangulation of compass sightings. This chart was a Herculean achievement of patience and precision. For all that, it was damn hard to read. I understood then the apocryphal story of the navigator plotting his position and turning to the skipper, tapping the chart and pronouncing grimly 'either it's flyshit, or we're in deep trouble'.

Despite the sea's collapse into lethargy, it forced itself into a trot at the entrance to Donaghadee Sound. My course involved a dogleg through the greatest concentration of soundings yet, pencilled annotations, a rubber's smear, flyshit, numerous * (rocks which never dry) and Rid Rk +, Bush Rk + and, most alarmingly, Governor Rks ++++++. I cast eyes over my instruments and took a few compass bearings, but it was only when I tried to work out the magnetic variation that I realised this chart wasn't old, it was antediluvian. There in miniscule copperplate was the someone who had mooched here – *Surveyed by Comm^R R. B. Beechey, R.N., as-*

sisted by Lieut A. G. Edye & MR A. B. Usbourne, Master R.N. – and his mooching date: *1853, updated 1915.*

'Yacht *Weasel*, yacht *Weasel*... '

I pricked my ears at this unlikely grouping in a matter of minutes, but returned to the problem in hand. At any point on the globe there is a variation between the direction of True North and the reading a compass will give - Magnetic North. An exception to this is if you happen to be standing on the North Magnetic Pole, a point which wanders about and is currently near Ellef Ringnes Island in Canada's frozen Arctic Ocean. Here a compass becomes lost. For centuries Magnetic North has loitered to the west of True North but the difference is decreasing by about ten minutes a year and in 2046 (at this particular location in the Irish Sea) the two will briefly equate, before Magnetic North continues on its eastwards slide.

In keeping with all things nautical, the variation is slightly different at every spot on the planet, so each nautical chart plots the specific variation at several points across the area covered. For my current position the chart showed a variation of eighteen degrees and twenty minutes west (1915), decreasing by nine minutes annually. Thus I had almost a century of nine-minute annual increments to convert into degrees.

In my youth blackboard dusters were regularly thrown at me by a Mr Wilkin who confused his inability to teach arithmetic with my inability to understand it. Somehow I missed out on long division and never recovered the loss. Thus my schooling had not adequately prepared me for following Comm^R R. B. Beechey's recommended route past Governor Rks and through Donaghadee Sound. But there – bless the Commissioners of Irish Lights! – were red and green buoys to mark the passage. I swung the tiller round, watched the rudder shed a trail of capering eddies and raised the binoculars to check that *Ceana*'s bow was now aligned on the next mark. Beyond lay Ardglass, a harbour littered with rocks, more like a quarry bitten out of the coast. I rolled in on a burst of surf and rounded a breakwater where fishing boats were gathered in gossipy huddles. I considered joining them for a free night but they are notorious for keeping unsociable hours and using yachts as fenders, so I moved to the adjacent marina. Even 3.5 knots proved too fast as I swung *Ceana*'s bow round sharply and headed for a semi-vacant berth.

'Can't stop', I yelled, realising reverse gear had failed and I was brakeless once more. 'Fend me off!'

Considering the ruination of *Celtic Rival*'s cocktails, her crew of two were magnificent. A G&T was sacrificed as the owner braced himself to protect his hull, and his wife, rooted to the spot in shock, happened to be in the perfect position to catch my warp.

By chance, my neighbour on the other side was Robbie. He'd arrived that day from Workington in an ex-oilrig lifeboat, a twenty-foot long orange peapod containing a generator, washing machine, tumble drier, oxy-acetylene kit and industrial lathe. He was an engineer and fixed my problem in five minutes. I cracked open beers and threw a celebratory party. *Celtic Rival* declined to attend.

That night Force Eights prowled the Irish Sea, and scarcely let up for three days. Perfect weather for Castle Ward, twenty miles distant, a monument to strife of the matrimonial kind.

Castle Ward

blarney *noun*. cajoling talk, flattery. *verb*. to beguile with flattery. p.p. **blarneyed**. - **blarney-land** Ireland [from the belief that bewitching eloquence is bestowed on those who kiss a certain stone at Blarney Castle, near Cork].

There are two notable castles in blarney-land where the gift of persuasive talk failed. In 1636 Anastasia Archdeacon (*née* Gould) planned a surprise for her husband who was abroad for several years while serving with the Spanish army. He'd left her in charge of their estate, five miles south of Cork. What was a paddock on his departure was a castle on his return. Monkstown Castle, also known as Castle Mahon, is a fortress set within four towers and is now regarded as one of the finest examples of the seventeenth century great-gabled house. Her husband was outraged at her extravagance and accused her of mismanagement. Anastasia triumphantly produced the accounts which showed that, because she'd insisted on being the sole supplier of food and clothing to the workforce and struck a particularly advantageous bargain, the net cost of the project was precisely one penny. Captain Archdeacon was not to be appeased and, miffed by her success, he never forgave her.

Castle Ward is the other. I changed into my kilt and hitchhiked to the edge of Strangford Lough. The road was a low rollercoaster choked by hawthorn blossom. Each time the van I was riding in mounted a rise and became airborne for a second I could see folds of green pasture ahead, boxed and yet empty, the promised land for some herd or flock yet to arrive. Castle Ward reared out of its demesne (a peculiarly Irish word and relic of the Normans, meaning the private policies of a large house) at the end of a long drive. A queue had formed at the side entrance and I joined Brad and Meryl from Wisconsin. It seemed every other couple were from America.

'It's the Eerack thing', Meryl explained. 'We don't feel too safe going many places now. We were kinda worried even coming here.'

'But ah think it's right what our boys are doin', Brad added. 'That Saddam's a monster.'

I didn't feel like debating the Iraq *débâcle* and turned to an information board where I read about the wife of the 3rd Viscount Bangor, 'known in family terms as "the Extinguisher" for her withering demeanour'. The tour was led by none other than the Extinguisher herself, though her badge named her as Margaret Denny.

'Castle Ward was built by Bernard and Anne Ward in 1760. He was an MP for County Down and was rewarded with the title of Baron Bangor, later Viscount. He'd … I'll tell you once, and once only, ladies and gentlemen, *NOT* to touch any of the exhibits or furnishings' – and Brad froze, shot between the eyes, as his finger traced a relief whorl in the wallpaper – '…inherited the estate and family lead mining fortune. Lady Anne had her own money and brought ten thousand pounds into the marriage…'

This last was a pertinent fact because it gave Lady Anne power. When it came to designing their new house, they couldn't agree. Bernard favoured the classical look. Anne considered that frowsty and passé. Smitten by the sharp spiky angles of Horace Walpole's home on Strawberry Hill in London, she was hell-bent on Gothick. Neither would yield, so they split the plan down the middle. Everything on the sunny south side of the building's centreline, from foundation to roof peak, inside and out, would be his; Classical. Everything north of the centreline, the view side, from roof peak to foundation, inside and out, would be hers; Strawberry Gothick.

'The house was once described as a mixture of, and I quote, "English stiffness and Irish good nature".'

At first our horizon was of rectangular sash and case, low relief stuccos of cherubs, oak panelling and faux doors whose sole function was symmetry. Then we passed through a rectangular door, and two feet later – crossing the great divide – another door only this time a peaked arch. In the realm of Irish good nature the windows were lancet with lozenges of glass divided by lead. The oak panelling had been painted blue. No little cherubs here but a violin, a straw sombrero, a basket of flowers – the real things – which had been dipped in plaster and fixed to the wall. Above us was a ribbed, vaulted ceiling which reminded me of a fleet of hot air balloons, but Betjemen caught it better: 'like living under cow's udders'.

I can't remember who had the cases of stuffed birds of paradise, Bernard or Anne, but they probably now outnumber those found today in Papua New Guinea, or the ten red squirrels, two to a case, each wearing striped shorts and gloves, each a cartoon sequence of a boxing match from the initial courtesy contact to the loser lying felled on the floor, but it was probably Anne. Part of the problem was the Extinguisher's pacemaker. It was on fast. 'Bad heart, I'm afraid', she explained, directing us up the servants stairs while she disappeared into a secret lift, materialising hale and hearty to greet the first breathless arrivals and rush us round the next room. Some of Brad and Meryl's compatriots were equally as old as the Extinguisher and several looked less robust, but they were never offered the secret lifts. Still, they would have been well insured, one would imagine.

Of course, the inevitable happened. Neo-classical and Strawberry Gothick are incompatible. Atriums don't go with udders. English viscounts blow Irish livewires' fuses. Bernard and Anne parted shortly after the house was finished though they never divorced. She retired to the spas of Bath and he remained in his half of the house.

Their eldest son, Nicholas, was classified as a lunatic and the youngest son, Robert, devoted much time to preparing booby traps to kill him. He forced Nicholas to make a winter journey in a carriage he'd meticulously soaked with water the night before in the hope of inducing pneumonia. He removed a manhole cover on one of Nicholas's favourite walks but to no avail and, undoubtedly his best effort, weakened the banisters outside his eldest brother's bedroom. Unfortunately a footman leaned on them first and fell three floors to his death. After that Robert gave up and resumed his career as colonel of the local militia. The fifth viscount married off his daughter, Bertha, in exchange for a stuffed Russian black bear he wanted for the hall where it was installed with a tray held out to receive visiting cards. (With hindsight, the aureoles and squirrels were probably his). His wife, Mary, was a respected scientist and illustrator, and needed no further distinction, but her untimely death in 1869 accorded her one. On that day she was riding a mobile steam contraption built by her cousin when she slipped and fell under the wheel, thus becoming the world's first recorded car accident fatality.

Partition, divided interests, murder plots, stuffed history, charm and eccentricity; it was all terribly iconic of Ireland herself.

Dublin

When Joshua Slocum became the first person to circumnavigate the world alone in 1898, he had no autohelm, no Global Positioning System, no engine, no radio, no self-tailing winches, not even a jam cleat to secure a rope with a single-handed tug. He relied on sextant, knots and fifty years' seamanship. This was an awesome achievement at the time but it appears all the more so now, viewed from a modern yacht choc-a-bloc with electronic aids and hi-tech 'essentials'. In his longest run of 2700 miles from Thursday Island to the Keeling Cocos Islands, his sail trim was so perfect he only had to lay hands on the tiller 'for about an hour'.

'It was a delightful midsummer sail', he continues breezily in *Sailing Alone Around the World*. 'No one can know the pleasure of sailing free over the great oceans save those who have had the experience…there was a great deal of fun in it.'

My own voyage, I reflected, wasn't going quite so well. After two weeks at sea I was still too green to believe I could cope, too distrustful of my boat, too tyrannised by a fear of ++++++ and the weather to open myself to the pleasure of sailing free. Each morning I'd wake up with my stomach a tangle of anxiety. Wind, tide, waves, storm, malfunction, miscalculation, Man Overboard… my mind invented headlines constantly. 'Sailor Missing Off Ardglass.' 'Yachtsman Feared Dead.' 'Buoy Sinks Yacht Man Rescued.' Even on calm days, the calmest of days, I worried ('Tanker Collision – Exclusive Pictures').

Then I would try to hide in Joyce. I was approaching his forsaken home.

* * *

I arrived in Dublin on the sixteenth of June, a bloodhot godfrying priestparching day makingyou think of drinkanddrinkanddrink and. Bloomsday.

Things weren't going well between me and Joyce. True, his imagery was electrifying. His abuse of grammar was invigorating. His stream of consciousness style was decades ahead of its time. But why so much of it, why so boarskullhard to read? I found myself skipping chunks of *Ulysses* twenty pages at a time with no loss to the plot, or more accurately, still searching for one. My edition of *Ulysses* has 702 pages. By page four hundred, the hero, Leopold Bloom, has been to the pub, attended a funeral, bought threepence worth of kidney and masturbated. I grant you that this could be considered quite a busy schedule considering the entire story is of one day in the life of Bloom, but dragged out over *four hundred* pages? Yet *Ulysses* is considered 'one of the greatest and most celebrated works in modern literature'.

Joyce was born in Dublin in 1882 but grew to detest Ireland as a claustrophobic hell of suppression, tedium and Catholic zealotry. Like W B Yeats, J M Synge and other contemporary Irish writers, he moved to Paris and joined the bohemian set. He returned to Ireland once, to bury his mother and elope with a Galway chambermaid, whom he married in London twenty-seven years later. Nora Barnacle was to require all the tenacity suggested by her unusual name in their subsequent wanderings across Europe.

Joyce wrote *Ulysses* over seven years in Zurich, Paris and Trieste, finishing it in 1917. The work was considered base and obscene, its characters obsessed with sex, its descriptions of bodily functions (the two pages on Bloom's bowel movements, for example) shockingly explicit. His battles against the censors lasted fourteen years. The breakthrough came in 1933 when the ban in the United States was overturned. Random House rushed the book through its presses and sold 33,000 copies in ten weeks. *Ulysses* was now adjudged as emetic rather than aphrodisiac, revolting rather than contaminating. By this time Joyce was already riding high on the accolades of his other works.

His literary success was not reflected in his personal life. The tragic derangement of his daughter, who was to spend more than forty years in institutions for the insane, was the family's most closely-guarded secret. Lucia Joyce grew into a tall striking woman with dark hair and predatory blue eyes. Joyce was fascinated by her imagination and considered her a 'blocked genius'. Gradually he became disturbed by her promiscuity which soon developed into a complete lack of sexual boundaries. What appears to have tipped Lucia over the edge into mania and violence was her failed seduction of the man she became infatuated with, Samuel Beckett. She was diagnosed as suffering from a form of schizophrenia called 'hebephrenia' which is characterised by extremes of 'adolescent-type' behaviour.

By the time Lucia reached her late twenties, the family could no longer cope. She was in a mental hospital in Brittany when war broke out. The Joyces fled to Zurich, leaving their daughter behind to her fate at the hands of the Germans. The hospital was allowed to continue its work and Lucia remained in occupied France during the war, being transferred to Zurich when it ended. By then Joyce had died, in 1941, and her mother chose not to resume contact. On Nora's death in 1951, Lucia was moved to St Andrews Hospital in England. She died there in 1982, aged seventy-five.

* * *

There was in Dublin, I was told, a Joycean Society, where a group of acolytes met each week to analyse a few paragraphs of the master's works. I felt I had to track them down. They were hard to find. Bloomsday, the anniversary of James and Nora's first date, did not set Dublin alight but glowed in a scattering of corners where readings were staged, breakfasts were taken in period costume and an unusually large group of elderly, walrusy men went bathing at Sandycove where the novel begins. Eventually I found them one evening in a splendour of Georgian bricks on North Great George's Street. Here were doors flanked by white pillars and fan windows, and wrought iron balconies suggesting that Dublin's climate might sometimes permit people to sit out and enjoy them. Fifty yards down the street it was a seedier world of rubbish and street dealings. Paddy's Pets, Parnell Blinds and Kane's Wallpapers were losing ground to Alilang Korean Restaurant, the Bollywood Takeaway and Lithuanian/Russian Hairdresser Kirpykla. Chinese signs proliferated and dingy doors offered cut-price international phone calls and instant loans.

I pulled the brass door knob of number thirty-five and the entire mechanism came away in my hand. A wino climbed up from the basement, scaled the spiked railings and landed by my side. He was in the process of asking for money when the key holder strode up in a great coat and chased him away.

'You're most welcome', he said, and led me upstairs to a room with filigree plasterwork as delicate as snowflakes. The author stared down from several portraits and his name was a repetitive stutter in glass-fronted bookcases.

People gradually arrived, a dozen in all split equally between the sexes, aged between fifty and seventy. For the most part a tweed and cashmere set who I imagined lectured at Trinity, ran Dublin's museums or were married to the Mercedes franchise. The exception was called Robert, a thirty-year-old with shoulder-length blond hair and studious, Lennon glasses. We sat around a mahogany table where two lamps were raised endearingly on piles of books; one gained its four inches on *The Dubliners*, *Finnegan's Wake* and a couple of analytical works, and the other on Volumes 1-3 of a critique on *Ulysses*.

I whispered to Robert: 'Are you all academics?'

'Good God, no! We're just ordinary folk. I'm a trade unionist, seconded at present from my usual job as a tax collector. Just imagine how well I go down at cocktail parties – trade unionist, taxman *and* Joyce devotee!' His laugh was rich and earthy. 'We just admire him and want to get the most out of his works.'

'How long has the group been going?'

'It started in the eighties. Sometimes twenty turn up but it depends what we're reading. It's always less for the *Wake*.' He smiled. 'Took us seven years to get through it last time!'

Everyone opened books. To my embarrassment I realised I'd forgotten my copy of *Ulysses.* 'I'm sure we can lend you one', the Chair said reassuringly, and there was a flurry of activity around the bookcases. After a long hunt a blank was drawn.

'We can do it in Japanese or German', a woman explained, 'but not English, it seems.'

'The Japanese *love* Joyce', said another. 'I don't know why. I don't see how anyone could translate Joyce into *any* other language!'

'The Italians love him too', a man added. 'But not the French. But then the French don't like anything that's not French.'

At last an English copy was produced. They had covered roughly one-third and had reached two pages of non-sequitors, nonsense and words compacted into pile-ups. We read these pages to ourselves and then took a line in turn and read it out loud. A discussion followed in which it was revealed that each line was a phrase lifted from a subsequent passage and gathered not for sense but rhythmical effect.

It's like an orchestra tuning up, someone said.

Or an overture. Verdi uses exactly the same technique.

It's like a plane taxiing before take off.

We took turns reading again, each voice now an instrument in the orchestra. We'd recognise our parts later when the fragments of tune became a story. When the story comes they trace Bloom's movements through contemporary Dublin. None of the pubs are still going except The Clarence. They debate whether the Jewish and Italian shops are Joyce's fiction. No, the Italian ice cream and chip parlours were there in his time. What about this term 'wink the other eye'? It came, we are told, from a popular ribald song of the time. Everything is analysed and given relevance or meaning. In a quiet moment I make my only contribution.

'Somewhere Joyce says that barbed wire was invented by a

nun. Is it true?'

Within seconds someone has found the quote, one line in a book of seven hundred pages. Chair consults a tome, Gifford's standard interpretation. The last word on every word. No, we conclude, it is not true. Barbed wire was patented in 1874 in the United States by Joseph Glidden. No mention of a nun. Does it matter? No. The possibility is a grotesque delight.

In an hour and a half we covered six pages. Then we retired to Groomes Bar for a pint. I was so blitzed I could scarcely utter a word. I realised I'd missed the point with Joyce. In looking for a good storyteller I'd settled on the wrong man.

'The brilliance of *Ulysses* is the richness of language and the inventiveness of technique', Robert concluded. 'It has to be. God knows, it's not a thriller!'

* * *

I tried to relax in Dublin but the city's pace was relentless, like being trapped on a choppy sea. Not even the glassfibre cows which had taken up residence at strategic spots could placate the furore of the traffic. It was quieter in the pedestrianised Temple Bar, the city's 'Cultural Quarter', where the fragrance of coffee wafted among vendors squeezing carrots, picnicking backpackers, mime artists and buskers; but there was a corrosive background sound, the persistent rustle and chink of tourist euros slipping from fingers. Foreign earnings evaporated in the hip-heat of the place.

Away from the centre I made the mistake of touring Kilmainham Gaol, a pre-independence bastille for political dissidents and an inevitable depressant which made me want to apologise for being British and still alive. It was during the Guinness tour when half-stoned on statistics – 'sold in 150 countries...ten million glasses daily...thirty-one Irish pubs in Berlin...the biggest bevviers outside Ireland? The Spanish...' – that I realised I was in the wrong place again. Where I should have been was in the queue for the Book of Kells.

* * *

It's not a big book, thirteen inches by nine. Once it had 710 pages but thirty beginning and end folios have been lost, probably stolen, and the remaining pages were rebound into four volumes in 1953. Four monks created it on Iona between the seventh and ninth centuries, each taking one of the gospels in Latin and copying it in a distinctive hand and style. It is one of the oldest pieces of writing extant in the world and is classified as an 'illuminated' manuscript. Colours radiate with the brightness of slides. Dazzling creatures stalk the pages and steal the show. Clearly the monks had time to let celibate imaginations run riot. A mixture of fear, devotion and the exuberance of the *bon viveur* fills the pages. Perhaps we've the pagans to thank for that. In order to win them over the ascetic Christians adopted and adapted their festivals. It was not simply a one-way exchange and some of the epicurean's delight and colour infiltrated the new order. The Christians took the image of that most primitive of deities, the sun, and superimposed it on their own symbol to produce the celtic cross. It's believed they also followed the patterns of pagan dances and converted them into the basic swirls of their art and knotwork – an intriguing though not wholly convincing theory.

The monks appear to have been weak negotiators and some of the one hundred and eighty-five calf skins they used in making the book were clearly substandard. Their quills came from geese and swans, and their brushes from the fur of pine martin. For ink they relied on the female gall wasp and the 'oak apples' she produces. When the wasp injects her eggs into an oak shoot, a spongy gall of black dye forms on the tree. This was mixed with a medium of gum and water and was vastly superior to the alternative, lamp soot in the same medium, which adhered poorly.

The monks had to be careful not to absentmindedly suck the ends of their brushes for many of the pigments were lethal. Before them they would spread an array of powders and a dish of egg whites as a binding agent, mixing the colours as required. They bore testimony to an impressive global economy. Blue came from lapis lazuli and the world's only known source at the time was a remote mine in northeast Afghanistan. Yellow was orpiment, highly toxic arsenic sulphate. White lead or chalk produced white, copper yielded green and red lead one of two shades of red. The other, kermes red, came from the crushed bodies of a pregnant Mediterranean insect, *kermoccus vermilo*.

For most of its life the Book of Kells has been a fugitive: in 804, running from Iona and the accursed Vikings to the monastery of Kells, County Meath; being stolen and buried in a bog for three months in 1007; evading pillage by Cromwell's troops in 1654 and finding sanctuary in Dublin's Trinity College. Which is where I found it. Such was the pressure of people behind me that I was only able to lean over it for a minute. It was enough. I can see those colours still.

Arklow

I awoke in the night with a start. Lying on my coffin-shaped bunk I listened to the wind rampage through Howth marina, sounding like a low-flying Tornado, thrumming a thousand halyards. *CLANK CLANKclankclankCLANK CLANK...* Marinas are, of course, ideal amplifiers to make a casual breeze sound ferocious, but this was no breeze. I switched on the anemometer and '20 knots' glowed in neon red. In the shelter of the marina! It was 3am. I concentrated on the racket. Underground trains were now rushing past, car brakes were squealing, an Indonesian gamelan band had struck up on the port quarter. I could hear growling dogs, whiplashing, water rollicking down a chasm, the shrieks and squeals of playgrounds. For ingenuity of intimidation, it was some performance.

4am. The show ended. 'Small boat warning, westerly 6, occasionally 7.' Twenty minutes later I was easing *Ceana* out of her bay of lamplight.

'Where are you bound for?' The voice belonged to an insomniac drinking coffee at his stern, holding a mug in three remaining fingers. For a moment I thought it was *Ceana*'s old owner.

'Arklow.' I noticed a dog beside him, a Jack Russell in harness. 'How does your dog like sailing?' I asked, hoping he wouldn't tell me about his hand.

'Fine. Won't pee on board though. Have to limit my routes to short dog-legs.' His accent came from the Dales. 'Don't cross the banks. Stay inside or outside them, but don't cross them. And look out for salmon nets. Like trip wires all over the place.'

I waved thanks and headed off, hearing him call one last time, 'Remember, don't cross the banks...' before his voice was consumed by the throb of fishing boats queuing at the harbour narrows as the first hint of dawn coloured the horizon.

Bent under two reefs *Ceana* swept along at eight knots, cutting a V through the boisterous Irish Sea with all the confidence I was lacking. This, I had long ago determined, was man's optimum speed. It was the pace of the long-distance horse-rider, dog-sledder and cyclist. It synchronised with our nomadic biorhythm and soothed our soul. Eight knots. Ten miles an hour. Slow enough to observe and think, fast enough to cover ground and obviate tedium.

Perfect.

I soon overhauled Ireland's Eye. It's a curiously-named island, a corruption of Irelandsey (the suffixes -ay, -ey and -ea are Viking or Saxon words for 'island', as in Lambay, Guernsey, Chelsea) with nothing to backup its declared self-importance. I left it behind along with its larger neighbour, Lambay, another great unknown though many Second World War servicemen and women should thank or curse it for its omelettes. Every season 60,000 seabird eggs were sold to Britain from this island alone, and an equal number from Rathlin. Lambay's were considered superior, less fishy as the gulls mixed their diet with pickings from Dublin's dumps.

To my right Dublin Bay opened, revealing Joyce's Martello tower at Sandycove as a splinter in urban sprawl. Dirty mopheads of cloud moved in partially cloaking the land which was rallying itself in preparation for becoming the Wicklow Mountains. Beyond Bray a conical volcano rose out of scree to a summit of pink granite. The Great Sugar Loaf (500m), I guessed, but there was no shortage of possibilities with Prince William's Seat, Fairy Castle, Two Rock Mountain and War Hill lurking in the vicinity. Lime and leek greens mingled on their lower slopes, giving way occasionally to yellow slashes of cut silage, too gaudy to be real, more like orpiment from a monk's brush. Then appeared the first of the caravan sites that were to exclaim 'ПППППППП…ПППППППП' at regular intervals. 'BEACH!' in the language of banality. It was only when I noticed the streets of old Wicklow gathered in a fold in the hills and compared them with the housing estates on either side, that it struck me where the planning authorities were going wrong. Old Wicklow was wood, New Wicklow was desert. Why was there no regulation that made avenues of trees mandatory in all new housing developments and caravan sites? It seemed such simple and cheap therapy.

I chose to go inside the banks. They lie a few miles offshore where you'd expect the sea to be sixty metres deep. But Kish Bank, followed by Bray, Codling, India and the twelve-mile long Arklow Bank are rogue bits of sand posing as water. Over them the depth drops to one or two metres. The backbone of the Arklow dries out. In calm weather they disappear and suddenly snag your keel. In an hour you can be high and dry. In bad weather they turn to cauldrons of surf. The tides are wholly complicit. In ebb and flow they set against the shallows and pull or push you in. They have their own little quirk on this stretch of coastline, flooding simultaneously from the north and the south, then heading east towards the Bristol Channel and then ebbing simultaneously to the north and south. They are not particularly strong but at any stage of their routines they endeavour to feed you to the banks.

Ahead twenty-eight trawlers interwove their wakes as they ploughed a particular patch of the seabed, the particular patch that marked my safe passage between shallows. Several times I had to pull the tiller sharply round when one broke out of the pack and threatened to block my way. As they were men-at-work and I was man-at-play it was up to me to steer clear but their movements were as anarchic as bagatelle balls. They were Greencastle and Derry boats dredging seed mussels in an intense three-month season, offloading them each evening in Arklow. From there they would be trucked north to Lough Foyle, returned to the sea for two years' maturation in logged sites, then dredged up for the second time in their lives and sold to France. Little did I suspect at the time that it would be this cycle that would take Ceana into a head-on with a mussel boat.

I fiddled with compass and dividers and made a show of checking my GPS but I couldn't fault it and traced my progress through tracts of white between the danger zones of yellow. Numbers flickered on the depth gauge and confirmed my position on the chart. Things were going splendidly and I was able to nurse my charge through the hazards to a monolithic factory which marked the entrance to Arklow harbour. I'd covered forty miles and notched up another survival. It was shortly after breakfast.

Arklow's two shopping streets ran uphill and ended in fields, thereby connecting the two industries in which it dabbled. They had been designed to provide farmers with Guinness every two hundred yards (seven pubs) in-between filling a shopping bag with fish hooks, fertiliser, food, clothes and gravestones.

'Sure it's a fine car that', remarked an old man with a bicycle that looked even older. His gaze was fixed on a softly-humming blue Porsche Carera. I stopped, charmed by the Irish informality with strangers, and struggled to interpret what some regard as the least attractive Irish accent. It appeared to bounce over potholes from deep in the throat. 'D'you tink it ud be de petrol or de diesel?'

'I think it would be the petrol.' In the accent of starched linen.

'And it wudn't be havin uny problem wid gettin to suvunty, now, wud it?'

'No problem at all, I imagine!'

'De trouble is, we're not havin de roads to muck the use o it.'

He pondered the dream machine anew. 'Well, tanks a million, boy!', and off he set pushing his bicycle, smiling broadly.

The greengrocer's was run by two brothers close to retirement age and closer to God.

'Yer most welcome here, so y'are, God's mercy on you', greeted one.

'Are ye enjoyin the lovely weather, bless God?' asked the other.

'We haven't had too many like this, God be praised.'

It was shortly before closing time and they were off to swim in the sea, a fitness thing they did every day. Their closing time was flexible, depending on late shoppers. ('What's half an hour here or there, praise God'). They threw in an extra orange with my order and advised on the best bananas.

'Now these are lovely sweet, bless God.'

'But these are bigger an a bit cheaper, thanks be to God.'

So I bought twice as much fruit as I'd intended and departed with a thousand blessings. Added to my million thanks this seemed a lucrative tally for my first twenty minutes in town.

I steered clear of The Four Seasons Floral and Headstone Centre but lingered long enough to note that headstones were available from fifty euros upwards. Scanning concentrated sentimentality soon became unbearable. Feeling wretched I scribbled down the epitaph carved on the chest of a pink stone teddy bear - *A daughter is a special gift / One that's meant to stay / Our hearts broke in two / When God took you away / Mummy & Daddy* - and fled to the newsagent's.

The *Wicklow Times* summarised the state of the nation. Inflation was rampant. Civil servants' salaries were lagging far behind sprinting prices and a promised pay rise had been postponed indefinitely. Dublin's 'rip-off prices' were a disgrace many feared would cripple the whole country's tourist industry; in a pub in Temple Bar two Wicklow girls had been charged €9 for mineral waters with a dash of blackcurrant. Sister Stanislaw Kennedy, a leading social activist, was speaking out for women who, she believed, still bore the brunt of Ireland's poverty. Much followed about the latest motorcycle accidents (three a week seemed to be the norm), and Arklow's determination to find funds for a fulltime litter warden and a skateboard park. Advance warning of Tir Nan Og Primary School's open day was given prominence and a three-page spread suggested ideas for giving homes a revamp (attic conversion, paint colours, weary kitchens). A single paragraph informed that the subjugation of Iraq was going well.

On the edge of town I hitched a lift to Bunclody. The driver was Aemon McLarity, a civil servant driving forty miles to pay to have his old car oil recycled.

'We're not seeing many of those skirts around here', Aemon remarked.

Around Glendalough the road twisted through drystane dykes of epic proportions. On and on they went, uniform jigsaws of granite, their neatness and repair too consistent to be other than products of policy and grant. Remove the Friesians, the odd droopy-eared sheep and paunchy pony, and I might have been in the land of the Incas. It was hard to imagine how anyone could have found the vision and motivation to create fields when confronted by so much stone, though clearly walls were the only sensible thing to do with it. Yet their pride contrasted with the run-down farms at their centres. Small, shambolic buildings surrounded by mud baths stood as symbols of the hard graft that was excluded from the Celtic Tiger's prosperity.

'The IRA's always been big around Wexford and Enniscorthy', Aemon remarked, even though these places were a little to the south. 'Kneecapped a lad last week. Drugs. Not that they're anti-drugs, you understand? No. They just don't take kindly to any competition to their own dealers.'

A shotgun to the back of the knee. I assumed that was synonymous with amputation. Done in some anonymous lane among hedgerows, such as these before me. And did the perpetrators leave their victim to drag a trail of blood in the quest for help, or did they play the Samaritan and call an ambulance? And how, I wondered, did they conscript knee-cappers? How did they sell the idea of pulling the trigger? I didn't care to dwell on those thoughts. Instead I concentrated on the view. But now our descent was through hedges bloated by the unconfessed events that had taken place behind them and glades of broadleaf dark with suspicion. Even the redolence of honeysuckle and elderflower which assailed us at intervals was now tainted with treachery. I thought of limps. Of Sir Walter Scott limping (as a legacy of polio, not kneecapping) this way in 1825 heading to Glendalough on a whimsical pilgrimage to sleep in 'St Kevin's Bed', a remote cave used by the saint in the sixth century. He found it intolerable but his visit helped launch Glendalough as a tourist destination.

We limped – the car was playing up – into the hamlet of Shillelagh, little more than a spraggle of terraced houses on a bend of the road, but immortal as the origin of Ireland's primitive war club. I expected to find a dozen shops dangling black mallets over their doorways, but there appeared to be only one window in Shillelagh which offered the goods, and to the exclusion of all else. They were small, substandard affairs barely strong-enough to brain a trout, and the shop looked permanently closed. Clearly Ireland's enemies had shrunk, then the shotgun had arrived.

'Bunclody Welcomes Burkina Faso'

Burkina Faso's flag was everywhere. It rippled as bunting over the stream which tumbled down the main street in crafted cascades. It fluttered in the trees of the village square. Red and green stripes plastered windows and lampposts. If you came from Ouagadougou and entered a Bunclody shop, you passed through a halo of your home colours and couldn't fail to be reminded of your equatorial roots. The Special Olympics were on, and Ireland had designated villages within commuting distance of Dublin to be hosts to specific countries. Wexford had drawn Poland. Roscommon had got Uganda. Burkina Faso must have seemed a natural choice for Bunclody.

I wondered what Burkina Fasons made of the place. Its stone bungalows stood rooted in permanence, apparently immune to time. Its streets were the preserve of neatness and peace. Bustle would be an offence here, noise a heresy and to chase a ball along a pavement, I imagined, would provoke a reprimand for endangering the shuffling lanes of door-to-door domestic routines. Clean water flowed into Bunclody and out of Bunclody, unmolested, uncontaminated, for its visual effect, for the pleasure of its company. Then beyond the last house extended undulating fields where stock lived the lives of Reilly, pampered to excess. No mosquitoes, scorpions or snakes in Bunclody. There again, not much sun either.

There were no Burkina Fasons in the place that day. They were all in Dublin at the Gaelic Athletic Association's prime venue, Croagh Park, for the opening ceremony. I watched the celebration in a pub committing both heresy and offence. Loud, rowdy, mobbed. Mafia-styled bouncers guarded the door. Maybe in other personae they were knee-cappers. People crushed round tables and stood jamming the aisles. Handfuls of drinks were raised like Olympic torches as their owners wormed passages back to their friends. Liquid sloshed down sleeves and over shoulders. The smoke screen only thinned at groin level. I found a perch in a corner and resigned myself to being wedged in for the evening, and forced to eavesdrop.

'...and there was Sean, he went in that car accident, and John, can't remember what took him...in fact, when you tink on it, of the tree of em, there's only Paddy Anderson left on his feet...'

'...can't get no railway sleepers nowadays, sold em all to England in the footanmouth. Got to buy em, *buy* em, you hear, from bloody Poland...'

Above me a TV screen glowed brightly then dimly through the murk. The Burkina Fasons were parading round the track waving their flag at 75,000 spectators whose colours hurt the eye. Seven thousand athletes from one hundred and sixty countries were taking part. It was the first time the event had been staged outside the USA. When the parade was over, rock stars U2 took to the stage and *In the Name of Love* swept the arena, led by Bono who looked bluebottle-ish in tinted shades. He left the stage before the song ended and returned leading a small, frail, white-haired, black man.

That evening there were two moments when The Gin Mill went silent and all faces turned to the screens. The first was when Nelson Mandela started to speak. The second was not when Bertie Ahern followed; no one gave a damn about the sheaf of notes he laboured through. No, the noise only began to go down when a posse of Greeks trotted in with the torch. Voices fell away as it was passed in turn from Uzbekistanis, Ivory Coasters, Chinese, Americans and El Salvadorans. Suddenly all was quiet. Everyone in the pub seemed to be holding their breath. Ten-year-old David McCauley now had the torch and was a lone figure mounting the steps. No one in the room moved. The boy lent forward and held out his arm. Nothing. You could hear Ireland holding her breath. Then a flame leapt high into the summer sky and The Gin Mill erupted.

When the cheers died down: '...bloody charade...'

'...and d'you have any idea what it's costing...?'

'...millions...the hypocrites...it's cost millions. And what's Ireland ever done for her own special needs people? Fook all. Fook all, I tell ya. Bloody charade.'

The Greatest
Sailing Feat in Ireland

≈

Tommy Doolan, Commodore of the Wexford Cruising Club, put it on the line. His moustache outlined each word in boldface. 'There are two great sailing feats in Irish waters. The first is to enter Wexford.'

I'd met him the previous day for advice on how to do this, without realising the magnitude of the undertaking. He described twenty-eight dog-legs through sandbars on a five-mile route which had to be started at a precise time and completed within ninety minutes to make safe use of the tide. Now I was approaching that crucial time. An hour earlier I'd reduced sail to creep across the only gap in the shallows, the Rusk Channel, which went down to 2.4 metres despite being two miles offshore. To my left was Moneyweights Bank and ahead, Lucifer Bank. Patches of uniformly textured water were broken all around by islands of surf. Nervously I looked for landmarks which might offer a cocked hat of bearings but the coast was a belt of coniferous green, so low and featureless it might have been heaped seaweed. The sea slapped *Ceana*'s hull and set in motion a chortle which ran the length of the boat, and intrigued two immature gannets in grey worsted. Above them clouds were twisting themselves into noodles. The whole world was warped.

In 1788 things were very different here. The first attempt to register shipping activities in Ireland shows Wexford had a deep seaway and was a port to rival Waterford in importance, each averaging a turnover of one ship every nine days. It was from Wexford that the *Thames*, a paddle-steamer built in Glasgow, made the first ever motorised crossing of the Irish Sea in 1815, and eventually reached Plymouth. Belching black smoke it caused alarm everywhere it appeared. Two pilot boats and several salvage cutters put out to effect a rescue only to be left trailing in the paddle-steamer's wake. Royal Naval officers at Portsmouth viewed the contraption with amusement, predicting it might be useful as a tug for their men-of-war but beyond that it would have no future. Some time after this the sands shifted, the approaches silted up and Wexford was abandoned.

'When you reach Dogger Bank you should see the first marker buoy. *Don't* turn west towards it until you see the perch on the is-

61

land with the ruins.'

The first marker duly appeared, a sun-bleached orange, but I could see no island with ruins. I took in some of the foresail and scanned the islands through binoculars. I was close to the shore now. There was almost as much sand in view as there was sea. Suddenly ruins appeared and there was the spindly iron pole, the perch. I swung the tiller about and headed for the buoy.

'Stay close to the buoys. Pass within six feet.'

The second buoy lay only a hundred yards away. The depth meter was set to read the clearance below the keel in feet. (When in danger I feel happier in imperial.) '1.8' it now said.

'The second buoy marks the shallowest spot. It's in twenty feet of water but if you stood on it and fell off, you'd hit your head on the bar. *Stay close in!*'

The water was now bright green. Odd stones and clumps of seaweed raced past. They looked about six inches under the surface. Swept forwards by the tide I was going faster than I wanted. Thirty yards away surf was breaking. A frightening sight. And I had to steer straight towards it, not flinch, until I reached that buoy and then turn hard to starboard.

1.4   1.2   1.2   1.1   0.9...

My bow was a boat length from exposed sand when I reached the buoy and executed the turn. My knuckles were white as I gripped the tiller, feeling a slight surge of relief that I was now past the shallowest part. Then my eye turned to the depth gauge.

0.8 0.8 0.7 0.7...

My God! Eight-and-a-half inches of water under the keel! Bail out! ...But how do I turn? ... I need to leave the channel to swing round ... Jesus, what do I do?

'The channel is marked every year because it changes. Those markers can become obsolete overnight. It's a bastard. *It can move anytime.'*

0.7   0.7   0.8   0.8   0.9   1.1   1.1...

When in doubt, do nothing. It was only a fear of worse shallows to either side of me that prevented a hasty retreat. Then a new complication appeared. A crossroads. Rival markers. Appealing because they took a more direct route. Currently I was sailing to Wexford by heading away from it.

'Don't be tempted to follow other buoys. Some fishing boats have laid their own routes, but they may have a smaller draught than you.'

1.4   1.4   1.2   1.1   0.9   1.3...

For an hour and a half there was no respite. Just tense muscles, the immanent expectation of a grating rasp underneath as we came to a sudden stop. Ninety minutes of glancing from depth gauge to buoy, from one horror to another. But eventually I made it.

'And the second great sailing feat in Irish waters?' I asked that evening in the sailing club.

'The second is even harder.' Tommy Doolan leant forward over his pint. His moustache revealed the high water mark of Caffreys. His expression was solemn. 'The second great feat is to leave Wexford.'

* * *

This wasn't new territory to me. When I was twelve my family went on holiday to southern Ireland and we rented a cottage near Wexford. We expected it to be vacant but it wasn't. About fifty sparrows lived in the thatch and not one of them slept beyond 5am. Fortunately that was about as much activity as we experienced in the country. It was 1966. The banks were on strike and caused commerce to seize, setting a pace of life ideal for capture by my Kodak Instamatic. There before me in black and white is a raggle-taggle vendor with donkey and cart. There are road menders, two of them, also with donkey and cart, filling holes with gravel and ladling on tar from a barrel. There are two ladies having a picnic in a baby Austin. Because it commands the best view they are parked on a humpback bridge on what was, and still is, the main R742 Blackwater to Curracloe road. There I am upside-down kissing the Blarney stone. We hardly had to queue. There was no rubbish collection in those days and we didn't know what to do with our accumulation. 'Just throw it behind a hedge', we were told. But we couldn't. Not even as a vague atheist and loose Episcopalians could we despoil a beautiful Catholic land. When the holiday was over we hadn't enough cash left to buy petrol but the Irish never entertained the slightest suspicion of cheques drawn on an obscure Scottish bank.

But that was then, and this was now. I liked Wexford. Partly because you always feel an affinity for a spot you've walked on before, particularly when your feet were forty years younger. I liked its tight grid of streets, and shops avalanching goods over the pavements. As I sat munching fish and chips I enjoyed watching the tide and river Slaney play with moored boats, making them swing like the shadows of sundials, making them strain at their warps as the surface creased around them. I liked being the only visiting yacht in the harbour, and flew my saltire proudly (I'd been advised not to fly the red ensign in Éire – this region in particular was a republican stronghold and the one carrying all the guilt and shame of the Norman invasion). What I didn't like was the group of youths who peered down at me from the parapet of the harbour wall and show-ered empty cans and carry-out cartons onto my deck before bolting. This was the only hint of strife in the world. Not even the Iraq war could touch me here. I almost missed the newspaper report of six soldiers killed in Basra. I dreaded seeing my nephew's name but the coverage was so brief, no details were given. It was not Ire-land's problem. It might have been a political coup in Cameroon for all the relevance it held. It was someone else's ghastly mistake, and I couldn't fault Éire for that. And besides, Wexford had turned mini-Poland as its bit for the Special Olympics.

Perhaps because I should have felt more at home here, I felt even more of a stranger. I strained to recognise the bridge I'd fished from at night all those years ago, hoping for a crab but hooking a conger eel which had taken half an hour to kill with a passer-by's help, but couldn't. No wonder, it had gone. In ten weeks they had demolished and replaced it with a new one, a quarter-of-a-mile long, prefabricated in Holland and lifted into place by Europe's larg-est crane. From barrel and ladle technology to this was some shift.

The Second Greatest
Sailing Feat in Ireland
≈

1.1 0.9 0.7 0.7 0.5 0.5 0.5 0.8 1.1 2.1 2.6 2.9 3.4 3.6...

Whales

39 40 42 41 40 42 41 42. Meters. Out at sea again. Rosslare is behind me. To my left the Tuskar Rock lighthouse rises thirty-three metres, a lonely silhouette against the polished savannah of the ocean. It makes you think: *How audacious to test such a precarious monument against storms! How ingenious to win! But for how long?*

To my right a squad of wind turbines fan lazily on Carnsore Point. An illusion of cavorting triangles is semaphored in the overlap of their blades, and then they move out of alignment and stand as fourteen individuals like so many Mercedes insignia held aloft. I glance behind me and four hundred yards away a black fin is waving. It must be three feet high and flops this way and that. But for the lack of urgency it might be a plea for help. A friend used to call it a 'lolling-about shark', though a more common adage is the 'room-sized monster with the pea-sized brain'. It is the unfortunate ingredient of China's shark fin soup; the enormous, harmless, somewhat dozy, basking shark, cruising along with mouth agape. Twenty tons of water a minute pass through its gills as it sieves plankton. Very little else is known about this shy creature but it is believed to disappear each winter and hibernate in the depths beyond the continental shelf. The one before me sinks, as if its buoyancy has just given up, and is gone without a splash or an eddy or a burp to suggest it was ever there.

Usually one shark or whale sighting must suffice for many days, or even weeks, but today is different. I'm on the edge of two seas, leaving Saint Georges Channel – though I'm always doubtful about cartographers who can't punctuate – and the Celtic Sea, *An Mhuir Cheilteach*. A few minutes later, the same distance away but this time to port, a pod of whales appear. Their dorsal fins are tall and behind them is a sharp downward curve of the back. I think the angle of the dorsal is insufficiently vertical but its size is pretty conclusive. I strain through binoculars to catch the give-away patches of white but these creatures are in no hurry and their undersides remain submerged. I'm convinced they're killer whales. They turn towards me and slip below the surface. Their absence is more threatening than their presence. I hold my breath and wait, but they too have disappeared. Nothing further disturbs the thin plane of my existence.

42 41 42 5.5 5.8 40 5.9 6.0 42 6.3 5.8...

This is unnerving. I take sightings and confirm my position. I'm where I think I am, where I should be. The chart shows clean water averaging forty metres in depth. Why is my sounder occasionally showing the bottom at five or six metres? Sometimes this instrument has fits of madness but only in water whose depth exceeds the range it can read. It has no problem up to eighty metres. It's never done this before. Suddenly I wonder...could the whales be travelling underneath me? Matching my slow speed and weaving about, breaking in and out of the sonar's beam? I peer over the side but can detect no shadow. Yet it's the only logical explanation. I feel a thrill of excitement and more than a little anxiety. Killer whales are among the fasted recorded swimmers, reaching speeds of 35mph. They are also amongst the most intelligent and playful of our fellow mammals. Who knows what games sea creatures play with us?

* * *

In 1843 a pack of killer whales initiated a hunting partnership with the inhabitants of Eden, a whaling township south of Sydney in New South Wales. For the next eighty-seven years the pack gathered in Twofold Bay at the start of each season and led the boats to humpback whales which they would mortally wound. The whalers would finish them off, allow the killers their reward of tongue and lips, the only parts that interested them, before towing the carcasses home. The leader of the pack became known as Old Tom. In 1930 Old Tom's body was washed ashore and the pack never returned.

Despite having killed whales for centuries we still know remarkably little about these leviathans. We know their physical dimensions but even these statistics defy credulity. The blue whale tops the scale at a length of up to 100 feet and a weight of 150 tons. Its heart is the size of a Volkswagen Golf and each pulse pumps ten tons of blood. To dissect the larynx (effectively the vocal chords) of a humpback whale you'd need a chainsaw and a crane. The Southern Right bull has the world's largest testes, each weighing a ton. The head of a mature sperm whale contains 500 gallons of the purest oil, believed to be a mechanism for balancing its equilibrium when it dives, which it does to flamboyant excess. In 1991 a bull sperm whale was recorded at a depth of 6500 feet off the Caribbean island of Dominica in a dive lasting one hour and thirteen minutes.

Hydrophones dipped at almost any point in the ocean are filled with the constant calling of whales. Depending on the species, whales produce sounds in three distinct ranges of wavelengths, each determined by the distance the sound is to carry and its purpose. The lowest range is infrasound. These are slabs of rumbling which last about two seconds and are emitted constantly in perfect regularity. They are too low to register in a human ear and must be raised in pitch and speeded up sixty times for us to hear them.

Infrasound is believed capable of penetrating thousands of miles of ocean, *and returning* – this is the important factor. Each whale is simultaneously listening for its own voice and logging the distance, texture and shape of the echo. How each whale recognises only its personal signal is a mystery. The internal mechanism for producing sound is also poorly understood. No air is released so it is assumed that a device like two bagpipe bags squeezes air from one sac to another past the larynx. However it's produced, infrasound enables the great whales to map the edges of continents and the contours of underwater mountains. The oceans are not dark voids through which they blunder but a landscape of minutely-defined features through which they navigate with all the familiarity of home. Blue whales can live for up to two hundred years. Two centuries of map-reading and living by their wits represent a formidable accumulation of experience, hence whales are revered as guardians of the world's wisdom by the Inuit and depicted as the symbol of knowledge on Indian medicine cards.

The mid-range frequencies are used by whales for communication. They span lows and highs, rising in pitch the closer a companion comes when the need to 'project' their voice diminishes. These sounds produce all the colour and vitality of conversation and rank among the most complex calls of any species. Individual killer whales identify themselves with an audio 'signature' which is repeated by the addressee; a format identical to that used by ships making radio contact. Regional families develop their own distinctive dialects so that the language of a pod off Vancouver Island is noticeably different from that of a pod in the Sea of Japan. However, the supreme exponents of underwater communication are the bull humpbacks who sing to attract a mate. Divers who have come close to these shy creatures describe the impact of their sound waves as like having your chest pummelled violently enough to make you feel faint.

Their songs encompass about fourteen 'notes' and each song can last twenty-four hours. The pace is relentless. They will repeat songs indefinitely without a beginning or an end and change on a whim, as if they've suddenly recalled an old favourite. Different populations of whales sing different songs. Typically, a sequence of five to fifteen notes is produced and then repeated to form a phrase. More and more phrases are added and these build into themes which can be repeated any number of times, but the sequence of phrases and their relationship to each other is always the same; thus these are not temporary, impromptu compositions but memorised structures. These types of song are the most common but new evidence suggests there may be some selection process whereby females favour the improviser. Bulls have been overheard breaking all the rules and launching into spontaneous outbursts of what researchers can only describe as 'jazz'. Different frequencies and songs appear to have different roles: low frequency tunes may attract females from far away while higher frequencies, which don't travel so far, tend to be more intricate and may be intended to woo the female with their subtlety and panache when she gets closer. We can only guess at what they're saying.

And finally there are the high-pitched clicks used by sperm whales, killer whales and dolphins, amongst others, for locating their prey. Not only does sound travel further in water than in air, but it moves four times faster, at a speed of one mile per second. A sperm whale descends into total darkness to hunt for its staple prey, giant squid, and here it needs to produce short-range sonar which provides very rapid echoes to plot the movements of the chase. Dolphins have perfected the high-frequency range of clicks to overcome what is known as the 'Doppler effect', changes in sonar wavelengths resulting from their speed in the water and the agility of much faster prey. Race against dolphins in a sail boat and you'll hear their orchestrations through the hull.

But if whale sounds travel hundreds of miles, what about the sounds humans make underwater? I had just passed Rosslare which in summer is host to one hundred and thirty shipping movements in and out of port *each week*. What effect do these thundering engines have on marine life? What about the geological explorations around the globe which detonate large explosions for seismic surveys? Clearly whales still frequent this area but research around the world on the damaging effect of sound pollution indicates the problem is serious and growing exponentially. It will, scientists believe, soon thrust itself into human consciousness and become a major environmental issue.

Over the last sixty years the ambient level of man-made noise has increased three to five decibels every decade; that is, at least two to three orders of magnitude. This equates to a voice that was once discernable across a playing field now having to advance within an arm's length to be heard. The same increase has occurred in the seas. Whales live considerably longer than sixty years so in one whale's lifetime they have experienced a drastic reduction from an ambiance of clarity to one filled with acoustic smog.

Salt and Emerald

The qualities of water which enhance the abilities of sea creatures to communicate over long distances also work to exacerbate
the problem of noise pollution. Both temperature and pressure have
radical effects on how sound travels though water. Sound waves
bounce off the surface and are deflected down to the depths until
they hit a layer of colder, denser water which deflects them back up
again. In terms of communication this is ideal as it confines the energy of the sounds to a narrow plane in which they can travel further. But noise pollution is also trapped within this channel and
maintains its cohesion rather than entering a wider orbit of disper-
sal.

We tend to think of the oceans in terms of almost incomprehen-
sible immensity. We believe there is unlimited space there for creatures to relocate to a less disturbed habitat. This is simply not true.
The specific environmental factors which permit a species to survive and the genetic programming which has conditioned its behaviour for millennia can restrict its population to small regions. (Even
an airborne nomad as liberated as the albatross is at risk. Grey-
headed albatrosses fly around the globe and can complete the journey in six weeks, but it appears they feed exclusively in just a few
locations). Whales *do* now take what evasive action they can from
noise pollution. Records show they've forsaken a traditional migration route near shipping channels around Hawaii. What is not
known, however, is what the long-term effects of noise pollution will
be in places where whales have always congregated for specific
purposes such as breeding or feeding. If they are driven away from
these places, the future of an entire species may be at risk. Northern Right Whales are now believed to number less than two hundred, and their migration routes and gathering places are specific.

When I lie in my bunk at night in some remote anchorage,
sometimes I hear a ticking like a clock, only faster. I know what it is.
I've got up before and looked into moonlit distance to identify this
invasion. It's an outboard motor, perhaps 25-horsepower, and it's
half-a-mile away. My hull is not designed for hearing, my human ear
is not particularly sensitive and yet this sound is clear, incisive and
irritating. I would experience marked discomfort if it rose to 120
decibels. Sea mammals are believed to tolerate up to 180 decibels.
Higher levels maim and kill. A 25-horsepower engine half-a-mile
away will wake me from sleep but it is feeble in the scale of noise
compared to a 50,000hp super tanker or a chain of 260-decibel
seismic explosions: particularly to creatures who live by their ears
and can hear over a thousand miles.

70

Potted History No 2

Between Kilmore Quay and the Waterford estuary, at Bannow Bay, my route traversed the point where Richard FitzGilbert de Clare, the Earl of Strigoil, entered Irish history. I was about to meet the Normans.

Around 1150 was a time of confused nationalities and, in general, unwieldy personal names. The king of England, Henry II, was a Norman and thus French: French-born, French-speaking, resident in, and also king of, France. Taking a notion to add Ireland to his realm, he followed the quaint practice of the period and sought permission from the Pope. Pope Adrian IV happened to be an Englishman (the only one ever to hold the office) and in 1155 he sanctioned Henry's request 'to enter the island of Ireland in order to subject people to law and to root out from them the weeds of vice... to enlarge the boundaries of the church... to proclaim the truths of the Christian religion to a rude and ignorant people'. Given the comparative states of the two nations the invasion should have been the other way round, but Henry's propaganda prevailed. He was, however, too preoccupied with other wars to contemplate rooting out weeds on a new front. In 1166 an Irishman offered to do it for him.

In Ireland, two warrior kings were engaged in a fierce feud. The loser, Dermot MacMurrough, fled to France and asked Henry for help. The king offered no money or troops but had nothing to lose by providing a letter urging his subjects in England and Wales to support the Irishman. With the unwritten promise of land and booty to be won, Dermot had no difficulty in persuading one of the mightiest Norman leaders to gather an army and accompany him to Ireland. Richard FitzGilbert de Clare, known as 'Strongbow', landed at Bannow Bay in 1169 and within a year both the Norse and Gaelic-Irish forces had been defeated. Henry immediately leapt on the bandwagon and arrived with his own army to claim the country's fealty. It would take another eighty years for Ireland to truly (though never fully) become 'Norman'; the longest and most bitter process of colonisation had begun.

It began well. The Normans were the first to establish a central administration in Ireland. They built cathedrals, founded orderly towns and brought coins into general use. In their wake came a freshening influence of religious orders: Dominicans, Franciscans, Augustinians and Carmelites. A new legal system was introduced (the basis of the one existing to this day) and a period of stability ensued; yet only in the regions where their authority was undisputed. As colonists go, they were among the best. Indeed some historians maintain that it is one of Ireland's tragedies that the Normans failed to complete and hold on to their conquest. But their numbers were insufficient, they received too little support and their achievements were the by-product of a disinterested kingdom rather than an integral part of its plan. By 1300 the Normans were losing territory to a revived Gaeldom, and being assimilated. The coronation of the Scot, Edward Bruce, in 1316 was in overt defiance of the colonists. By 1400 the only area safe for the French/ English occupiers was a small area centred on Dublin, known as 'The Pale'. To venture 'beyond the pale' was considered reckless or extreme behaviour.

For the next century England was too preoccupied with other conflicts to bother much about Ireland. To maintain an adequate army to subjugate the country was too expensive, so an ineffectual government was entrusted to Anglo-Irish lords. Only when Ireland appeared a direct threat to her security did England react with a punitive expedition. In 1494 came the first of many draconian measures to crush resistance and eradicate the Gaelic culture. Bans regulated everything from politics to the wearing of 'coats made after the Irish fashion' and 'any hair growing upon their upper lip, called or named a *crommea*'. Significantly, no attempt was made to outlaw the speaking of Gaelic. The re-conquest began in earnest under Henry VIII, who adopted the title 'King of Ireland', and continued under the Tudor dynasty until Elizabeth I completed the task.

Gaelic earls, whom the English called 'Irish enemies', continued to rule their localities though under nominal homage to Henry, along with another distinct group of regional powers, the Anglo-Irish lords, former Norman nobles who had gone native and, in English eyes, were 'rebels'. Gaelic resistance gradually diminished, culminating in a heroic last stand in 1594 when the earls of the northern counties of Ulster almost wrested control from England and offered their country to Spain. Almost, but they failed. The year 1607 marked the 'Flight of the Earls' when over ninety Gaelic leaders went into exile on the continent. Ulster had fallen and Ireland was at last conquered. It is no irony that the Ulster of today is the staunchest pro-British fraction of the country when it was formerly the kernel of anti-English feeling. Indeed it was precisely because of this that the next ruthless experiment in subjugation would be staged in the north: plantation.

The idea of evicting people from an area and replacing them with an implanted population of proven allegiance and conformist practices was seen as an instant solution to colonial insurgency. It had been tried before in Ireland, in 1583, unsuccessfully, but the new phase of plantation which began in 1609 was on a much larger scale and would continue for the rest of the century. What added impetus to the purge was the new element of religious hatred. Henry VIII's most divisive legacy was the Reformation which left Ireland despised not only as a rebellious colony but now also as a Catholic state. Protestant England realised that control of Ireland was crucial in order to prevent her enemies, Catholic France and Spain, from using this wayward neighbour as a gateway to invasion.

The City of London undertook the rebuilding of war-ravaged Derry, re-christening it 'Londonderry' and Protestant English and Scots flooded in as they did all over Ulster. Catholics were ousted but the plan to confine them in segregated communities was never carried out. Instead, they became scattered throughout the poorest lands or were reduced to the lives of serfs. No Catholic could own land east of the Shannon. By the time Cromwell had exacted brutal retribution for Ireland's support of Charles I, one-third of Irish Catholics had been killed, 30,000 had emigrated, thousands had been shipped as slaves to the West Indies and 20 million new acres had been transferred to Protestant settlers. In 1670 an exchange took place in which 20,000 Irish Catholic girls were forced into new lives in England, and 20,000 Protestant girls were sent over from England to replace them.

England's instability as it vacillated between Protestantism and Catholicism was mirrored in Ireland. When the last Catholic monarch of the united kingdoms of England and Scotland, James II, was deposed and replaced by William of Orange, it was to Ireland that James came to gather forces and try to win back his throne. His failure to do so is still the source of provocative celebrations in Protestant/ pro-Britain/ Unionist/ Loyalist Ulster to this day. The annual Apprentice Boys marches commemorate Londonderry's survival of a three-month siege by the Jacobite forces. The other much harped-on-about and painted victory was the pitched Battle of the Boyne the following year. Here James's 25,000 troops (7,000 of them French – England's worst nightmare come true) were routed by the 36,000 men led by William. An irony was at work here which makes the defeat all the more galling for contemporary Catholics: as a result of France challenging the Vatican's power, the Pope of the day was backing William and not James. The Protestants won the Battle of the Boyne with the Pope's blessing.

Ireland was now decisively divided between a privileged Protestant minority and an underprivileged, to the point of destitution, Catholic majority.

The eighteenth century was one of Catholic suppression. Penal laws were enacted which barred Catholics from administrative roles and many legal and civil rights, including the right to vote (unless they were landowners which few were except the Anglo-Irish, the old 'rebels', and they lived in constant fear of losing these few privileges). Industry was created for Protestants in Ulster, but the rest of the Irish were reduced to scraping a living from the land. Politics were not the sole cause of their poverty, though, as the Catholic church continued to exact tithes that its followers could ill-afford. Out of these dismal times emerged the first of the freedom fighters for whom Dublin would name her central streets, men such as Charles O'Connor and John Curry. They were followed by Daniel O'Connell, Wolf Tone and many others. Gradually things changed. Britain was realising that Ireland's discontent could not be held at bay for ever.

A traveller in 1777 put his finger on the thorn:

> ...We keep the Irish dark and ignorant, and then we wonder how they can be so enthralled by superstition; we make them poor and unhappy, and then we wonder that they are so prone to tumult and disorder; we tie up their hands, so that they have no inducements to industry, and then we wonder that they are so lazy and indolent.
> T. Campbell,
> *A Philosophical Survey of the South of Ireland*

Two events shook Britain out of its lethargy. In 1778 the American War of Independence ruptured the colony. Britain had insufficient troops and withdrew forces from Ireland which left the Protestants in Ulster feeling vulnerable to Catholic insurrection, particularly when France and Spain joined the American side and threatened to broaden the conflict to both sides of the Atlantic. Volunteer forces sprang up and a tradition was born of taking up arms in organised forces for political purposes and 'community defence'. Many Irishmen saw the Americans as fighting a war for them, and when Britain lost, and then the Bastille fell in the French Revolution of 1789, suddenly anything seemed possible. The Ulster Protestants were digging in against any erosion of their power and privileges. The Orange Society was formed in September 1795 to counter the competition for land. Catholic unrest was growing more vocal and more organised. Meanwhile Britain tried to placate Ulster and maintain a status quo, all the time realising it was untenable. For a few years she renounced all claim to legislate for Ireland but the country was too divided to rule herself and such an easy retreat from years of abuse was impossible. The more indefensible measures of the penal act were gradually relaxed and Catholic emancipation was conceded in 1829. For the first time a Catholic could give evidence in court and enjoy recourse in law, go to school in a dedicated building instead of the illicit 'hedge schools', take a craft apprenticeship and own a horse worth more than five pounds.

The momentum for radical change was increasing when a national disaster occurred and devastated the country: the Great Famine.

Yola

I spent the night in Kilmore Quay, the most expensive marina in the country, tied up between two fishing boats, *Turtle* and *Platypus*.

'Are y'all right?' called the *Platypus* man as I arrived.

'Are y'all right?' called the marina keeper as he caught my line.

'He's after got it at the stern', the *Turtle* confirmed. 'I'm after getting the bow.' And: 'I doubt ya'll not be movin' now less it turns curkite', when the process of tying up was complete.

'Are y'all right?' greeted Michael O'Leary, the curator of the grounded lightship that had been turned into a museum nearby. By this time I was convinced I had to be looking far from all right.

'Yola', Michael explained. 'It's a special dialect they speak around here. Strange words and expressions. There's words going back to Norman times that's spoken nowhere else in Ireland. You heard of Chris de Burgh, the singer? He was born here. Family owns Burgh Castle. He's Norman. Place is full of Norman castles, Norman surnames. Now this minister, Jacob Poole, he compiled a lexicon of Yola. Found it to be a mixture of French, High German, Irish, Manx, Chaucerian English and Old Saxon of the Bristol Channel.'

'Can you speak it?'

'I'm an O'Leary, Irish. I'm in the minority here. But I can count to ten.' He stiffened like a child asked to recite his homework. 'Oane, Twye, Dhree, Voweër, Veeve, Zeese, Zebbem, Ayght, Neene, Dhen.' The words were delivered slowly and drawn out. I might have been listening to Dutch. 'Yea, Jacob Poole. You should check him out.'

Jacob Poole was born in Growtown in 1774 and inherited the family estate when he was fifty. By all accounts he was a kind, amiable man, and generous with his good fortune. He was not a minister but a farmer, latterly living off his estate and spending his time bird-watching and writing copious notes on the customs and dialect of his neighbourhood. By then the region of spoken Yola (meaning 'old') had contracted to the Baronies of Forth and Bargy, with a population of 40,000. A century earlier a Dublin historian, Stanyhurst, derided the speakers of Yola as speaking a gallimaufrere *(a* 'mingle-mangle') of languages that was 'neither good English, nor good Irish'. Poole's glossary, containing such words as *ihuske* (a flock), *palsk* (a kind of cake), *curkite* (adverse or contrary) runs to only 1700 words and is frustratingly sparse on pronunciation and grammar. Nevertheless it remains the one and only guide the world has to Yola.

I didn't linger long among Kilmore Quay's artefacts. By then I was fired up on Yola and found the exhibits too depressing. Every coastal museum I visited devoted too much space to shipwrecks. A map plotted the downfall of a small selection of ninety-six between Arklow and Hook Head, the notorious 'Coastline of a Thousand Wrecks'. There was the 1400-ton clipper *Pomona* carrying 373 passengers and thirty-six crew outward-bound from Liverpool in April 1859. The captain confused his lights and, thinking he'd cleared the Tuskar, turned for America. The crew commandeered the only lifeboat and were lost when it was dashed against the hull before it could be cut free. In all, 388 died. Captain Charles Merryhew's body was found tied to the mast. Several days after the accident a salvage crew came across the bodies of a woman and her seven children who still clung to her in death.

Two hundred and twenty ships were wrecked in this area last century, and more than 600 in the previous one. Kilmore Quay was not a place for the nervous sailor to tarry.

The following day I rounded the black and white bands of Hook Head lighthouse, the oldest in Europe except for the Pharos of Corunna in northern Spain. It was my third week of voyaging and I was a quarter of the way round the country. *Ceana* took me into brackish water, the estuary into which – appropriately – one quarter of Ireland drains. I was heading up the River Barrow for the emigration ship of New Ross.

Emigration Ships

In 1858 Patrick Kennedy gathered his possessions into a *Luggage Allowance for each Statute Adult* of ten cubic feet and took ship for America. A few miles downstream from New Ross he would have seen the homestead he had just abandoned at Dunganstown. The keening of his own wake would have still been sounding, for the emigrant's departure was accorded the full ritual of death. How fortifying it would have been at this departure to have known that one hundred and five years later, on the 27 June 1963, his grandson would return and visit the site of the Dunganstown steading (all trace of which has disappeared) as the incumbent President of the United States of America.

Emigration has cast a long shadow over Ireland's past and predates the Great Famine (1845-51), the event which witnessed two million people forsake Ireland in a single decade. Perversely it was in the 1720s from Northern Ireland, which invariably reflects the opposite trend to the rest of the country and remained relatively unscathed by the widespread exodus from the south throughout the nineteenth century, that large-scale emigration first occurred. Religious persecution of the Presbyterians forced large numbers to flee to the New World where they set up the forerunners of the Scots-Irish Associations that remain so prevalent to this day. From 1770 to 1815 it is estimated that 4000 people emigrated each year, now predominantly from the south for reasons of poverty and the political suppression of Catholics. From 1815 to 1845 that figure rose to a million. Then two million in ten years, and the haemorrhaging of Ireland's youth and vitality flowed freely for the next sixty years to a degree unparalleled by any other country in Europe.

NUMBERS OF EMIGRANTS PER 1000 OF POPULATION					
	1851-1860	1861-1870	1871-1880	1881-1890	1891-1900
IRELAND	14	14.6	6.6	14.2	8.9
NORWAY	2.4	5.8	4.7	9.5	4.5
SCOTLAND	5.5	4.6	4.7	7.1	4.4
ENGLAND	2.6	2.8	4.0	5.6	5.6
SWEDEN	0.5	3.1	2.4	7.0	4.1

For the most part the emigrants went to Britain and America. So overwhelming were the numbers of Irish in places like Liverpool, Manchester and New York that prejudice took root and employment posters often added a postscript, 'No Irish Need Apply'. Emigrants from a town or district launching their lives into the unknown tended to follow those friends or neighbours who had gone before, thus Irish districts replicated themselves as enclaves abroad. Emigrants from the Donegal Island of Aranmore eventually settled on Brewer Island in Lake Michigan and links between the two communities remain strong to this day. The more adventurous, or possibly wealthier or desperate (and many of them came from Northern Ireland) chose Australia as their destination. A voyage to Sydney lasted anything up to six months and ships set sail reserving the right to choose between the Cape Horn and Cape of Good Hope routes depending on the weather at the time. One in five passengers died during the passage.

*   *   *

New Ross occupied a steep bluff beside a river and was in the late stages of a personality crisis. It was redressing itself from the centre outwards in flower baskets and loudly-coloured tourist boutiques but seemed at a loss to know what to do with the sandstone warehouses which had been robbed of their centuries-old function and occupied the town's prime water frontage. From the main street the zeal for re-branding diminished rapidly. Eight shop premises were for sale in a secondary street and derelict sites abounded with full grants on offer to developers. That New Ross had been a centre for emigration seemed cruelly evident.

I walked down to the dock and bought a ticket for the *Dunbrody*, a 458-ton three-masted barque reeking of pine and hemp. My ticket was a facsimile of the contract between William Graves & Son, shipowner, and Catherine Koogan, a twenty-year-old passenger, dated 18 March, 1849.

> I engage that the Parties herein named shall be provided with a <u>Steerage</u> Passage to <u>New York</u> in the Ship <u>Dunbrody</u> with not less than 10 cubic feet for Luggage for each Statute Adult, for the sum of £3.10.0 including Head Money, if any, at the place of landing, and every other charge. Water and Provisions, according to the annexed scale, will be supplied by the Ship as required by law, and also fires, and suitable hearths for cooking.

SCALE OF PROVISIONS AND WATER THAT WILL BE SUPPLIED TO EACH ADULT BY THE SHIP. Per week. Issued not less often than twice a week: 3½lb. of Biscuit : 3½lb. in all of Flour, Oatmeal, or Rice or a proportionate quantity of Potatoes (5lb of Potatoes being computed as equal to 1lb of the other articles above enumerated.) 3 quarts of Water per day.

So in 2003 I paid €6.50 (£4.68) to wander round the *Dunbrody* for a couple of hours, whereas in 1849 Catherine received full board and passage to the New World for the equivalent of €4.86.

At a time when farm labourers were paid one shilling a day, Catherine's fare represented seventy days' work, though probably closer to several years of saving. The regulations allowed one person, crew and passengers included, per five registered tons or Ten Clear Superficial Feet of deck area. This worked out at a 'bunk' measuring seventy-two inches by eighteen inches for each adult but there was no stipulation that each bunk had to be independently defined. In practice the sleeping spaces for four people were lumped together in sections six-foot square which ran the length of the steerage deck on two tiers. Children counted as Half Statute Adults and therefore two were lodged in an adult's space. Babies under the age of one didn't count. Strangers had to sleep alongside strangers, often having to lie in the vomit, urine or excrement which flowed across from the sides or dripped down from above.

The food rations were pitiful, the voyage a slow process of starvation. Only in good weather would the stove on deck be lit and passengers take a turn to cook their meal, always harangued by the press of those waiting behind. In bad weather, which was most of the time, they had to eat their rations raw and cold. Only in good weather were they allowed on deck for a brief period of respite. The reality behind any dreamy thrill of 'taking passage to New York' was up to fifty days' confinement below deck with 350 others in the fetid stench of a turbulent ship. Occasionally buckets of sea water were passed down for washing, but without privacy personal hygiene was impossible and soiled clothes had to be endured for weeks. The only means for the emigrants to relieve themselves was in a line of buckets on deck. Epidemics were rife. On the worst crossings the mortality rate rose as high as fifty per cent. The dead were buried at sea.

Up one deck, life was considerably better. First-class passengers paid £25 for a place in a four-berth cabin. They mingled with the officers and ate with them, and were free to go on deck as they liked. The captain's pay was not recorded but the First Mate received £5 for each trip, and the cook and ordinary crew, £2.50. The cook, however, was docked a day's pay for every meal served late.

The *Dunbrody* was built in 1845 in Quebec because there was not enough suitable timber in Ireland. Despite having official space for 350, she averaged 176 passengers per trip, but sometimes exceeded her capacity as the regulations for Half-Statute Adults provided convenient grounds for confusion. For thirty years she carried emigrants one way then sailed down to South America for a backload of guano. There was often still guano lodged in crevices and corners when the next consignment of emigrants boarded.

The *Dunbrody* was built as a project to bring unemployed youths and trainees in traditional crafts into partnership with New Ross's shipbuilders. She's a beautiful ship. Her rigging is immaculate, interior polished and pristine, her supplies neatly stowed in bags laundered white, and she smells, as I've said, wholesomely of pine and hemp. Naturally, we must be protected. The true ambience of history is too offensive to recreate, too opposite to the feel-good factor demanded, too injurious to the precarious self-image of civilisation we prefer to believe. Of weevils, vomit and clothes rotting in excrement there was no sign. Merciful this may be, but such a sanitised treatment of history holds the past safely out of reach in a realm somewhere short of make-believe. It becomes instantly forgettable, as impersonal as semaphore. Half a ton of guano probably would have done the trick.

Hazards

A week until the only entry in my diary, a meeting with Dervla Murphy. Before dawn I left my anchorage, a few miles from Waterford town centre, and played a spotlight over the slobland of the King's Channel to find my way out. The beam startled a heron which took flight and its shadow turned into a pterodactyl with a life of its own.   Every so often the warbling whistles of curlews built up into hysterical duels and then faded, only to start mysteriously from some prompt of their own divination. Their calls seemed urgent; as if silence stole souls and could be repelled only by singing their identity through amorphous night. My engine grumbled on low revs as the River Suir's current carried me towards the sea through nine miles of mud.

Waterford had been a pleasant interlude. Gripped by the fervour of the Munster Hurling Final, every car fluttered the blue-and-white stripes of the home team from their side windows. The place was choked with cars and beset by winds.

'Yer better aff jaywalkin', I'm tellin ye', advised a local as I waited to cross the main street. 'Ye'll catch a chill waitin at them pedestrian crossins.'

The breeze constantly nagged my kilt. It spun polystyrene cups in corner vortices and sent shivers through floral displays on the city's splendid river frontage. But the wind, traffic and all the energy of the metropolis seemed to subside after the home side's defeat. Waterford were the defending champions but not even a late redirection of the silotar through the goal posts by Sean Og hoAilpin was enough to defeat archrival Cork. Waterford's population dejectedly went back to work, doing what it was best at and had done for three centuries; blowing glass.

As I sailed away points of light from the shore – farms, houses, factories – extended into poles which lanced *Ceana*'s silhouette, but these faded as dawn broke over Legoland. This was Waterford's container port, a suburb of gaily coloured boxes. The names emblazoned on the sides might not be of household familiarity but they represented the oligopolies of maritime transport, the standard wrapping of goods exported in the global economy: Hanjin, Maersk, Lysline, P&O, Norfolkline, Cobelfet, European Containers, Danzas, Bulkhaul, Bruhn, Powerbox...I viewed them with animosity. Every year 100 million of these containers are carried on the seas and an average of 0.1% fall overboard. This may seem a fair record but 10,000 lost containers, each measuring eight feet square by forty feet long, now represent a serious threat to small-craft. Superships such as Japan's *Mol Encore* cram 2070 of these containers into their holds and stack a further 2508 on their decks. They could shed a dozen and not notice. It would be a simple expedient to fit vents and ensure that lost containers would sink, depending on the buoyancy of their contents, but this is not done. Containers can float for months, if not years. They litter the world's oceans, not uncommonly becoming waterlogged and attaining neutral equilibrium a few inches below the surface.

I hugged the shore as a freighter approached. The flag of Panama flew from the stern, and above the bridge, as the traditional courtesy to the host nation, the green, white and orange of Ireland. It made me think of Thomas Meagher. I'd hunted Waterford's streets for a statue or plaque in his memory but found none. It seemed a gross omission for one of the city's most remarkable sons. Born in 1823, he developed into an outstanding orator who spoke out against British rule. He was a leading instigator of the ill-equipped uprising of 1848 which resulted in his capture. Found guilty of treason he was sentenced to death by hanging, drawing and quartering; an execution little used since medieval times and so brutal for the 'enlightened' era that it shocked the nation. Queen Victoria intervened and in 1849 the sentence was commuted to five years' exile and hard labour in the penal colony of Tasmania.

Meagher escaped in 1852 and made his way to America. Here he received a hero's welcome among other ex-patriots and became an influential lawyer. When the Civil War broke out he personally raised and led a force of 15,000 men for the Union cause, fighting at Bull Run, Seven Pines and a crushing defeat at Fredericksburg where he was wounded.

In 1865 he was acting governor of Montana when he fell off a boat on the Missouri River and drowned. Although he had been drinking his death was considered 'mysterious'. He was forty-three. Not least among the achievements credited to him in his short life is the design of the national flag: green for Catholic Ireland, orange for Protestant, and between them a band of white for the peace that might hold them together.

Below my own Irish flag I watched the ship and its balanced boxes pass. Rogue containers, however, were not my main concern this morning. There were other hazards about. I spotted the first of them just as life seemed as good as it can get, with a bacon sandwich in one hand and a mug of coffee in the other. On autohelm. 5.4 metres clear under the keel, Duncannon fort standing where it should be as a tall sandcastle off the port beam. Suddenly I saw them. A row of floats the size of apples strung across my route fifty yards ahead. Simultaneously I glimpsed a distant fishing smack heading towards me with a figure gesticulating at the bow. Down went sandwich, down went mug but fouling on a hank of rope, over-turning and emptying contents over sandwich. I disconnected the autohelm and swung the tiller round. For a moment the net seemed inescapable, the rudder too slow to respond but then the bow turned and I heard the floats rattle along the hull.

Now I was looking for them, I could see that floats extended across almost the full width of the river. I was incredulous. This was the main shipping channel for Waterford! Maersk and Hanjin would-n't put themselves out for a salmon net, so I assumed I was an un-expected arrival in a known schedule of traffic. On and on the floats went. In dismay I watched the depth drop. The fishing boat drew level on the far side of the net, the man at the bow waving me fur-ther into the shallows. By now I could make out the orange buoy that marked the end but it looked impossibly close to the shore.

'How much depth over there?' I yelled.

He couldn't hear over his engine's din . Still he waved me on.

'HOW MUCH DEPTH OVER THERE?' I was now down to a me-tre's clearance, on a falling tide. If I got stuck, I'd never get out. *Ceana* would be laid flat on the sand, fill on the incoming tide and become a RNLI poster.

'ENOUGH!'

This was pure optimism. He had no idea of my draught and was only concerned for the integrity of his net. I needed five feet and four inches to float, and I was currently in seven. It was Wexford all over again. I rounded the buoy with a foot to spare and told-you-so smirks on the fishermen's faces.

More coffee and a soft ginger nut, the top one always being the sacrificial layer to damp. Dirty clouds hung low and harboured squalls underneath. They dangled from sinews and swept left and right. I reduced sail, tightened my sheets and made bumpy pro-gress in a wind which matched any change in direction to meet me head on. The coastline slowly panned past and I looked out for Bal-lymacaw inlet, spotting a straggle of houses at its entrance. Here a farmer found a strange bird in 1834. It was exhausted. He tried to revive it on fish and potatoes but it died. Today, stuffed and mounted, its remains stand in Trinity College, Dublin, as the last great auk recorded in the British Isles. The species had been among the first wildlife to be accorded legal protection in 1794, but the measures came too late.

County Waterford's fields had turned black when they weren't hidden behind cliffs the colour of wet bricks or storm-chewed promontories where signal towers from Napoleonic times still stood. Bays opened to reveal Dungarvan and Youghal behind a weft of surf, looking just as hostile as the pilot advised. Youghal, Youghal... there was a story connected with the place but I couldn't grasp it.

Then another panic of nets ahead. They parcelled the sea. I gazed at their hopeless puzzle. It was impossible to make sense of them. I'd already learned that if a buoy was white it usually took off as you approached and turned into a gannet. But these were orange. I dropped sails and crept forward under engine, guessing which pairs might be linked and which were innocent lobster markers. Officially the gill-netting season lasted from June to mid-August, and nets could be out during daylight hours only. Here in the south their length was restricted to a maximum of 800 feet, but a newspaper reported the confiscation of a string of nets fourteen miles long. My shirt was damp with perspiration and my nerves jumping by the time I won through.

A century and a half earlier these fishermen would have been after a different quarry in a different place. The Newfoundland cod banks were the place to be and each spring 8000 men gathered in Waterford in the hope of getting work on 200 boats. The lucky ones would spend the summer hauling in 100-pounders (unbelievable sizes by modern standards) which would be salted and sold to Europe. Salted cod kept for over twenty years. The fishermen returned for Christmas, and Waterford became a riot of money and disorder. Gill-netters led a quiet life by comparison and compensated for it by tripping up yachts.

As I passed through the bottleneck entrance to Cork harbour, a natural basin ranked second to Sydney as the finest boat haven in the world, the heavens opened. I'd never seen rain like it. I might have drifted under a waterfall. Drops landed with such force they killed the wind, flattened the waves and hammered like hail on my deck. The noise was deafening. Thin glass stalagmites rose momentarily from the surface before being shot to pieces. A container ship a quarter of a mile ahead dissolved into a hint of discolouration. It was like starring through bubblepack. For five minutes it seemed to be Armageddon by water, then it stopped as suddenly as it had begun. The sun came out and I grabbed a mooring far from the bustle of the port, up a river among mature oaks and beeches in Drake's Pool, where the great man (supposedly) once hid from the Spanish. It felt like I'd crossed the Atlantic and arrived in New England.

That evening I remembered the missing piece from Youghal.

Mystery Ship

On 4 December 1872 the barque *Dei Gratia* – whose owners were Irish, the Fleming family of Youghal – was in mid-Atlantic, nineteen days out of New York bound for Gibraltar. The sea was disturbed after recent storms but a breeze held steady from the north and the *Dei Gratia* bore south-east by east at nine knots on the port tack. The Azores lay 400 miles to the west.

Around 1.30pm Captain Morehouse noticed a two-masted ship about six miles distant travelling in the opposite direction on the starboard tack. She was square-rigged on the foremast and absurdly under-canvassed. As the gap closed a glass was raised to reveal no-one at the wheel and no sign of life on deck. Morehouse launched a boat and sent the mate and two sailors to investigate. It was now 3pm.

Only when they rounded her stern did her name come into view. The *Mary Celeste* was making between one-and-a-half and two knots. She was completely deserted.

They boarded with difficulty. Overall the ship was found to be in excellent condition. Her unused sails were furled, her rigging showed some disarray but was mostly intact, her hull was sound and her interior orderly. She was well provisioned with food and water. Her cargo, barrels of industrial alcohol, was still lashed securely in the hold.

Clearly she had suffered storm damage. Two sails had blown away. The ship's compass and binnacle had been knocked over and broken after a lashing had parted. Two hatches were lying on deck, leaving the interior exposed to rain and heavy seas. Three and a half feet of water were measured in the hold – a considerable but not dangerous amount – and 'a great deal of water' remained between decks. Clothing and bedding in the cabin nearest the main hatch, the captain's, was damp. Yet the *Mary Celeste* was seaworthy and could readily be made comfortable. (The *Dei Gratia* men pumped her bilges dry in a few hours and had her ready to sail the following day.) There was no obvious reason why she should have been abandoned.

The last entry in the log had been made on November 24, ten days earlier, when the ship's position was noted as six miles north-east of St Mary's (Santa Maria) in the Azores. This small island, almost completely ringed by cliffs, is the southernmost of the group. Ships travelling from New York to Gibraltar found the Azores an obstacle directly on their track and either went round them to the north or south; if to the south, there was no advantage in cutting through the tail end of the island group, exposing a ship to a reef on one side and the cliffs of St Mary's on the other. Yet the *Mary Celeste* appears to have taken this route, as if wanting to be close to land. When found by the *Dei Gratia* at 38° 20' North, 17° 15' West, she had travelled almost 400 miles southeast from her last logged position, and then turned northwest, heading vaguely back to New York.

Her wheel was not lashed. This vital fact has induced many to assume that she must have covered much of the distance under some degree of control, being abandoned only shortly before being found. If this were the case, then why did she make such poor progress and why were no entries made in the log?

A small boat appeared to have been stored on fenders over the main hatch, without any obvious means of launching it, but it was gone. There was no evidence of violence or a struggle, nothing to suggest piracy or a mutiny. The ship had not been knocked over or run aground. Yet something had happened, suddenly enough for no messages to have been left behind and yet without causing panic. In the captain's cabin the bed was unmade and what looked like the impression of a child still indented the covers. Opposite stood a polished rosewood harmonium, a bookcase and a small table supporting a sewing machine. The ship's safe was intact. When it was opened several weeks later it was found to contain personal effects: money, jewellery and gold trinkets of modest value.

The mate's cabin was equally neat. A chart on the wall logged the ship's progress. The crew's quarters in the fo'c'sle presented a scene of normality. Clothes lay folded in individual sea-chests lined up on each side. Notably they contained oilskins and tobacco pipes; the last items any sailor would voluntarily forsake in an emergency. The fire in the galley was out and its ashes were cold. No food was lying around. Pots and pans had been cleaned and stowed. The evacuation had taken place during the brief period of inactivity after one meal had ended and before preparations for the next had begun. The only obvious item that was missing, they noted, was the ship's chronometer.

Now with a salvage claim to pursue Morehouse divided his crew between the two vessels and continued on to Gibraltar where the Admiralty conducted an official inquiry. Its investigation revealed that the *Mary Celeste* was a New York-based brigantine of 206 tons, listed in the 1871 American Lloyd's Register. On this particular voyage (to Genoa) ten people were recorded as constituting the ship's compliment. Captain Benjamin Spooner Briggs was in command of a crew of seven, and on this occasion he took along his wife, Sarah, and two-year-old daughter, 'Sophy', for the trip. They were never heard of again.

It was readily appreciated that the entire *Mary Celeste* 'mystery' hinged on the testimony of the crew who found her. The captain and men of the *Dei Gratia* ('thanks to God') were cross-examined and their accounts, given under oath, were put under the gravest scrutiny, without any reasons to doubt them emerging. The ship was impounded and subjected to a more meticulous search.

In addition to the missing chronometer, it was recorded that the sextant had also disappeared. These two instruments were the essential items of navigation at the time. Without them, no mariner could plot a route across an ocean or have any idea where his ship was on the face of the hemisphere. There was no sign of the ship's cargo documentation, register or navigation book, and a more detailed inspection of the barrels of alcohol revealed that one had been breeched.

The prosecution's initial case, presented without much conviction, was that the crew had raided the hold, consumed the contents of a barrel and murdered the captain and his family in a drunken spree. They had then taken the navigational equipment and made their escape in the boat. For months, and indeed years, it was hoped a survivor would turn up and solve the mystery. This never happened and the file was left open. Nevertheless immediate action had to be taken and in the face of the uncertainties the crew of the *Dei Gratia* were awarded a paltry £1700 in salvage. The *Mary Celeste* was released and a new crew delivered her cargo (valued for insurance at $36,943) to Genoa. Of the 1701 barrels, aside from the one damaged and known to be empty, a further nine had leaked dry - a remarkably low wastage for the times, and possibly a very pertinent clue.

The mystery caught the imagination of all sea-faring nations and the *Mary Celeste* became a *cause célèbre* attracting ever more bizarre solutions in the absence of any plausible one that could square the facts. The crew might have been plucked from the deck by a giant squid, or sucked up by a tornado? Or possibly they'd landed on a sinking island? Or been eaten by sharks while having a swim? Yet the most obdurate theory was the drunken mutiny; it too was fatally flawed as industrial alcohol is highly toxic. The following is probably the guess that comes closest to the truth.

The *Mary Celeste* makes reasonable time to the Azores, averaging eight to nine knots despite some heavy weather (reported by several sources in this sector of the Atlantic at the time). Captain Briggs chooses the southern route round the Azores. On 24 November it's discovered that one barrel of alcohol in the hold has ruptured and the fear is that others may have done the same. The hold is now full of fumes which are potentially highly explosive. Briggs is aware that a spark caused by moving barrels could destroy the ship but the weather is too violent to take any remedial action. He alters course to pass close to St Mary's.

The next morning, 25 November, the weather is greatly improved and the sea moderate under a gentle breeze. It may have stopped raining (the meteorological station at Ponta Delgada in the Azores recorded 29mm falling between noon on the 24th and noon on the 25th – it also noted 'calm with light winds' in the morning but by afternoon sudden, gale force winds struck the Azores). Unaware of the impending storm and desperate to safeguard his ship and family, Briggs gives the order to evacuate the ship while the hold is being vented.

The two hatches are removed. To ensure a draught he does not heave-to (stop the vessel) but reduces sail to maintain a speed of a couple of knots. The foresail, lower and upper topsails are set to starboard to draw, while the foretopmast-staysail and the jib are set to port to hold her head to the course. The wheel is not lashed as this might provide overly-efficient steerage and make re-boarding the vessel difficult should the wind get up. He is only intending to leave the ship for an hour or two. It must now be fair as the crew do not take their oilskins. No one is allowed any luggage but Briggs takes his sextant, chronometer, navigation book and ship's papers in case the worst happens. In his haste he omits to make any entry in the log. Rather than uncoil a tow rope, the crew pull down the main peak halyard (a strong rope about 300 feet long) and use this, knowing they can replace it later.

At first all goes well and the small boat is towed by the now deserted mother ship. Suddenly the weather turns. The *Mary Celeste* speeds up but steers erratically and causes the tow rope to chafe on the stern. The small boat is unable to regain the safety of the ship, the tow breaks and everyone is lost in the ensuing storm. The *Mary Celeste* continues at two to four knots, weaving an erratic course but averaging a southeasterly direction for eight or nine days. Then comes a more violent squall which drives her into the wind, her foresail and upper topsail blow out and she tacks onto a northwesterly course. The jib and the foretopmast-staysail are now in a position to draw and the yard on the lower topsail would work round and also act as a driver. Within a day or so, the *Dei Gratia* chances on her.

As a theory it fits the known facts but fails to be wholly convincing, relying as it does on some fairly irrational behaviour by an experienced sea captain. Despite the passing of over one hundred and thirty years, we still cannot say with any certainty what befell the crew of the *Mary Celeste* on, or around, 25 November 1872.

As for the celebrity ship herself, she survived for another twelve years with an 'unlucky' reputation. She met her end on the Rochelais reef off Haiti on 3 January 1885. The weather was benign, the day bright. The steersman saw the reef and changed course to avoid it. Captain Parker ordered him back onto the original heading. All hands survived but the vessel was lost. The captain died before his charge of barratry and conspiracy came to court. Unfortunately for the owners of the cargo, the *Mary Celeste* did not sink immediately. Her heavily-insured freight was found to be worthless. They admitted culpability and settled out of court. In 2001 the wreck was found and some trove recovered.

International Code of Signals

C aptain Morehouse's initial attempt at communication with the *Mary Celeste* was by loud hailer, but it could have been by flags. The first International Code was prepared by a British Board of Trade committee in 1855. It used eighteen flags in combinations that represented 70,000 signals, and could also be transmitted by semaphore and Morse. Today, despite having been rendered almost obsolete through the supremacy of VHF radio (and the abandonment of Morse in 1999), the Code is still updated and retained as a reserve means of communication.

You can say almost anything with flags, and say it a lot more concisely than with words.

AX1   [From a Ship to a Helicopter] Shall I train my searchlight nearly vertical on a cloud, intermittently if possible and, if your aircraft is seen, deflect the beam up wind and on the water to facilitate your landing?

Some signals could spoil your voyage:

VY   One or more icebergs or growlers have been reported.

4   Stop. I am icebound.

OW   There is a minefield ahead of you. You should stop your vessel and wait for instructions.

AJ   I have had a serious nuclear accident and you should approach with caution.

How many people, I wonder, are aware of the correct *international* way of pronouncing numerals over the air? Here's a small selection. (Each syllable should be emphasised equally).

0	NADAZERO	(NAH-DAH-ZAY-ROH)
1	UNAONE	(OO-NAH-WUN)
2	BISSOTWO	(BEES-SOH-TOO)
6	SOXISIX	(SOK-SEE-SIX)

However, the fattest section of the International Code of Signals, by far, is devoted to medical matters. There's very little human suffering that cannot be conveyed precisely and quickly by flags. In fact, it's a wonder the government hasn't introduced the Code into the National Health Service.

MDG   Pain is a dull ache.

MCG   The breathing is wheezing.

MGM   Emetic has been given with good results.

MIT   Patient has persistent hiccough.

MLB   Patient has delusions.

MLE   Patient has had much alcohol.

MMR   Patient has single hard sores on penis.

MOU   The buttocks are coming first [childbirth].

MPP   Treatment has been effective.

MPR   Patient has died.

Finally, for Scottish Nationalists, it's distressing to note that Scotland's flag, the saltire, is an international signal for a dismal message: 'My vessel is stopped and making no way through the water'.

Of Kilts

On securing an anchorage it was my custom to swap trousers for kilt and to row ashore for the discovery of Ireland as an identifiable Scotsman. From the perspective of a landlubber I looked relatively normal approaching in the dingy – an Arran jersey attached to oars – but when I stepped out, the sight of a cylinder of Scott tartan above wellies invariably brought frozen stares.

My kilt worked a charm for hitchhiking. Traditionally Ireland was a hitchhiker's paradise. It was the accepted custom to hitch rides, to give rides. You saw figures with a hand out everywhere, mostly men in tweed jackets heading to or from the pub. Tony Hawk famously tested the national spirit to the extreme in his book *Hitching Round Ireland with a Fridge* (1998).

But even in Tony Hawk's day something had changed. Compos had entered the game. An epidemic of fraudulent compensation claims was sweeping the country. Insurance costs were soaring. The government had vowed to get tough and introduce ten-year sentences as a deterrent. Yet still they persisted. A woman was suing Dunne's Stores for €38,000 claiming she'd fallen on a 'jerky' escalator. She lost her case after it was proved she'd disregarded a notice banning any form of pram and was trying to balance a child in a buggy with eight grocery bags attached to the handles.

The majority of Compos won their damages and lawyers had jumped on the bandwagon by actively seeking cases to represent. On the roads the fear of litigation by a passenger involved in an accident had all but killed the ride-giving tradition. I hardly ever saw another hitchhiker now – the odd foreigner in summer – and it seemed you needed either a fridge or a kilt to be successful.

The reactions to my kilt often left me perplexed.

'There's a man in a skirt', a youth in Cork shouted.

'It's a kilt', I explained. 'I'm from Scotland.'

This produced no visible response. Such a lack of familiarity with the term 'kilt' was the norm across Éire, particularly among the very young. Yet kilts appeared in obscure village festivals. Kilted pipe bands entertained the crowds at the Special Olympics. Kilts were far from infrequent intrusions into modern Ireland's life but remained 'skirts' in the eyes of the young.

It was only later when I revisited Northern Ireland that a possible explanation occurred to me. Could it be that south of the border the young connect pipers and kilts with Loyalism and Unionism north of the border? That a generation exists for whom the kilt carries no association with Scotland but is a symbol of mild ridicule for those who continue to divide their nation?

Laundrettes

It is a sad fact of Irish life, and a glaring business opportunity, that Éire has only a handful of laundrettes. It has laundries where you reclaim your clothes the next day beautifully clean and folded - but this is not cheap. The world's oldest yacht club, the Water Club of the Harbour of Cork (1720), did not have one, did not even understand the concept of one.

I asked Mr Kidney, Crosshaven's butcher ('Kidney's – Lamb, Beef, Chops'), a dumpy, jovial man in blue and white stripes who clearly enjoyed his Happy Families caricature. No, he said, there wasn't one in town. Cork might have one but he doubted it. I stocked up on sausages and bacon, and had a beer in the company of 200 Toby jugs and a wall of boxing gloves in Cronin's Bar. As I stood chatting to the owner's daughter, Jolene, about washing machines and the national dearth of laundrettes, as one does, she smiled sympathetically.

'Just got to go and fill some glasses over there', she said.

When I next looked down my bag of dirty clothes had gone. I felt awful. I offered to pay her twice the fee of a laundry, but to no avail. Ireland's like that. God bless the Irish.

Potted History No 3

Despite alarming unemployment and a steady increase in emigration to America, Ireland experienced an unprecedented population explosion in the first half of the 18th century: five million souls in 1800 grew to 6.5 million in 1821, and over eight million by 1841. Congestion on the land became intense, and dependence on it, almost total. Eighty per cent of the population occupied fifteen per cent of the land. Forty-five per cent of holdings comprised less than five acres.

What made a population boom possible under such an adverse allocation of resources was the potato, and every humble Irish mouth consumed a staggering ten to fourteen pounds of boiled potatoes every day.

Hugh Brodie, in his book *Inishkillane*, conducted a nutritional analysis of this diet. As long as it was supplemented by a daily pint of milk (which was common fare), the result was flawless; probably much healthier than a fast food diet in contemporary Ireland. Potatoes and milk in these quantities provided 3852 calories, where 3000 are recommended by the Food and Nutrition Board of the National Research Council in the USA. The breakdown is:

		10lbs potatoes + 1 pt milk daily	Recommended daily intake
Protein	gm	64	70
Calcium	gm	2.63	0.56
Iron	mg	21.75	8.4
Vitamin A	units	3500	3500
Thiamin (Vit B1)	mg	45.06	1.26
Riboflavin (Vit G)	mg	1.60	1.89
Niacin	mg	22.67	12.6
Ascorbic acid (Vit C)	mg	1741	52.5
Vitamin D	units	280 (winter) 764 (summer)	280 (excluding effect of sun)

Potato blight (*phytophthora infestans*) struck the seaboard of America and Canada in 1842 and crossed the Atlantic with the 'back-loads' of immigration ships: mainly flax seed but also pota-toes. It was incorrectly believed to be a disease and therefore early remedies proved ineffective. It is in fact a fungus which blackens and rots the crop, and is highly infectious. At its peak it spread across the country at a rate of fifty miles each week.

Blight struck Ireland several times from the 1830s onwards. What made the attack of 1845 so different was that its effect was total and it was followed by five consecutive years of crop failure and particularly harsh winters. Starvation came in the company of a rapacious entourage: 'famine fever' (actually two diseases, typhus and relapsing fever), the 'bloody flux' (bacillary dysentery resulting from diets of raw turnip and seaweed), scurvy and 'famine dropsy' (now called hunger oedema).

Perversely – and to the inexcusable shame of Britain's politi-cians and the majority of Ireland's landowning families – throughout the famine Ireland remained a food exporter and the area under cultivation actually increased by a million acres. The crops that the great landowners raised for export were not redirected to sustain a starving population but continued to be sold in Britain for profit. For three seasons the British government refused to grant aid, believing unswervingly in the work ethic and private enterprise. If the lazy Irish worked, they would have money for food. The laws of supply and demand would create a market. This was the credo of the day. But there was no work, no money, and no food to buy. The Quakers in particular proved heroic in their efforts to bring relief.

The government realised the extent of the disaster too late, and even then insisted that all aid would be linked to work projects. By December 1846 nearly half a million were employed in building roads, railways and canals at a cost of £30,000 a day, and a staff of 11,500 were needed to administer the schemes. The following month the government abandoned the projects for direct relief. Hundreds of thousands had already died, the land was deep under snow, crowded 'coffin ships' were plying the Atlantic with emigrants too weak to survive the journey, and still more were crossing the Irish Sea. By June 1847 it was estimated that 300,000 destitute Irish had descended on Liverpool, a city whose pre-famine popula-tion had been 250,000. By 1849 the workhouses held 932,000 peo-ple reduced to beggary.

Much has been written to depict the scale of the horror; but even the bare statistics reveal with chilling clarity why the Great Famine lives on in Irish memory, why, like Scotland's infamous clearances, it seared the psyche of a nation. Between one and one-and-a-half million people died; one million emigrated; a further two million emi-grated over the next two years. In less than two decades Ireland's population halved. Much of her energy, intellect and enterprise went with the departed, leaving a poor demoralised nation. And worse, emigration became a pattern of growing up. By 1923, 43% of those born in Ireland were living outside the country, compared with 14.8% for Norway and 14.1% for Scotland, two other countries of abnormally high emigration tendencies. In recent census returns, forty-four million Americans claim Irish roots and of these eleven million are of 'unmixed' Irish ancestry. One in five Londoners owns Irish blood. The figures for Australia are even higher, one in three, making this the most 'Irish' of countries outside the homeland. Éire's population today is 3,800,000 with just under half of them living around Dublin, and it remains by far the most sparsely inhabited country in the European Union at fifty-one heads per square kilometre (Greece being second with seventy-six).

It is indeed a diaspora eloquent in achievement, indecent in magnitude.

Prison

I heard first the sound of oars, then the thud as one hit my hull, then the shout. 'Lo there! Kin ah come aboard, like?'

It was evening. Flights of duck were returning upstream and late participants in Crosshaven's rush-hour were doing the same on the far bank of the river. The current was at full flow and a raft of foam had taken shelter at the stern while an assortment of flotsam raced past. I'd just settled down with a beer and Dervla Murphy's *Wheels Within Wheels*, but I'd been expecting a visit from my neighbour. Close up, his appearance held all the promise of misfortune that had been hinted at from afar.

He rose into view above the gunwales, rheumatism and uncertain balance slowing his progress. A centre-parting in hair smeared flat to the contours of his skull, eyes whose blue was hard to read in the depth of their shadows and a broad nose which made me think of boxers. The rest of him was a peppery tangle of beard.

'Alastair.'

'Jim.' He extended a muscular forearm quite out of proportion to the rest of him. Rims of colour at the elbow revealed he was wearing at least three layers under his beard but his outline indicated a skeletal figure. His hand transmitted a trembling tic. Sun-dried skin threatened to split around his smile. Before me stood a castaway.

'Looks like you've got problems with damp. Is it a leak?' All day a mattress had been slung over the boom of his Folkboat. His clothes looked damp. Freshly-laundered, I felt a fraud. My usual state was closer to his, and I felt the gulf widen as I handed him a beer and his eyes took in *Ceana*'s comforts.

'Leaks! Ah've more bloody leaks than boat.' He sat on a bunk and reclined against a cushion. 'Nice boat yev got.'

This was the only occasion the interior of my boat received a compliment, but it was understandable from the owner of a Folkboat. These old twenty-five footers are wooden classics that are tough and seakindly but terribly cramped inside. They breed hunchbacks, mariners who take a week ashore to unfurl and reclaim their full height.

Jim had been a crane driver in Newcastle when the Bohemian urge took him. 'Nineteen eighty, it was', and his face lightened to show that twenty-three years hadn't all been hard nor devoid of sweetness. 'Me and the wife jacked in the jobs, sold the house, took to the Broads, did the odd job, like. But there weren't mooch variety there, in canals. So we bought a camper van. That was a bit of all right, fer a time.'

They toured Britain and sunny Europe, squatting here and there, just hanging out. Then that paled. It was all too mundane. Particularly for the wife. (She had no name, just a role and the definite article.) They sold the van and bought a horse and wooden caravan. But that was too slow, the horse too much work and a responsibility they discovered they didn't want. They parted company: horse, caravan, the wife, Jim.

'Ah bought maself a forty-foot boat, an ah'll tell yer this fer nought, she were a beauty. Sold her three year ago, an ah wish to hell ah still had her…' he nodded over his shoulder, 'instead of that loadashit.'

He talked, talked like he'd rediscovered his voice. He came to Ireland in 1989. Hadn't sailed much but dossed around harbours. He could afford wine in those days. Chilean was best. He swore it was the only wine to travel well and keep on boats. As his money dwindled, he tightened his belt. Then he had to downgrade. From forty feet of fibreglassed comfort to twenty-five of wooden loadashit. For three years he'd been attached to the river bed here. His coal stove proved ineffectual against the relentless ingress of water. He felt damp all the time. The owner of the north riverbank had befriended him and allowed him to tie up against a private jetty for 'drying out' sessions. He lent Jim a dehumidifier. Occasionally he found work for him in his sawmill.

'Ah'm sick of it. Ah jist cannae hack another winter here. You know what winter's like in these parts? Can rain fer five days on the trot. Not even nice rain. Here it's…*spiteful* rain. Like it's got it infer you. And wind! Fuck, the wind!'

In Waterford, he said, gale force winds were recorded on one hundred and sixty days of the year. A gale every two days. Cork, he reckoned, was worse.

'Last winter ah was rowin back to m'boat when this gust came outta nowhere and flipped me inflatable over. Man, that water was liquid ice. Ah managed to swim to another boat but it was locked so ah sat fer three hours till the wind went down. Ah thought ah was dead.'

Now he was shrinking, retreating into himself despite knowing he possessed no shrine against despair. Fear lent the blueness of his eyes a vulnerable beauty. He was worried about the shakes in his hands. Rheumatism was encroaching, his knees and wrists ached. Twice he'd been admitted to hospital with 'damp on the chest'. No, he repeated, he couldn't take another winter here.

'Tried to sell m' boat, but nothin doin. Who the fuck's going to buy a leakin wooden boat? Ah'm advertisin right now. A swap. A boat fer a camper van. Ah've got to get to the sun, man. Just got to get to the sun.'

Bad Days at Charles Fort

C ork ought to have been magnificent. Situated on an island between rivers and overlooked by a wooded bluff, it had everything going for it. St Finbarr's cathedral reared up on arches and
poked three spires into the air, giving the place a good start. University Park kept the momentum going but beyond that it fizzled out
into degenerate housing and industry. The central streets were being dug up in a show of civic muscle-flexing and any sense of identity was being lost to homogenous modernity. Yet it remained difficult to gauge whether modernity was creeping outwards, or decay
expanding inwards. Seedy warehouses glared menace across
streets at new offices and hotels. Supermarket trolleys, crocheted
with weed and twisted into works of art, had penetrated into Cork's
heart and were gathered on the riverbanks, poised for their final
assault. If they could cross the seething traffic, I reckoned there
wouldn't be much resistance.

I managed to get through to Dervla on the third attempt. Her
phone was a carefully controlled interference in her writing routine.

'Come in four days' time. That would be lovely!'

'I'm not the sort of guest that needs entertaining.'

'Don't worry, none of my guests get entertained.'

With time on my hands I went to Kinsale, Ireland's most southerly town. Here was the charm that Cork lacked. I was to find its
brightly painted houses and burgeoning flower-baskets replicated
across much of southern and western Ireland. The neatness of the
decoration and the intensity of colour were contrived to a point of
tweeness, but it made a welcome change from the lethargy found in
much of 'Bonnie Scotland'. Irish villages on tourist trails made an
effort to look impressive, took pride in their appearance whereas all
too often their Scottish counterparts greeted the visitor with indifference, or determined neglect. Kinsale was a tonic for the senses, not
only visually but also in its role as the 'gourmet capital' of the country. More restaurants per foot of pavement are found here than anywhere else in the country, and the seagulls are the fattest. They
hang around the rooftops like bloated weathercocks, twisting their
necks, eyeing the rubbish bins and cackling each time a backdoor
opens. They siesta with the rich in the marina. When pickings are
lean they glide the mile to Charles Fort for a sandwich. They would

have been there in 1703 when Alexander Selkirk boarded the *Cinque Ports* in Kinsale, unwittingly bound for his five-year ordeal as a castaway and eventual fame as 'Robinson Crusoe'. And they would have been there some thirty years earlier poking around the fringe of the wedding banquet that went so terribly wrong.

Charles Fort is one of the finest star-shaped forts in Europe: the landward walls are fortified by earthworks that must have exacted a brutal toll on human labour. The seaward walls align themselves on vertical crags, a theatre ripe for tragedy. It was built in the 1670s, and attacked twenty years later by William of Orange, still riding high on his success at the Battle of the Boyne. John Wesley preached here in 1749. A British garrison was stationed at Fort Charles as late as 1921 but when the troops pulled out, the buildings were severely damaged during the civil war.

The first governor of the fort was Colonel Warrender, a harsh man known for a heavy hand in punishment. He had a plain but vivacious daughter called Wilful. At this time only six soldiers in every hundred were allowed to marry, as marriage was not considered beneficial to the army's interests. These marriages were chosen by lot whenever 'vacancies' arose, and were officially recognised, being termed 'marriages on-the-strength'. On-the-strength wives always had to share the general barracks, a woollen blanket being rigged up as the only gesture to privacy, but they were allowed to accompany their husbands on campaigns. Soldiers who married off-the-strength had no rights. They were not allowed to sleep out and their wives were forbidden from entering the fort or accompanying them on tours.

Naturally officers were above such restrictions and Wilful became engaged to one, Sir Trevor Ashurst. The wedding was a dazzling affair and Colonel Warrender spared no expense. During the evening the married couple slipped out of the celebrations to take a stroll along the battlements. Wilful leant over a wall and spotted some flowers growing at the base of the crags. She hinted that she'd like them. Sir Trevor accompanied her back to the festivities, then sneaked out to assess the logistics of the task. He soon realised it was beyond him but he persuaded a young guard to make the descent on his behalf and promised him a handsome fee. The guard agreed on condition that Sir Trevor would take his place so he could not be accused of deserting his post.

They had thought the errand would take half an hour but the descent proved trickier and took longer, and Sir Trevor, exhausted by the day's events, fell asleep with his head slumped forward on his chest. Colonel Warrender happened by and was so incensed on finding a guard asleep on duty that he immediately drew his pistol and shot the man. When Wilful, still in her wedding gown, discovered her husband's fate she leapt to her death from the fort's walls.

It is easy to imagine the poor guard grinning as he appears over the parapet ('Done it, sir!'), and worth recalling the Colonel when you think you've had a bad day.

Encounters

I hitched to Dervla. In each car I entered, Ireland and the world repositioned themselves in tinted vignettes.

Car one. I'm passing through Tipperary's horse stud country with a farmer who dabbles in breeding thoroughbreds. He's forty-eight, bestowed with eloquence and words flow in the manner, I imagine, his horses move. With minimal punctuation. He looks as shrewd as a gypsy. 'Oi've got meself eleven foals roight enough and there's some roight gooduns there oi'm telling youse. Now if youse gets one goodun in three youse doin well and oi haven't done bad meself over the years. Oi've found meself this buyer from the Argentine he is and he's got three off me in the past and they must have done all roight because now he's askin for three more. So oi gets me a deposit and sends them out but save my soul getting the money that's the hard part. The June final payment has passed and he tells me there's been a little problem but it'll be all roight so he's told me to meet him in Spain and he'll have the rest of the money then so oi'm taking meself a little holiday and oi'll pick up the money then and it'll be fine. Sure oi like the man and oi trust him. The money'll be there all roight, you'll see and oi've never been to Spain to see what it's like.'

Car two. I'm standing by the road in my kilt. A car stops but before I reach it a woman gets out. She's in her sixties, confident and her clothes are exceptionally well-cut – something I'd never normally notice. She asks 'Can I take a photograph of you?' Her accent is Canadian. Somehow, and I've no recollection how but perhaps she was pre-empting any grounds for confusion over stopping, we get onto the subject of her husband. He's absent for the day, delivering a keynote presentation at a conference. She emphasises 'keynote' as if idiots galore address conferences but you must be special to do the keynote bits. He is, she says, an academic, an urban climatologist. I've never heard of this profession. 'He studies how a city affects the climate around it.' She's used to blank faces, and continues. 'In what ways climate changes on encountering a city as opposed to crossing, for example, a plain. He looks at thermals, moisture release, temperature changes, water flows and things like that.

How skyscrapers and streets create wind tunnels and eddies.' They live in Vancouver, she says, but her husband is working in America a lot these days, mainly for the army. He's been exceptionally busy since nine-eleven. 'They're very concerned about a gas attack. If terrorists release poison gas in New York, for example, at this point, that point and over there, where will the gas go? How do air currents circulate the city?' She smiles, sadly. Even to my Philistine's eye her clothes do look very, very expensive.

Car three. The same lay-by. It's on a hill overlooking the Glen of Aherlow. Below me, Ireland lies in a thousand pieces like unlit stained glass, crudely welded together. There are few cars. Despite a sign which assures me it's only twelve kilometres, it does indeed feel a long way to Tipperary, or anywhere. Another car stops. Another lone woman. When the door opens she does not step out but drifts down, spills onto the verge like the coloured eddy the army is afraid of in New York. Peacock blue. In one movement she has settled on the grass and lit a cigarette, and is now lying back staring at the sky. Dire Straits rocks the air. After a while she turns to me, beckons me over. Cigarette? She withdraws a mobile phone and shouts a message. 'I'll be a bit late for work but I'm on my way.' She's into cloud-watching, she says. She's fifty-two and left Edinburgh twenty years ago. Her father is an eminent neurologist, and all her peers have 'done well'. She does not state, but owns through implication, that she has not. 'What brought you here?' I ask. 'What takes us anywhere?' she counters. 'What brings you here? Everything happens for a reason.' She returns to the clouds. As we drive to Tipperary, she offers no name but some of her past. She was an ex-dope hippy from Afghanistan and India. She runs a funky clothing shop called Vibes of Venus. Her daughter was twenty-one and had a six-month-old boy when she died suddenly. She adopted her grandson but grief and anger tore her apart. She lost all interest in life, couldn't wear colour. Without Mrs Dunleavy, the woman she rents her shop from, her business would have sunk. Mrs Dunleavy lives next door to the shop and, without anything being said, she took over running it. After a year colour returned. 'Her boy' is what keeps her going now. He's hard work but a source of fun and delight. We enter the shop. Krishna bells tinkle. We weave through a bazaar so congested that some garments will be worn out before they're sold. No one is there. Then a rail of wraps swings round on the back of a concealed door and I glimpse the privacy of Mrs Dunleavy's home. She shuffles to the kettle. She mentions it hasn't been busy this morning but she's made some sales. No excuse for lateness is given or expected. Nothing else needs to be said. In the silence of mutual support, Mrs Dunleavy makes us coffee.

Car four. An Englishman in his thirties takes me on. He married an Irish girl three years ago. He travels about doing something with computers. He does not feel he is accepted in his village. He frequently experiences racial abuse and fears he'll never be regarded as anything other than a 'fuckin English incomer'. 'But the last place I want to live in is fuckin England.'

Car five. Coincidence sometimes continues the same theme. I'm with a former rugby player. He played the game because he loved it but in the Republic, he says, your sport can brand you with your politics. He wants to see a united Ireland, but rugby is a British game and anyone who plays it must be pro-British, pro-Union; that's the perception. On many occasions he has been shunned in his life for his love of rugby. 'Real' Irishmen devote themselves to Gaelic football and hurling, and the Gaelic Athletic Association is a powerful lobby.

I think about this, the men in green who jink about the fields of Murrayfield, Twickenham, Cardiff Arms Park and Lansdowne Road and how I used to think they were the pick of all Ireland. I never suspected their talent had to be drawn from Northern Ireland, the Dublin Pale and a handful of minor clubs who dare to play despite insinuations of treachery.

Yes, he continues, we Irish are bigots. I don't know if we're any worse than other nations but we're certainly no better. 'Look at the current influx of Ghanaians, Nigerians and Asians. I think they're making our country more cosmopolitan and that's a good thing. Besides, now we need them. Once there was no job an Irishman wouldn't do, if he did any job at all, that is. The Irish navvy was famous for doing all the shit jobs. Now we've changed. It seems bad to say this but we need these immigrants to do all the lowest jobs we won't do ourselves. Yet people still abuse them, say they're taking our jobs.'

I ask 'Would you be happy if one of your children married an immigrant?' He replies that his concern is not about the mixed marriage but the upbringing of any grandchildren. He's a lapsed Catholic but if his son married an Asian girl and she wanted to bring up their children as Muslims, then this scared the shit out of him. No, he thought out loud, I could never accept that.

Car six. To lighter things: aluminium horse shoes. A young man in his twenties tells me about his job in Dubai where he's a farrier. His boss is a sheik who owns over a thousand horses and employs five farriers. For a race the horses are fitted with aluminium shoes. 'There's hell to pay if a shoe comes off.' I'm thinking of beheadings but the van stops and I have to leave. Prematurely truncated conversations are the most irritating aspect of this mode of travelling.

I stare in disbelief at an elephant. It's standing in a field chained to a post. It reminds me of a sacred elephant I once encountered in a temple in Kerala. A holy mark had been daubed on its forehead and on receipt of a rupee, which it handed to its keeper, the trunk rose and bestowed blessings, a benevolence I found insufferable coming from a creature fettered far from sunlight in a murk of incense. Between blessings it rocked from side to side, swinging its trunk, occasionally picking up hay and swishing the bundle in a ritual of movements cultivated to alleviate boredom, before the reward of eating. I will never forget my sense of horror on looking at the spot on which it stood. Worn deep into the stone were the footprints of centuries of bondage. Before me now, this might be that elephant. The memory fills me with indignation. Fosset's circus has come to Cashel.

Car seven. Two retired men are going fishing. They're well into their sixties, I guess. There's really no room in their van but the passenger scrunches next to the driver and we fit three in two seats. 'Now there was an article about fishin in Scotland I read recently. In the back, Jack. Reach over and see if you can find it.' Jack reaches back and I hear magazines spill. He produces a copy of *Health & Efficiency* whose cover depicts two naturists frolicking on a beach. 'Not that one', the driver chortles, 'that's quite different.' The magazine is tossed back and talk of fishing resumes. I can't help wondering if possession of *Health & Efficiency* is a confessable sin? In this era of internet pornography it seems a quaint relic of respectability. Almost a virtue.

A farming newspaper is on the floor, folded into a brick with the *Personal* column face out and I can read several square inches of ads. Debbie Master Clairvoyant is offering 'Psychic Therapy for Depression', while Ireena Psychic's declared speciality is 'Dating Heartbreak/Trauma'. She's followed by 'HORSES - Wanted For Slaughter. Owner can see them put down'.

I'm let out at the Vee, a viewpoint on the Knockmealdown Mountains. Dervla lives ten miles away on the other side. A dearth of cars forces me to walk most of the distance. To arrive any other way, I console myself, would be inappropriate. Better still would be to have a thorn in my foot.

[Around the age of seven]...I invented my secret endurance tests. These consisted of regularly inflicting on myself increasing degrees of pain, until I was capable of such feats as walking three miles with a sharp thorn embedded in the sole of one foot...I had simply discovered...that it was possible to repel certain kinds of pain...This entailed practising mental detachment from bodily sensations...Although the training course lasted scarcely three years I have ever since been almost wholly insensitive to what most Europeans regard as severe discomfort.

Dervla Murphy, *Wheels Within Wheels* (1979)

Dervla Murphy

For the last few miles the road was almost subterranean in places, sunk below hedges and trees which thickened into a wood of magnificent dimensions. It threw its canopy over Lismore's few streets. Here cottages were interspersed among shops and businesses whose only concession to time was the occasional changing of signs. Some gardens were unable to contain their flowers and they burst over the pavement. Where a parting in the trees allowed, Lismore Castle towered as a chunk of brazen Victoriana, a solidified pile of the Duke of Devonshire's wealth. Below it, out of sight, was Dervla's swimming pool. From April to September anglers paying up to £500 for a beat on the Blackwater River have the chance to catch sight of one the world's greatest travel writers, and undoubtedly its most prolific, furrowing their pools.

'She lives somewhere up there', a boy said, pointing through a stone arch which led into an ally. Rubble made the surface underfoot awkward and I felt slightly claustrophobic between walls like medieval defences. A door at the far end opened to my knock and three blond girls invited me to follow them.

A coterie of narrow passages led into a cobbled courtyard. Everything here looked as if it had been locked away for a century. A corrugated iron canopy, supported on wooden columns, jutted out from one wall, giving an impression of stalls. Sheltered underneath were wooden carts. Heavy use had burnished the cobbles. They shone though outlines of weeds. Virginia creeper sprawled along walls of crumbling mortar. At their base buddleia and convolvulus injected jolts of colour. Their fragrance hung in the air inducing a soporific sense of well-being. No sound disturbed the peace. Only a concrete bungalow set in one corner prevented me from believing that I was in a caravanserai on the Silk Route and that at any moment a line of camels would burst in and be led to their quarters.

'Welcome! Love-ly to see you!'

Dervla stood there in a baggy blue T-shirt, baggy trousers and bare feet. She was about five foot six inches and sturdy, with strong limbs indicative of a life of physical labour. Her neck was broad and muscular but now, aged seventy-two, she was stooped and walked hunched forwards, a slight shuffle, feet splayed out for better balance, her shoulders adopting a frozen appearance as she smiled and squinted up. She smiled a lot, an expression that surfaced without artifice but knew its power; surely the passport of endearment which has taken her so far. Her features were well proportioned, almost sexless apart from thick silver-grey hair cut short and coiffeured into a light set – a surprise to me, not expecting this of someone used to sleeping against a mule – so that something more universal than gender struck the eye at first. For a long time I couldn't define it, then it dawned on me that what distinguished this face that might have belonged to almost any well-tanned European, was its quiet effusion of wisdom. You could *feel* the aura of this person who, for forty years, had travelled rough in diverse cultures, looked, questioned, sought to understand, and then locked herself away in solitary meditation to make sense of it all and articulate it on paper.

'These are my granddaughters.' The odd missing tooth was revealed in their grins. 'The little ones are having a holiday with me. Come, I'll show you your room. You'll probably get fleas from it.'

She led me to the old cowshed. An old spring bed extended from a wall of white-washed breeze blocks. On one side there was a quarter wall of paperbacks, on the other deep shelves from floor to ceiling laden with a yellowing archive of past works and the myriad sources of facts travellers gather, distil, index and hoard. I longed to sneak a look into them but that struck me as a breech of hospitality. I resisted. Besides, they were probably more potent as symbols in my imagination. I consoled myself with the thought that I'd be sleeping beside a national treasure in the making. Next door was a shower with an art deco mosaic floor and a sink whose single tap never produced water. The loo worked but Dervla suggested that most guests preferred to pee behind the shed.

'This is my study where I happily lock myself away every winter.' She opened the door of another outbuilding. If this had also been a byre then it was the largest, three cows long by two wide. Antique bookcases lined one wall, a highrise of colourful spines intermingled with heaps of papers. Even in mid-summer it was a dark room, but it looked as though it would be cosy in winter with a fire in the hearth as a balm to creativity. Her desk was placed below the main window and at head height on the sill stood a model bicycle about eighteen inches high. Every time she looked up from her work the view of the courtyard would feature its silhouette. A ponderous electric typewriter occupied the prime position on the desk.

'Oh yes, I'm still on one of those!' she laughed. 'A golf ball type, it's an old favourite. It's getting so hard to get ribbons for it now. "d" and "o" are almost indistinguishable. I always feel sorry for my editor at Murrays having to cope with my typescripts, all the cutting and pasting, but computers are not for me.'

She spoke slowly as if each word had been weighed and measured, and each preserved her Irishness intact through lilt and long vowels. Her voice was deep and made me think of smoke and whisky. 'I just love getting back from a journey to begin writing.'

To do this she entered 'purdah' as her friends called it. The study door was locked, the phone was taken off the hook and she wrote for up to twelve hours a day. Long-hand first, then the wads of pages were transcribed through the golf ball. This was how some two dozen books had come into being.

'How has travel writing changed over the years?'

'It's got much better, much more stylish, but I haven't! I'm still the Victorian traveller, and I get criticised for it. But there again, I get lots of nice letters too.'

She'd met some of the past masters of the genre, mostly at book festivals which she loathed and refused to attend any more. She admired Freya Stark but had found her 'terrifying and very arrogant'. Patrick Leigh Fermor was charming and a marvellous writer. Bruce Chatwin: 'Arresting to look at, but there was something very unnatural about him'. Thessiger had sought her out on one occasion, never having met anyone called 'Dervla' before. 'When he discovered I was a woman, he lost interest at once!'

And the best contemporary travel writers?

'I admire Jonathan Raban but I prefer – and I can't decide between them – Colin Thubron and young William Dalrymple. But I don't read travel books by choice, only when I have to review them. I find them unbearable. Either they make you wish you were doing that journey and writing that well or else they're insufferably bad.'

'How did you get into this business?'

'Ah, that's a long story.' She led me back into the courtyard, the former town market, and into 'the cottage', through a small 1960s kitchen in which everything looked bashed and worn but serviceable. From this unlikely setting she produced an Irish stew to rival any in the land. I ate alone. Dervla excused herself and explained she ate only one meal a day, first thing in the morning. 'But it's a large one. It takes me about an hour!'

Afterwards we sat in her living room. The chairs were wooden. The most expensive one, she explained, cost £2.50. Two of them had cushions. Her bedroom was a platform, a mezzanine level jutting out as balcony draped with Persian rugs. It was reached by a chunky wooden ladder of the sort I imagined the Crusaders had in their arsenal when trying to recapture Krak Des Chevaliers. Very little wall was visible outwith the panorama of books which were arranged by country. A map of the Middle East dangled seductively from a rafter. Despite wearing a chunky sweater I felt cold and hoped Dervla would put a match to the fire set in the hearth, but she seemed immune to the evening chill and continued to sit in flimsy cottons and bare feet. The light faded but it was not until it was almost too dark to gauge facial expressions that a light was switched on. I had already ascertained that there was no hot water on call when I'd attempted to do the washing up. An immersion was switched on for a specified period each day.

'I don't believe in wasting time on such trivialities, washing up after every dirty dish. And no washing up after sundown, that's the rule.'

I felt a wimp next to her. She was tough and she intended to stay tough. Her home provided everything she needed but no pampering, and no time was wasted on its care when she could be learning the history of Mesopotamia. Dervla encouraged living, reading and writing over cleaning, maintaining and prettifying. We drank a friend's homemade cider, and she smoked Café Crème cigars; her two concessions to decadence. And bottle by bottle, I learned how the travel had taken her.

She was born in 1931. Initially the priest refused to baptise her 'Dervla', condemning the name as pagan. *Dearbhail* meant 'true desire' in Gaelic. Eventually a compromise was reached and she was christened with the Latinised form, Dervilla Maria Murphy.

Nationalist blood ran thick on her paternal side and her father had spent his twenty-first birthday in Bedford jail for Old IRA activities. Unable to afford a honeymoon he and his bride moved to Lismore on their wedding day. He was to take up the post of county librarian for Waterford. Being Dubliners they met with a cold reception. In his first year he was stoned three times. The previous incumbent had been a popular man who'd held the post for almost half a century. He'd left a collection of nine books.

Her mother was in her early twenties when she developed rheumatoid arthritis which, by her twenty-sixth birthday (and Dervla's second), would leave her wheelchair-bound, never to walk again. Both her parents were 'utterly without material ambition' and money was always tight. Increasingly any savings went on trying to find a cure, or relief, for her mother's condition.

'From my father', Dervla wrote in her autobiography, 'I had inherited a certain shyness or gaucherie or tendency towards self-effacement...Unwittingly my mother gave me an inferiority complex I was never to outgrow.'

From the moment she could walk she exhibited a highly independent and adaptable nature, and was never at a loss to entertain herself. By the age of six she was 'a proficient and dedicated masturbator' until a sense of guilt forced the abandonment of this habit and she turned to the world of her imagination. The amount of time she spent on her own alarmed one aunt, a child psychologist, but her parents better understood her contentment and isolation. She spent hours in the surrounding woods which she filled with magical animals, most notably an omnipotent dynasty of teddy-bears who inhabited an ancient elm. Intuitively she had already decided to become a writer.

Her schooldays under nuns whom she regarded as 'superstition-sodden autocrats' were undistinguished except for a total ineptitude in languages. Finding netball and hockey too tame she founded a secret rugby club, and began her private explorations into pain endurance. Much of her childhood, it seemed, was a series of self-imposed challenges. Then came the present that was to become her key to the world. On her tenth birthday she received her first bicycle. It was second-hand, as was the accompanying atlas. Soon afterwards, she resolved to cycle to India.

'I have never forgotten the exact spot, on a steep hill near Lismore, where this decision was made. Half-way up I rather proudly looked at my legs slowly pushing the pedals round, and the thought came - "If I went on doing this for long enough I could get to India." The simplicity of the idea enchanted me.'

The following year she did a trial run, a fifty-mile circuit in one day. Dervla always credits her mother's moral support as the vital element in realising her early dreams. Yet perversely, just as the young girl's ambition reached to infinity through her mother's enthusiasm, so her mother's infirmity imprisoned her. These became the dark years, sixteen of them. Dervla found herself housebound as sole carer. In winter she was never out-of-doors during daylight. Despair set in, eventually resulting in a nervous breakdown. 'While my mother lived', she recollected, 'I could nowhere find freedom.' It was around this time, aged twenty-nine, that she switched from sherry to whiskey. Her mother died the following year.

'I was nearly thirty and had achieved - it then seemed - nothing. As a daughter I was a failure, as a woman I was ageing, as a writer I was atrophied, as a traveller I had only glimpsed possibilities.'

Free at last, she cycled to India.

In Old Delhi a chance encounter with Penelope Betjeman persuaded Dervla to send an account of her journey to Jock Murray, doyen of London's renowned house of travel publishing. With no expectation of success, she parcelled up the dog-eared fourth carbon copy of her manuscript. Back came the reply, 'Accepted! Come and see me when you're in London. Jock.'

'At once I knew that I had arrived at the predestined end to a much longer journey than my cycle to India.'

Dervla Murphy

I had caught Dervla between trips to Siberia. Her last one had gone badly. She'd got up for a pee in the night, forgotten about a hole outside the door, tumbled in and spent a fortnight recovering in a hospital somewhere near Lake Baikal. She was going back to complete her itinerary. However, her book was written and she was out of purdah. 'This is the time I enjoy my friends. I've old friends coming next week...love-ly...my holidays!'

We all went for the daily swim. The three granddaughters, three terriers (Guinness, Spit and Nipper), one of her cats (Felicity, Frances, Ferdinand, Fortune or a fifth whose name I've forgotten) and me. With secateurs we trimmed the Duke of Devonshire's brambles on our way to the Blackwater River.

'That's the teddy-bear tree!' Dervla suddenly exclaimed. 'This is where I sat as a child looking up into it. Each branch was a country, and each leaf a town and the bears were always squabbling!'

We changed into our swimming gear under a cow's scrutiny. Dervla swam half-naked and soon disappeared from view. For the first minute the water was invigorating. By the fourth minute I was worrying about my male integrity and had had enough. Dervla cruised back almost half an hour later.

A group of friends arrived for lunch. She laid out soup, quiches, cheeses, tomato and couscous salads and slabs of bread fit for Easter Island faces. Despite her prolonged immersion in the calorie-sapping Blackwater, Dervla maintained her fast.

One guest ran his own business installing special windows. He'd fitted bullet-proof glass to the American Embassy in Dublin, and blackout glass to Shannon airport for the duration of US forces passing through on their way to Iraq. Those present expressed shame at Ireland's compliance with Bush in this 'mad' war and his flagrant abuse of power. They'd all attended protest marches. Dervla had taken her grandchildren along and they'd carried placards reading WHY BOMB IRAQI CHILDREN?

'The Dublin protest was huge', Dervla explained. 'Such things give me a glimmer of hope for the world. I've read that European armies are finding it harder to find recruits. That too is hopeful.' Her face turned weary. 'I have to cling to little glimmers of hope now.'

Another of the guests was a nurse who'd done aid work in Tanzania, Laos and Bosnia. Yet another had moved from Northern Ireland after enduring two years of harassment for being a Catholic in the small 'Protestant' port of Kilkeel. One evening this woman was visiting a neighbour when a friend burst in to say her flat was on fire. The Ulster Defence Force had put a fire bomb through her letterbox. The fire brigade 'got delayed' and didn't arrive until it was too late. She lost everything. What was left of the house had to be sold to a Protestant housing association for a pittance. There were no other offers. 'Yes I was bitter. I wasn't an activist or anything like that. I don't even understand how they knew I was a Catholic, but for them that was enough. I'd done everything I could to get on with people and lead a quiet life. I gave up after that and moved to Lismore.'

She and her husband now ran courses in traditional skills. This week they were building a Celtic roundhouse, next week it was tin-smithing, then thatching, then tool-making with an Iron Age foundry. I sensed the window man was slightly discomforted by the depth of morality and green-consciousness exhibited around the table. Ireland would have felt the same when it passed under the spotlight. Its health system was berated as being in chaos. So were its roads. Unlike Spain which had joined the EU at the same time and had used its grants wisely to create a superb road system, they said, Ireland had squandered it on studies and surveys and multiple consultations on projects that never happened.

'We've had too much wealth too quickly', the nurse said. 'Our biggest problem is we know our rights but we've yet to learn our responsibilities.'

'The Irish rebellion against authority is a colonial kick-back', the window man added. 'For centuries we were always suppressed and never allowed to own anything, so naturally people fought the system and bled it for what they could get. Now we're in control but the attitude persists that It's OK to cheat the state. When our beloved Charles Haughey was found to have lined his pocket while in power most people thought "Good on him! I'd have done the same!" We've got a whole mindset to change there.'

Dervla pitied the younger generation. 'There's no longer any continuity with the past. That's a tragic loss of connection and identity. And what terrible moral dilemmas these generations are going to have to face. The trouble with medicine and science is that being able to do something now is taken as the right to do it.'

Conversation scintillated, Café Crèmes turned to ash, cider flowed. On my way back to *Ceana* the following day I realised I'd not done two things I'd particularly hoped to do: wash some clothes and dry out the silica gel bags I stored with my concertina. In retrospect the oversight was wholly forgivable. They simply never occurred to me. You visit Dervla Murphy for the illumination of travel not the fulfilment of your domestic chores. I can't remember how many countries we travelled. I was left trailing a restless spirit whose desire to understand has become a need born in opposition to the world's ignorance of, or willing blindness to, what it's doing to minority cultures and the rich lessons it might learn from them.

Lusitania

og. A common scourge of this coastline. The Roches Point lighthouse rumbled as I crept out of Cork Harbour sending me scurrying to check my chart. Far to the south the Bay of Biscay was upset and sending missives to slop against Ireland. I motor-sailed into a boisterous swell wanting to clear the shipping lane before yielding speed for the peace of wind. *Ceana* lurched and yawed and all her trappings became pendulums trying to catch me unawares.

Once round the Old Head of Kinsale we fell onto a broad reach. Although the motion remained the rise and fall of a merry-go-round, the sight of a full sail bent to its task and Fleming holding us on track added exhilaration to the discomfort. I watched how my boat handled these waves, some now rearing up to one-third of her length. Her weight and design gave her an attitude that inspired confidence. I felt immense pride in her. She possessed an uncanny ability to read each wave and know when to yield, letting the brute energy find no resistance, and when to hold her own and outrun the point of danger.

Occasionally she got it wrong. A breaker would thump against the topside, toss us askew and envelope the cockpit in water while I braced myself for the expected calamity. This sailing game seemed as ticklish as robbing banks. Each successful venture left you elated but convinced that your luck had to be running out. Sooner or later you were going to get caught.

I was now in the Lusitania Current and close to the wreck for which it is named. The *Lusitania* lies 295 feet below the surface of the Celtic Sea, twelve miles south of the Old Head of Kinsale. The outline of her name is apparently still legible on her stern. Her detached bow sticks up at forty-five degrees. Her broken hull rests on its starboard side and conceals the entry point of the torpedo which caused the first explosion at 2.10pm on 7 May 1915, just as passengers were finishing lunch. Almost immediately a second explosion occurred which has ever after remained a mystery and source of speculation. The world's greatest ship at the time of her launch – almost 800 feet long, 30,000 tons and the first vessel to be fitted with four propellers – sank in eighteen minutes. In 1993 an American salvage team sent down three manned miniature submarines.

Clearly recognisable in the images they brought back were a lady's shoe and a shower room with its fittings encrusted but looking serviceable.

'The steamer turns to starboard', Kapitänleutnant Walther Schwieger, commander of U-20, wrote in his log at 1.45pm on that May afternoon, 'directs her course towards Queenstown and makes possible an approach for a shot. Ran at high speed to gain position directly ahead.'

When U-20's torpedo scored a hit just below the waterline, Germany ended what had been regarded as an honourable convention of war. Until then it had been the practice – incredible as it may seem to our world of unbridled ruthlessness – that submarines would not sink civilian vessels on innocent passage without first giving a warning. Submarines would surface within communicating distance of their enemy's ferries, fishing boats and cargo boats, signal their intention to attack and allow time for evacuation. Once their target was destroyed they were expected to rescue all who had been on board. The *Lusitania* was the first to be refused that courtesy.

Some accounts declare that the Admiralty withheld reports of sinkings off the Irish coast from the *Lusitania* on the pretext that an outrage against an American civilian ship, and the most famous liner of the day, would precipitate greater American aid in Britain's war effort. This claim is without substance. Germany had already announced that it considered all ships in British waters to be legitimate targets in a war zone, and this warning appeared in New York's newspapers on the morning of the *Lusitania*'s departure. Her captain, William Turner, was certainly aware of the danger. However it was believed that the ship's exceptional speed would protect her and Captain Turner could not have envisaged the scale of submarine activity off the south coast of Ireland. His destination was Cork's harbour, formerly called Queenstown but later renamed Cobh, an obvious attraction for submarines. During the week of his passage across the Atlantic, twenty-three merchant ships had been torpedoed.

The *Lusitania* was built on the Clyde and launched in 1906. Within a matter of months her record-breaking dimensions were superseded by her sister ship, the *Mauritania*, but the *Lusitania* was faster. She held both Blue Ribbands and broke records on five occasions. Captain Turner was a highly experienced master but at the time of the attack he was closer to the shore than Admiralty recommendations, not adopting a zigzag route and was running at reduced speed. In reality there was probably little he could have done to avert the tragedy.

What caused the second explosion shortly after the torpedo struck has never been established. It was not a second torpedo. Raymund Weisbach, the torpedo officer who fired the shot from U-20, was asked about this when he visited Tralee in 1966. 'I fired one', he replied. Was the *Lusitania* breeching her neutrality and carrying a secret cargo of munitions? Was it, despite contrary testimony from boiler-room crew, an engine explosion? Or was it, as seems most probable, coal dust from the empty starboard bunker being thrown into the air and ignited by the torpedo's blast? Had this much more destructive second explosion not occurred, the *Lusitania* might have floated for long enough for more people to have been safely evacuated. Of the 1,959 people on board, 1,198 perished. Many were too afraid to jump when the stern, the last part to sink, was raised a hundred feet over the sea. Captain Turner was thrown clear from the bridge and survived for three hours in the sea, being among the 761 who were rescued.

The Germans struck a medal in honour of the achievement and further added to the outrage felt on both sides of the Atlantic. The Allies based a propaganda campaign on this medal and produced a replica denouncing the Germans as heartless murderers. The replicas became popular and 300,000 were distributed. For months afterwards the *Lusitania*'s deckchairs continued to be washed ashore, and American support for Britain substantially increased.

The Cape

I was now almost at the southwest corner of Ireland, heading for Crookhaven. (The Irish have a knack for names.) The fog cleared intermittently but returned each time I approached a headland. Once a fisherman overtook me, gave a friendly wave and promptly laid a kilometre of net between us. After this came two wheelywaws (black-headed gulls) flying malevolent, close-cutting shears across my bow, their beaks opening and closing continually as if silently cursing. They were followed by the first storm petrel of the season. They are my favourite seabird. Barely bigger than blackbirds and not dissimilar in colouring, they flit among the waves, seemingly able to grab a moment's rest in the lee of a crest before allowing the wind to carry them where they're going. To be so small and to find the weather always a convenience, this is the storm petrel's achievement.

County Cork made the odd appearance, a grey sponge which sharpened into fields thrusting up at crooked angles. Ruined watch towers stood on the edge of this broken land, above guano-stained cliffs and reefs where the surf erupted; two whites straining to touch. The general desolation was reflected down below. I hadn't closed a hatch properly and each time the deck was awash the sea had slopped into the cabin. My bunk was soaked. The constant battering had dislodged clothes, books, notes and charts from shelves and they lay plastered to the floor, washed by a ripple of liquid like photographs in a developing tray. Being cold, wet, and invasive are some of the sea's less attractive traits.

While clearing up the mess I came a little closer to Doolic Rock than intended. I looked through a porthole and wondered what that tall white geyser could be. The wind had backed and tricked Fleming. His only point of reference was the wind on his foil. Under fickle conditions he was easily duped. I realigned him and we were safely through another phase of the bank robbery. (If you can get away with it, I recommend a close call on Doolic Rock in a heavy swell). I returned to sifting through my papier mâché collection. Something about a damaged map or chart cuts me deeply. It's an affront to my wellbeing. I laid them out as if they were dying companions. I tucked my notes over the curtain rail, draped clothes over the storm jib. *Twenty Years A-Growin* had survived unscathed on a lifeboat of

Sailing Directions South & West Coasts of Ireland. For the rest of the voyage, from Dawros Bay to The Conversion of Measurements would remain a solid brick.

Just to the north of my position was a small pocket of water unique in all Ireland. Lough Hyne lay a quarter of a mile inland, roughly at mean sea level, at the end of a magic river. Twice each day water flowed from the sea into the lough for four hours, then the river reversed and water flowed out for eight. Within this gigantic rockpool existed several thousand species of marine creatures and plants: seventy-three species of sea-slug, seventy species of sponges, twenty-four species of crabs, eighteen species of sea-anemones, and sixty-five per cent of the seaweeds found around Ireland. One of the sea-slugs, *Dicata odhneri,* only half-an-inch long is known only here and in a few bays close to Naples. What makes this phenomenon possible is an unusual variety of habitats defined by temperature, salination, thermoclines and slope gradations from shallow to deep.

On my horizon the Sydney Opera House had moved in, painted itself black and run aground. On the chart it called itself 'The Stags'. The breeze which had helped me clear the early hazards now hindered me from plain sailing[1] to them. I was about to strike my furthest south and 'round the corner'. But it clearly wasn't going to yield easily, this climacteric point. As I tacked this way and that through a sea studded with orange buoys, the Opera House kept its distance. I lay back and tried to enjoy the sun's warmth through two jerseys and oilskins.

Several hours later the Opera House allowed me to pass and the tide abandoned its resistance. Soon I was doing a breakneck seven knots and the rigging was strumming. At latitude 51° 27.6 N I reached my furthest south. I raised a glass to all who shared this line with me; the inhabitants of Warsaw, Kiev, Irkutsk, Calgary, southernmost Hudson's Bay, northernmost Newfoundland and Wimbledon.

Ahead lay Clear Island, also confusingly known as Cape Clear.

---

[1] This term for an easy passage is a corruption of 'plane sailing'. During the many centuries when the sextant and chronometer were the only reliable instruments of ocean navigation, complex calculations had to be made using the declination of sun, moon, planets and stars. On long ocean crossings the computations for route planning became much harder because of the curvature of the earth, necessitating the use of spherical trigonometry. If, on the other hand, the route was broken down into a series of many short sections, the curvature of the earth became insignificant and the much simpler planar trigonometry (the measurement of distances and angles using straight-sided, flat triangles) could be used. Ships using this method were plane sailing.

'The island', according to my guidebook, had a population of 130 people, thirty-three tractors, thirty-two pushbikes and three pubs on a hill known as 'the stations of the cross'. What use bicycles were among gradients that would burn through a set of brake pads in an afternoon, I was at a loss to understand. In the days of sail blue-water captains from the Atlantic would heave to here and take on a pilot for the confines of the Irish Sea and English Channel. Pilots would race out to be the first to secure the job. The unlucky ones would return with a snippet of foreign news as their consolation. Thus Cape Clear was the first place in the Old World to hear that the American Civil War had ended.

I turned off before the island, passed through the Gascanane Sound, whose central rock is lethal to those trying to count Cape Clear's tractors, and entered the island-covered Roaringwater Bay. To starboard Sherkin Island's layers glowed ginger in the evening sun. Ahead rose the copper dome of Mount Gabria, the first mountain I'd seen from the sea since Wicklow, its tint betraying the metal that was mined from it 5000 years ago. Then I caught a whiff of peat smoke and felt a surge of excitement. Archetypal Ireland was about to begin.

I entered Crookhaven's tongue of water in a wash of golden light. Marconi's old radio station momentarily broke through as a silhouette whose edges were sharpened by lasers. Then the critical moment passed and the sun was gone, leaving me in the cold. A headland rose to seaward and a hole had formed in its point. Through it I could see for miles. To a dark finger which pointed up from a clenched fist on the horizon. It was, my chart confirmed, five miles away. The Fastnet Rock.

Fastnet

> I can think of no other edifice constructed by man as altruistic as a lighthouse. They were built only to serve.
>
> George Bernard Shaw

The Fastnet rock is the most southerly piece of Ireland a boat can collide with, and many have done so over the centuries as it lies on the trade route between England's most important ports and North America. Until 1818 this coastline was unlit for 150 miles between Hook Head and Mizen Head. The authority charged with the responsibility for lighting the whole coast of Ireland went by the name of the Ballast Board. The Fastnet rock was the obvious location for a lighthouse but for the fact that nobody could conceive of how one could be built or maintained on such a precarious toehold subject to the full fury of the Atlantic. So a lighthouse was built on Cape Clear but it was frequently obscured by fog and shipping continued to be lost. Eventually the Board realised the impossible would have to be attempted.

The name Fastnet is of Viking origin, believed to signify a fang. In Gaelic it is called *Carraig Aonair*, 'lonely rock'. During the nineteenth century it acquired a more poignant sobriquet, the 'Teardrop of Ireland', as it was the last view of their homeland for tens of thousands of emigrants. Eight years after engineers succeeded in constructing the present lighthouse on this inhospitable rock, its signal, one flash every five seconds, would be the last land light many on board the *Titanic* would see.

The first (1849) structure was a novel experiment with a cast-iron spire. It endured but inspired no confidence. In 1899 the Board decided to use Cornish granite for a tower which would be fifty-two feet in diameter at its base. They blasted a level area, not on the rock's summit but on a shelf six feet *below* the high water mark, and built diminishing circles of granite to a height of fifty-seven feet before making the door. The final tower was 160 feet high.

What distinguished this construction was the size of the blocks used and the ingenious method of fitting them together. The full height of the tower was reached in just eighty-nine courses, each block weighing an average of three tons but some exceeding five. Dovetailed joints were sculpted at top and bottom so that each course locked into its neighbour. In addition the external face had to be angled to fit the tower's graceful profile. Such was the precision required that the Fastnet lighthouse was built three times: firstly at the quarry in Cornwall where each block was numbered; secondly as a dress rehearsal at Crookhaven, the port which would be the depot for the construction team; and thirdly on the Fastnet Rock. In this last effort, all 4,300 tons of granite was raised into place in 118 working days, spread over five summers. Widely regarded as the most elegant of its kind, the Fastnet was lit in 1904.

Today the light is 1,823,000 candelas, visible under clear conditions from twenty-seven miles[1]. The optic floats on a trough of mercury to keep it level. It runs almost without friction. The original clockwork mechanism, long obsolete, required a weight of 290 pounds falling at the rate of forty-nine feet per hour to rotate the light at three revolutions per minute. (The flash is achieved with lenses and prisms). The weight was wound back to the top every forty-five minutes, a strenuous five-minute hoist. Three keepers worked four-hour watches in rotation and one was replaced every fortnight, weather permitting, which it often didn't. Each man was required to bring his own provisions for the duration of his stay. If he ran short the Lighthouse Board provided an emergency stock which was available for purchase.

The Lighthouse Board's regulations on food strike some observers as curious anomalies. When Wallace and June Clark were sailing off northern Donegal in the 1970s they dropped in on Inishtrahuill Island and were invited to tea by the three keepers. 'On the tea table were three loaves, three butter dishes and three sugar basins. We were pressed to use them in turn', Clark wrote in *Sailing Round Ireland.* This strict demarcation of provisions was designed to avoid grudges over food turning into conflicts, a very real danger among an isolated community of men living in close confinement. If each keeper had to supply and consume his own food, there could be no grounds for complaint over who was eating all the choice bits or more than his fair share. If keepers chose to share meals and their

---

[1] Lighthouses serve another important function besides defining their position by light or sound. They tell a ship how far away she is through the use of 'dipping tables'. As a ship approaches land the curvature of the earth obscures any sighting of it. The point when a mariner first glimpses a flicker of light as the top of a lighthouse momentarily rises above the horizon and then dips below, is called the 'dipping distance'. It is dependent on the height above sea level of the light (a fixed factor) and the height above sea level of the observer (a variable). Dipping tables are computed for each lighthouse. All the mariner has to do is estimate how high his or her eyes are above sea level when the first flicker of light is detected (maybe eight feet in my case on *Ceana*, perhaps fifty feet in Captain Turner's on the *Lusitania*) and read off the distance in miles from the table.

supplies they were free to do so, but any keeper who preferred not to had the regulations arranged in his favour.

This world has gone now. In 1997 the keepers of Ireland's last manned light, Dublin's Baily, packed their oilskins and walked out, their departures terminating remarkable chains of continuous human occupation on one spot. Fastnet was automated in 1989. Its reserves of diesel are sufficient to last eighteen months. Two back-up generators are on automatic standby and can be activated remotely but failing this, batteries will continue to send a signal at reduced power. A computer in Dublin monitors the signal sequence, the generator's revs, oil pressure, temperature and fuel level; even an intruder alarm.

In sailing circles the Fastnet has been well known since the race which bears its name was inaugurated in 1925. Starting with a circumnavigation of the Isle of Wight, it used the Fastnet as the outer marker and finished at Plymouth; a distance of 608 miles. With only minor modifications, the course remains the same today. The lumbering family cruiser continues to compete against the carbon-fibre and teflar streaks of monied technology, but can't hope to better the current record of 35 hrs, 17mins, 14secs set by the American 125-foot catamaran *Playstation*.

One Fastnet race stands out above all others. The mention of it inspires a hushed reverence and crossed fingers. The storm which struck the 303 competitors on 14 August 1979 began as an innocuous low off Canada. Its approach was predicted as rising to Force Six, which was nothing to worry about, only it underwent what meteorologists call 'explosive deepening', a rapid and unexpected drop of over 24 millibars in twenty-four hours. This is more commonly a winter phenomenon and almost always occurs over oceans. For it to take place close to land in summer was exceptional. At Forces 10-11 (64-75mph) this was categorised as a Very Severe Storm, causing waves estimated at up to thirty-five feet. As always, it was the breaking seas rather than the wind which posed the greatest threat to yachts. Rescue services were unable to cope with the number of vessels in difficulty. Seventeen lives were lost.

The 1979 Fastnet Race changed the regulations for yacht safety in much the same way the *Titanic* did for passenger safety though SOLAS (the convention for the Saving of Lives at Sea). It is still a standard by which storms and sea disasters are measured.

At the time of the storm Gerry Butler was twenty-nine years old and the assistant keeper on the Fastnet. I tracked him down. We spoke over the phone:

'There were three of us keepers as was normal, and there happened to be some tradesmen doing some work there too. In summer we'd be on for two weeks. In winter it'd be six, but you had to take at least three months' worth of food with yous. If the head keeper found yous with less he'd send yous straight back.

Yes, the Fastnet storm was bad but, golly no, it wasn't the worst I saw. I've seen some I'd say were eight times worse, yes, that would be no lie. But it was bad all the same. We were locked in the tower. The inside of the door had bars and wheels yous turned to clamp them shut, like a submarine yous could say, and we were locked in. In winter the sea buries the Fastnet. The tower's 163 feet high and the waves go right over the top. The whole structure vibrates and shakes. I joined the service at nineteen so by 1979 I'd already done ten years and two storms stand out in my mind.

The first time I felt the tower shake we'd been looking at TV in the kitchen which was about halfway up the tower. I heard this almighty explosion below us and then the water came roaring up the side and the TV picture went and we knew it had lost reception because the water was covering the aerial at the top. And all the time I was thinking, 'What's wrong with my chair?' because it was like it had turned to rubber. But it was a vibration in the stone. The whole tower was shaking and moving my chair about. But yous got used to it, the explosion, the shaking, the lost picture which came back when the wave had passed.

You see what was happening was the sea was breaking half a mile away to the west. It always breaks there and yous can see the surf coming. It builds up again and hits the tower at about thirty to forty miles an hour and plunges down and traps air at the base of the rock. The air is compressed and it bursts up and this is the explosion we hear and it lifts the wave over the tower. So it's not like the wave comes in as tall as the tower, no it's not like that, but this mountain of water is hurled over the top. It's a terrific weight of water and it makes the tower sway.

The tower was designed to flare outwards as it rises from the base, just at the bottom, to deflect the power of the waves but yous always got a rogue wave. Rogue waves gave no warning, no noise as they never formed an explosion because they hit the tower above the flare, and God I remember one. It must have been a monster because when it hit, the tower suffered such a jolt I was forced to take a step to keep my balance. And I was halfway up the tower, not even at the top!

The worst storm I remember was in December seventy-eight, the winter before the Fastnet storm. Now Reggie and me we'd seen the wind getting up and after tea we went out to take in some stanchions from the helicopter pad. He was a heavy-set man and he fought his way back to the tower but I weighed just nine and half stone then and I couldn't make it. Couldn't make any headway against the wind. There were railings that led to the tower and went round the back of it so I hauled myself along but they ended four meters from the door. Twice I tried to push towards the door and each time I was blown back. If the railings hadn't caught me, I'd have been away. I realised I had to haul myself round the tower more and hope that when I tried for the door again I could grasp hold of it as the wind took me past. I was blowing like a leaf in the wind, just like a leaf in the wind when Reggie lent out and caught me. 'Get in you silly bastard', he yells as a joke, but it was touch and go, really. Well, we locked the tower and I went to the workshop which was three floors up. I liked to spend time there, making models and things like that. I hadn't been there five minutes when a wave hit the side of the workshop. And moments earlier we'd been out there standing on the rock. That's how fast the sea can get up.

Well, I've never seen a sea as angry as that night. I went up to my bedroom and being so small I could open my window and squeeze into the recess beyond because the walls of the tower were that thick there was quite a space before the outer storm window. The storm window had a five inch square pane in it and through that I could watch the seas. They were huge. There was a moon out and I could see the waves coming and the biggest would block out the moon. And they were violent, absolutely violent. Yous wouldn't believe the power in that sea. The best description I can think of is that film, *The Perfect Storm*. Have yous seen that film? Well that night I saw seas just like it. And the next day it was a Sunday afternoon and it was the same. I went up to the light and there's a door onto a balcony and the seas were coming from behind and I stood in that open doorway and a wall of surf burst behind me. Maybe you've seen that poster, it shows a French lighthouse and a keeper standing in the doorway with a burst of surf hitting the tower behind him - well it was just like that with me only I was 163 feet up! No word of a lie, that's how it was.

But yous were asking about the Fastnet storm. Oh golly, I remember that awful night. I remember the conditions before, there was thick fog. It cleared about the time the race was starting. The skies had gone frighteningly dark and the wind was howling and it kept changing direction, from west to northwest, then back again. Now a westerly is the worst and when the sea's against it, it becomes like there's holes in the surface which a boat falls into. It becomes un-navigable. If yous take a line from the Fastnet to Mizen Head, then east of it is sort of protected. West of it and it's an unbelievable difference. Now these boats were struggling in the east area and then they crossed that line and hit what we call the Western Ocean Roll. That heave is always there, even when the surface is calm. When the wind gets behind it and starts to blow, then that sea rises thirty or forty feet very, very quickly. And I'll tell yous this, when the wind stops blowing it takes a fortnight for that sea to settle. That's how bad it gets. That's what these boats were going into.

Despite the weather the yachts kept coming. We had a big Aldis lamp and we had to shine it on the sails to read the numbers so we could record them. But after a while we stopped because the yachts had enough troubles without being blinded by us. Some of them came so close. I remember this one boat, huge it was, called *Golden Apple of the Sun*. She came so close I could have reached out and touched her. Honest, she was that near. Then I remembered an old fisherman in Crookhaven telling me that when a wave hits the rock and pulls back, it counters the force of the next wave and they sort of cancel each other out so there's a little patch of navigable water there, and that's what this yacht was doing. It was frightening and exhilarating to see. I don't know who was skippering her but he was a genius, it was really beautiful seamanship. God, yous needed good experience that night.

Jesus, we felt bad, witnessing all this and knowing there was nothing we could do. No, we didn't see any boats founder or any accidents, but we heard about them. Oh God that was the worst, all night we listened to the radio. Continuous distress calls, terrified voices pleading for help or others witnessing a disaster or dismasted yachts with no sign of life aboard and there was one of a man seen clinging to his mast waving for help but there was nothing the other yacht could do, and on it went, all night. All we could do was write down the messages and pass them on, knowing no one would be going to help. Valentia Radio issued bulletins and tried to reassure everyone but it was a horror, yes, that's the word, a horror. In all my years that was the most emotional night I ever had.

When daylight came the wind was still howling and the sea still raging but it was moderating. By then fifteen people had drowned. Yet you know, for days afterwards yachts came round. I found that amazing, that people hadn't abandoned the race, that they could still want to finish the course after all that had happened.

I'm a part-time attendant now, at Galley Head. When I was made redundant I hated it. What I loved was the time afforded us, God, yea, time to spare, time for reading and making things. I made models, of sailing ships mostly. I'd get every detail right. I did the *Cutty Sark*. Took me two years. Golly, I really miss that. But the Fastnet, that was something else. That was the worst night I spent. A horror, it was.'

Hungry Hill

At 6.30am I slipped my mooring and glided out of Crookhaven under sail. Two pubs and a sprinkle of houses faded astern, and Crookhaven was gone. It always seemed a furtive move, this departing in silence. The rustle of mainsail rising up the mast, a shivery hiss as the foresail unfurls, a splash as the warp is cast off, a winch's protest as sheets are tightened. Then nothing. Nothing save the occasional sort of gurgle a baby makes for want of a laugh as the boat picks up speed. I could hear myself breathing and a distant dog barking as we floated past other yachts whose occupants were asleep and unaware that three tons were on the move a few feet from their heads. I felt like an escapee tiptoeing away, buoyant on deception.

I had tides to catch, connections to make. Today I would be rounding Mizen Head, the start of Ireland's west coast, her wild side. She was giving me a kind introduction. The ocean was a toad skin with warts of light and dark. It undulated on a rhythmic pulse, orderly and precise, lifting us ten feet and lowering us with the courtesy of a medieval dance in which you're continually presented with a new partner. Without music we farandoled to Mizen Head.

Compared to the Fastnet, Mizen Head lighthouse was an apology, nothing more than a bungalow with a light below the sitting room window. It capped a small island with cliffs on all sides and shared a ledge with 20,000 guillemots. Sleep must have been impossible for the keepers. One foggy day in 1985 the keepers had a strange experience. First they saw a flare, very close. They went outside and heard voices coming from the chasm below. One man was lowered on a rope as far as he dared and there he came across the most prominent Irishman of the day, the taoiseach, the very wet Charles Haughey. He had just steered his yacht, *Taurima*, into the base of the rock and taken to a life raft along with several companions as *Taurima* sank. It took the coastguard two hours to hoist the first minister and his crew to safety. Not everyone approved of the rescue.

The breeze lightened and Fleming began losing his touch at the helm. His vane struggled to find enough movement in the air to power his arms and every few minutes he steered us towards chocolate crags. I took the opportunity of doing my washing, filling a tub with hot water and suds and scrubbing away in bursts between correcting Fleming's mistakes. By the time my clothes were rinsed and hanging along the guard rails, the wind had died and Fleming was asleep. I fired up the engine and soon socks, shirts and boxers were leaning out like pillion passengers.

I took a bearing on a tower on Sheep's Head as a squadron of shearwaters sped past, black and white boomerangs madly flapping their wings then relaxing into long low glides. The signal towers, whose stunted profiles stood on every promontory, had been built long before the phobia of Napoleon's invasion inspired a new wave of watch-keeping. These ones were raised after the Sack of Baltimore in 1631 when two Algerian ships descended on the town and carried off 117 people to lives of slavery on the Barbary Coast. There must still be Irish Arabs about in those parts, I supposed.

A breeze returned and pushed me up Bantry Bay, attractively furnished with hills, moorland and a fringe of greenery as dark as cucumber skin. That evening, with my washing stowed away (less one sock lost to peg failure), I came to rest in Ireland's most idyllic anchorage. Glengarriff Bay was a delight of islands, each a secretive haven of Scots pine screened off by rhododendrons. The largest comprised twenty-seven acres: Ilnacullin, 'island of holly'', a garden designed by Harold Peto and gifted to the nation. Seals slumbered on rocks looking over-inflated and immoveable, opening their eyes and yawning as boats shuttled tourists, who looked much the same, to Ilnacullin's Italian Garden and a bonsai collection whose prize specimens were planted three hundred years ago.

I lay on deck, drinking in this Hebridean landscape. I might have been at Shieldaig, Plockton or Inverewe. The shape and texture of the land was identical. The same dyes had been used. The same pungency of seaweed pervaded each breath. And enjoyment of it was equally transient. Within the hour I was clad in oilskins as the road to Puxley Mansion turned fluid under my feet. Lightning stabbed the horizon and soon my single-track road was in spate.

I thought it was a vision at first, a white cross of a size too large to be anything other than a miracle, but it was hard to see through the truck's window and a film of water. I couldn't ask, because the driver was telling a joke.

'So this father, you see, decides to have himself a little pep talk with his son. It's long overdue, you know, and he says, Well, son, now you're a teenager you probably smoke. I always told you never to smoke but I'm a smoker so I can't blame you. And I suppose you take a drink or two? Well, I'm not unknown in pubs meself...'

The cross mutated in each rivulet streaking the glass and refused to evaporate. It had to be enormous and, I guessed, at least a mile away on the top of Bear Island.

He was chuckling now, on the descent to the punch line.

'I imagine, son, you like girls? Well that's just natural too as long as you're not doing anything you shouldn't...'

A mile of lights and figures hunched under umbrellas marked the existence of Castletownberehaven. The longest place name in the country (along with Newtownmountkennedy in Co. Wicklow) was usually abbreviated, in marvellous Irish fashion, to either its first two-thirds or last half. Castletownbere, or Berehaven, was founded as a port for the export of copper ore and, according to my pilot, was 'one of the largest natural anchorages in Europe'. When the Anglo-Irish Treaty ended British rule over Southern Ireland in 1921 three strategic ports – Cobh, Lough Swilly and Castletownbere – were excluded from the handover and retained by Britain for a further eighteen years. My chart for the Beara Peninsula, however, gave a different picture. The approaches to this port were littered with the symbols of wrecks. Perhaps that was what the white cross was all about.

'But let me tell you this, son. If you ever have anything to do with the Gaelic Athletic Association, I'll feckin well stove your brains in.'

I laughed politely, feeling I couldn't seek clarification on the subtleties of his humour. I guessed it was his way of saying he played rugby.

'What you wanting to see Puxley Mansion for? It's a feckin ruin.'

'I read a novel about it.'

'Yea? We passed the old Hungry Hill mine some miles back. At Allihies. It must have closed fifty years ago.'

The rain ended and the gloom, which had turned a summer evening into a winter's night, lifted. For a mile I walked along a private road in the half-light, through occasional frenzies of midges, until Puxley Mansion's towers and arches stood before me. Even in ruin the building's former elegance shone. So many windows perforated its three storeys that it was a latticework. Vaulted arches, astragals and mullions cut lozenges in profusion lending the granite and limestone mass the lightness of a mirage, so that the mansion appeared not to be supported by the ground but hovering in the air. It looked desperately fragile. Trees and shrubs flourished in cracks. Steel ribs had been erected inside to arrest the inevitable. A low fence was all that prevented a herd of cows taking up residence. It was hard to tell which was the original house and which the Gothic extension that was so successful the rest of the building had to be remodelled to match it. Sad that the owner enjoyed it for just six years and then, despite being still a young man, left Ireland, never to return. But as a story, the Puxleys were a gift to Daphne du Maurier.

She was already famous following the success of her best-known books when *Hungry Hill*, her seventh novel, was published in 1943. She renamed the Puxleys the Brodicks, Puxley Mansion became Clonmere Castle, and Berehaven became Doonhaven. Her imagination filled out the details but five generations of family history provided the plot; the building of a mine, the exploitation of the miners, a feud with neighbours, tragic deaths, jealousies, alcohol and gambling addictions, and the final act of destruction by the IRA.

The Puxleys had married into a landed family in the area and were in financial decline when the third generation, 'Copper John', inherited the estate. When copper deposits in Hungry Hill were assayed as commercially viable, he imported Cornish miners in 1812 and started an industry which proved immensely profitable. Shrewd, ruthless and energetic, Copper John ran the business for the next forty-four years, increasing the payroll to 1300 and using force to suppress any protests over working conditions. It was Copper John's son, Henry, who took control in 1860, following the unexpected death of his elder brother, and converted the old house into Puxley Mansion. It was to be a gift for his young wife, Katherine. The work was finished in 1867 but Katherine died in 1872, aged thirty-six. Henry was so distraught he locked the door of Puxley Mansion and never returned. With properties in London and Wales, he managed the business from afar and employed caretakers to keep an eye on the ancestral home. He died in 1909 and his son, John Paul, returned once for a temporary residence of six months.

Du Maurier ascribes the final act of violence to John Paul (John Henry in the novel) being seen drinking in a bar with British soldiers in 1920. It is a chance encounter, endured as a courtesy but witnessed by nationalists and interpreted as fraternising with the enemy. The following day Sinn Féin set Clonmere Castle alight. The reality is only a little different. It was rumoured that Puxley Mansion was to become a barracks for the British Army. On 9 June, 1921, members of the IRA escorted the caretakers, a Mr and Mrs Albert Thomas, out of the building and set it on fire. It was not an isolated event. Between the years 1920-23 some 200 'big houses' of the Anglo-Irish ruling class, or the Ascendancy as they were called, were burnt to the ground, a figure representing about ten per cent of the stock. The Puxleys later sued for compensation, seeking £130,000 but being awarded £50,500. There was interest in restoring the ruins into a hotel or Jesuit College but in 1926, the remains of the mansion and 215 acres were bought for £2020 by a pub owner who chose to leave the stones as they were.

This is Puxley Mansion: luxurious family home for six years, frozen capsule for forty-nine, creepily resplendent skeleton for eighty.

Potted History No 4

The effects of the Famine largely bypassed the Protestant regions of Northern Ireland which was experiencing its own industrial revolution and increased prosperity. Belfast had grown into a giant of linen manufacture, shipbuilding and engineering. In the south people had no option but to cling to a ravaged system of agriculture in which mixed tillage was declining in favour of livestock. The minority north was divided from the majority south in every way: by religion, wealth, politics and civil rights.

In the south the Famine had concentrated grievances and feelings of betrayal into a nationalist movement, Fenianism, aimed at forcing Britain into ceding independence. The Irish Republican Brotherhood (IRB) was formed in 1858 to create an armed uprising but there were more than fifty years of thwarted missions and internal divisions before the move was made in 1916. New activists arose, notably Parnell and Davitt who founded the Land League. By withholding rents and defying eviction orders the League instigated a 'Land War' and produced the long-awaited revolution. (One landlord who held out against the League, Captain Charles Boycott, was reduced to a state of siege, unable to leave his property or harvest his crops, and his ostracisation added a new word to the English language). In 1881 the Land Act was passed, establishing security of tenure and a process for fair rents.

The next stage for the nationalists was Home Rule. Adding to the groundswell for reform driven by the Land League and the IRB there now arose new pressure groups: the romantic - literary movement (a force of such luminaries as W B Yeats, George Russell and playwright J M Synge), the Gaelic League and Sinn Féin (literally 'we ourselves') all of whom shared the independence ideals of the IRB but were committed to achieving them by political means, not violence. Unions developed in number and confidence and their strikes paralysed the country. When Britain retaliated with force a Citizens' Army was created to protect the strikers. With such determined and multilateral pressure for change, a bill for Home Rule was inevitable. It was passed, in name, in 1912, but no date for implementation was set *and it was not enacted*.

The majority of Catholic Ireland rejoiced at the news, yet a large part vowed to fight on for complete independence, and Protestant

Northern Ireland declared it would oppose the change ('Home Rule is Rome Rule') by every means available unto its last breath. It began immediate armament through gun-running from Germany and formed the Ulster Volunteers in 1913. In tit for tat measure Dublin formed the Irish Volunteers. Then came a new emergency: World War I.

Irishmen mainly from the north went to fight for Britain but in the south many saw Britain's weakness as an opportunity for revolt. The Easter Rebellion of 1916 was actually a small and relatively insignificant affair lasting only a week but the government's decision to hang ninety rebels (completing fifteen executions before realising its mistake) inflamed public opinion across the country and swelled support for Sinn Féin.

In the election of 1918 Sinn Féin swept to power and adopted a policy of passive resistance to press for a republic. Britain's response was to ban Sinn Féin as a political party. In doing this it underestimated the military capability of the IRB under the ruthless efficiency of Michael Collins and was unprepared for the guerrilla warfare waged by a new entity, the Irish Republican Army (IRA), formed from the remnants of the Irish Volunteers. Realising how desperate the situation now was, Britain brought in the 'Black 'n' Tans', a volunteer force still remembered for its brutality. The Anglo-Irish War ran its bitter and inconclusive course from 1919 to 1921 until a truce was called.

No political solution could be agreed so one was imposed. Ireland was to be split into two parts, the border being drawn between the twenty-six counties of 'Southern Ireland' and the six counties of Ulster which now became 'Northern Ireland'. Each part had dominion status, each had its own government and parliament, each had representatives in the British parliament which would retain control over certain key areas of administration such as security. It was the only workable compromise anyone could come up with but it was not a solution and it satisfied no one. The South was being offered a degree of autonomy; full fiscal and financial control but with Commonwealth ties and Britain's retention of her naval bases. Compared to the independent republic so many had fought for most considered it a miserable sop and a further obstacle to the united Ireland of their dreams. In the North, one third of the population was Catholic and opposed Home Rule because it would mean Protestant Rule. Even the Protestants (Unionists) were opposed because now their southern neighbour was being made an official Catholic state and they feared power being given to it, but they realised it was preferable to have their own government rather than the alternative of a Dublin one. The North accepted the treaty and its parliament was opened in June 1921. The South, under Sinn Fein's leadership, rejected the plan.

If Irish history was ever simple, now it became complex. Not only was Ireland divided into two, but new divisions within each sector arose. It is best to lay Northern Ireland temporarily aside.

Southern Ireland, or the Irish Free State as it was called, now found itself in a state of limbo. The old system of government had been rejected, independence was being denied and the terms of Home Rule were widely regarded as unacceptable. Feeling its hands were tied but forced to come to some decision its parliament, the Dáil, took the issue to a vote. Those in favour argued that Home Rule at least offered 'the freedom to achieve freedom', those opposed asserted that the Dáil had 'no right to ratify a wrong'. By the narrowest of margins (64:57) the treaty was accepted on 7 January 1922. British troops began withdrawing from the South, and Westminster, as naïve and complacent as ever, firmly believed that 'Ireland' had been cast off from British politics for good. The split Dáil proved representative of public passion and the country instantly dissolved into a civil war which lasted until May 1923. The supporters of the treaty won and slowly the Free State began the task of reconstruction and consolidation. In 1932 Eamon De Valera came to power at the head of a new party, Fianna Fáil, and began his sixteen-year leadership of the country by waging an economic war with Britain. It lasted six years. In World War II ('the Emergency' they called it, for it was not their war) the Free State remained neutral, believing Britain would be the loser. Independence was finally achieved in 1949 and the republic of Éire came into being.

She was still a poor nation. In 1911 Dublin had the worst slums in Europe and a death rate at birth even higher than Moscow's. Then the Civil War, Economic War, Depression and the Emergency, each accompanied by the scourge of emigration. Yet agriculture had made considerable progress and new industries were established, most markedly in concentrations along the Shannon. On the cultural front self-government brought a pretentious rash of puritanism which saw the Censorship of Publications Act introduced in 1929. Books judged to be of 'indecent or obscene content' (1200 in the first decade, including notable works of literature) were banned. A single line, for example a sentence mentioning a homosexual affair in Kate O'Brian's *The Land of Spices,* was enough to condemn a book. It took another forty years for this draconian measure to be modified. Today the Irish are a nation of readers. It's certainly the place to be a poet for more poetry books are sold per capita in Ireland than in any other English-speaking nation.

Salt and Emerald

The decisive turn of fortune occurred in January 1973 when Éire entered the European Community. Suddenly being poor man of Europe was an advantage as grants and aid flooded into the country. Large-scale industry, especially electronics, was attracted and the Celtic Tiger cub was born. In 2002 the Euro usurped the old Punt. Debate still rages as to whether this was a wise move and it is undeniable that price hikes rode the back of the change. Rural communities felt the difference most acutely as their wages seemed to lag behind, but generally Éire boomed and felt good about itself.

It was a very different story in the North.

Skellig Michael

Through a gap in the trees Puxley Mansion loomed into view as I cut through a rough chop and headed into the open water of Bantry Bay. Bear Island's rough grazing zipped by at a pleasing pace but then I rounded a spur and lost all protection. I hove-to and put in a couple of reefs but even then the wind pinned me at a drunken angle and water came foaming down the gunwales. My bow was now pointing a little to the north of Newfoundland, with no obstructions in between, and the sea was getting bigger. Soon the waves had tripled in size. They strode in one after the other parading their ocean pedigrees, burly thugs with pouting chests. I put in a third reef and altered course to 300°, which tucked me slightly under the lee of the land.

Fleming was in his element. He loved a gale, never seeming to tire of having so much power at the tip of his cogwheels. With the anemometer flickering around 25 knots, I'd changed his foil to the smaller 'storm' version and he worked away silently, his swivels, weights, gears and pinions twitching in mirror images of each other as he tuned the helm. I must have spent hours watching his intimate parts in an effort to fathom his engineering, to no avail. None of his conical meshes, offset angles or chamfered joints made any sense to me. Yet today I was just thankful that this art deco jumble of stainless steel was up to my task. I huddled in the shelter of the spray hood keeping a foreman's eye on proceedings, chewing the neck tie of my oilskins and wondering if I really should be out in this.

In such nervous moments I reread the pilot until I had my instructions off by heart. I hated consulting it. Wallace Clark called it the 'woe book', always giving the blackest picture of every feature it mentioned. My route was round one of the many appendages which stick out of western Ireland, separating Bantry Bay from another of equal dimensions – a long arm of the sea, really – misleadingly called Kenmare River. The pilot, in the cosy language of 1974, drew attention to a shortcut through Dursey Sound.

'Entering the sound from the south a peculiarity about which strangers should be forewarned is that having rounded Crow Head the bay presents the appearance of a cul-de-sac as the similarity of colour of the island and the mainland shores disguises the overlap. …strong tidal race…keep very close to the island shore going

Salt and Emerald

through the narrows, which are only one cable wide. Sound Rock with only 2 ft. over it at L.W. lies almost in mid-channel in the narrowest part of the sound thus limiting the navigable part to 80 yds. The N-going tide sets directly on the rock.'

The chart showed a farmyard of additional hazards. A Bull, Cow, Calf, Heifer, Horse, Sheep, Hog, Goat and Dog each had their own island. Lamb Head appeared to be well behind me, as was Flea Sound, but I'd have to watch out for Seal Rock, Gull Rock, Crow Head and The Cat. Currently I was right on course for the Bull's Forehead.

Two hours of heavy tacking between Bull, Cat and Crow took me into the optical illusion of Dursey Sound. The tide had turned an hour earlier and was picking me up, sweeping me faster into this dead end. Now lobster buoys were bobbing in its grip, being ducked under and springing up in rages of spray. Water coursed over rocks only a boat's length away making slurping noises and dragging seaweed taut as I clung to the shore in fear of Sound Rock. The engine was ticking over, ready to be engaged the moment steerage was lost. My usual world of five knots felt like a helter-skelter swirl of thirty. Everything was passing in a blur. A pier, a moored boat, a boy fishing, then rock, rock, rock soaring into cliffs and reducing the sky to a narrow trail. Suddenly the gap appeared, a slit of light parting the black. *Ceana* slewed sideways in the grip of an eddy. I thrust forward the gear lever and felt the propeller bite. By the time I thought of checking where Sound Rock must be, it was behind. Then I saw the cable car high above. A box so small it looked more like a dead sparrow hanging from a telephone wire. Dursey Island's only link with the outside world suspended six passengers over a void. As it moved with almost imperceptible progress it made Dursey Sound at sea level feel a lot safer.

The Vikings once used the island as a holding pen for captives before selling them as slaves in Scandinavia and Spain. Women in particular were in short supply both in their homeland and colonies. In contemporary Iceland where the population has been relatively isolated for centuries and bloodlines have known little dilution by visitors, genetic research shows that as many as forty-five per cent of women were once of Celtic origin. Today Dursey Island could do with being paid back. Sixty people lived on the island though I couldn't imagine what they did for a living. Their cattle took priority over visitors in the queue for the cable car. Most visitors came to walk a loop of the Beara Way and, I guessed, to see cows in cable cars.

'Don't be fooled', the Gaelic Athletic Association joker had told me, 'Dursey's a bitch. If it's OK on one side, it's always hell on the

138

other.' The trouble was, I didn't know his standards. I thought I'd just been through hell, but perhaps this had been its OK side? I braced myself for worse, but it never came. Sometimes you're your own worst enemy at sea.

* * *

Skellig Michael lies six miles off the coast of Kerry with no apparent chink in its cliffs for access. It is a cathedral of rock half a mile long and rises abruptly to 704 feet, its twin spires being separated by Christ's Saddle. Despite its isolation and austerity early mystics were struck by its similarity to other sacred sites. Towards the end of their occupation they named it for the patron of high places, Archangel Michael. Thus, in the pre-Columbian Church of 1500 years ago, this obscure rock joined Mont St Michel in Brittany and St Michael's Mount in Cornwall as a cornerstone of Celtic Christianity. Ever since seeing pictures of it years ago, I'd wanted to go there. Now I was so close. But to try and sail there alone was out of the question. The landing usually involved a leap onto a concrete ledge at the mouth of a cave. The cave swallowed waves and then spat them out causing a cross-current in the swell, demanding a highly manoeuvrable boat and a skill that picnicking around Ireland did not equip you with. In addition, the seabed gave no quarter to anchors. I'd take a tour boat.

The *Bealtra* was one of sixteen boats licensed to carry passengers to Skellig Michael, where a restriction of 200 daily visitors was enforced. By the time I reached her a sudden downpour had left me soaked. Sean was decidedly cool on seeing me step aboard in a dripping kilt. Neither did he flinch when Rachael arrived, a middle-aged Quebecoise wearing a light dress and bare feet. With five other passengers we sat in a cramped wheelhouse staring at plywood stained with what I hoped was fish blood rather than the effects of clumsy landings. A spaghetti of pink guts lurked under Rachael's seat. Sean was on the radio consulting with other skippers about the weather. His tone was pessimistic and he was considering cancelling. Eventually he decided 'to risk it'.

I felt queasy. *Bealtra*'s motion was alien to me. She didn't hold the water like *Ceana* but skittered about, rolling dreadfully, using her power to dodge the crests and surge through the troughs. We alternated between being pinned against the hull by gravity and being tossed into intimacy with the stranger opposite. Only Rachael was immune. She smiled continually. Her feet gripped the deck and she would stand up every so often to watch the antics of gannets, chuckling with glee, and then dropping to our level to offer comfort.

'Everytheeng you see and feel eze a mirror of yourself', she said during one particularly bad bout. 'Anger eze your teacher offereeng you a lesson. What you are angry about in oth-thers eze what you need to change een yourself. Every bad experi-ence eze an opportunity to learn and progress the qualitay of your life.'

'And what do you imagine the lesson is here?'

'You need to learn to let go control. To accept outside energee and go with the flow.'

'I'm already accepting as much outside energy as I can cope with.'

Rachael was a lecturer and consultant. Starting at the age of thirteen with an avowed goal of trying to solve the three riddles of the Sphinx she had embraced geometry, metaphysics, fire walking and South American healing rituals. She was now bent on bringing spiritual consciousness into corporate management. In her spare time she toured Europe, North America and Russia addressing conferences on 'The Scared Secrets of Egyptian Teachings'. Currently she was on holiday, visiting Callanish, Stonehenge and the Hill of Tara.

Had I not been in a revolving debating chamber, I would have enjoyed talking more to Rachael. But I failed my lesson, and then it was time to jump.

Sean was just in his twenties but he knew about boats. Twirling the wheel first one way then the other, interrupting his approach with bursts of reverse, he nursed the bow into the cave and held his position opposite a crude jetty. A man on shore held out his arm to catch us in turn when we responded to Sean's shout – 'jump!' – timed to meet the swell which carried us up and held the boat for a second within two feet of the land. Waves boomed in the cave and spray splashed around. Nesting fulmars watched with scant interest.

The start to this UNESCO World Heritage Site was unpromising. Modern man's contribution was a profanity of concrete spread underfoot, overhead and to the side for two hundred yards leading to a lighthouse. Then came a junction and rock-cut steps climbed heavenwards. For the most part these were the original steps created 1500 years ago. They rose in zigzags designed as penance through a landscape of tortured stone. Grey slabs as tall as a man stood angled in arrested stages of collapse, some eaten through, all gnawed into shapes suggesting both purpose and meaning. Even art. Around them was a swath of grass where puffins nervously guarded their burrows. Eventually the path led to scree and then a five hundred foot drop to the sea. This was Christ's Saddle. Way down below the tour boats, reduced to coloured dots, bobbed in the lee of the island as they killed time. To the right another path goat-hopped through crags to the hermitage where the monks had lived as close as they could to God.

They had built their beehive huts and oratory short of the summit in a recess to gain shelter from the eternal (and damnable) wind. In profile the huddle of buildings were closer to igloos with perfect curves and rectangular crawl holes at the front. Discounting some restoration, their state of preservation was remarkable. Inside they were surprisingly snug and dry, their cantilevered rocks having sufficient overlap and tilt to shed water. (This Stone Age architecture endured in some Scottish islands until 1890). Fine for a night. But a month, a year, a lifetime? The wind's moan filtered in and became trapped, at times circulating as a modulated chant, at times a dentist's drill. Beyond the entrance mist moved and smudged the limited view of walls and a Celtic cross, then erased it completely. For a time I was alone, reliving memories of Machu Picchu and the holy Chinese mountain Omei Shan, energised by the pilgrim's sense of awe and the tangibility of history.

Little is known of the lives of those who lived here. The small cemetery has not been excavated. Thirty anchorites at the most may have lived here, subsisting on fish and seabirds. Possibly they planted some crops. Rainwater was collected in a stone cistern. When the weather allowed they would have undertaken the hazardous pull to the mainland in a coracle. Drownings must have been frequent. Their whole existence was one of privation and austerity, inspired by Saint Anthony's Coptic Church founded in the deserts of Egypt and Libya. Skellig Michael's monastery was active for around 600 years from its start in the 6th century. Such was its fame that the Vikings risked destruction under its cliffs and plundered the island in 812 and 823, murdering some monks and carrying off others into bondage. The community recovered and as late as the 11th century the oratory was extended. A century later Skellig Michael had been abandoned.

Though not for ever. In the early sixteenth century it developed into a shrine to which sinners made annual trips to perform public atonement. Other islands also served this function and the words 'Penitential Station' are still printed against their names on Admiralty charts. Skellig Michael was among the most important. When the Gregorian calendar was adopted by the rest of the country in 1582 the Skellig held on to the Julian timetable. This anomaly gave rise to a new trade and the scurrilous 'Skellig Lists'. A tradition developed over centuries that marriage vows could only be consecrated during winter. Until as recently as the First World War eighty per cent of all marriages in rural Ireland took place between October and March. Marriages were expressly forbidden during the period of Lent but as the Julian calendar was one month behind the Gregorian, they could legally take place on Skellig Michael during four weeks of closed season on the mainland. Those who took the considerable trouble to sail out here were often lampooned as dilatory in their decision-making or desperate in their haste to tie the knot and the festivities enjoyed in isolation acquired somewhat scandalous notoriety. Around the country Skellig Lists were produced each year just before Lent, wicked and witty verse in which local characters were selected as matches and satirised for their faults.

Gradually Skellig slipped from consciousness. In August 1779 the privateer John Paul Jones was becalmed in the vicinity and almost lost his 42-gun man-of-war *Bonhomme Richard*. She was only saved from drifting aground by launching a row boat which towed the vessel clear. Most of the crew had been press-ganged into service and it took them some time to appreciate this stroke of fortune. They cut the tow rope and John Paul watched helplessly as they rowed to the mainland, and freedom.

The Skellig remained uninhabited until two lighthouses were built. Unusually, the keepers' families were allowed to stay with them. One couple had two sons, Patrick and William. They died around 1850, aged two and four, and are buried with the monks. Skellig Michael was the only world they knew. I looked for their graves but they too had melded into the grey.

It was time to go. Our two-hours had been shortened to ninety minutes owing to a deterioration in the weather. It was a rush to get back in time. Rachael only just made it with Sean threatening to leave her there.

'Well, what did you think?' I asked.

'Eet is mind-widening. And I've been communicating with Shiva. He's keen to reintroduce Celtic mysticism and invigorate druidism.'

I came away with lesser treasures, myself. Some pictures of beehives in the mist and a puffin which turned its back on me as the shutter opened.

Valentia

I had a very old man to see. He lived at Camp on the Dingle Peninsula. Against a forecast of gales and rain I donned oilskins and stuck out my thumb. The fifth car stopped.

'What do you see here?' Kieren asked, when we paused at a viewpoint on the Ring of Kerry, Ireland's most famous tourist circuit.

I looked down on a coastline of coves and beaches, on ribbons of grazing, houses that maintained the trend of the last ten miles and suggested either wealth or fanatical self-sufficiency, a bay of moored yachts and fishing boats, a village in colours that shouted too loudly and, in the distance, the headlands that led me back to Dursey Sound. *What do you see here?* I couldn't see the catch. Then a possibility came. It was all a little too pretty, too perfect. It wasn't a *working* landscape.

'Holiday Ireland?' I ventured.

'Not bad! What *we* see here…', he gestured to include his wife, '…is a social hierarchy blotting the landscape. Every house is a statement of its owner. That *quiet* village there – Derrynane – is an enclave of *old money* from Cork. Then there are the tribunal lawyers. Planning, compensation claims, you name it - everything in Ireland goes to tribunal and costs millions. The lawyers cream it off and build the expensive houses you see in the best locations. Then there are the alternative lifestylers, the tree-huggers and crafty folks, lots of foreigners, who home-build these one-off eccentric designs, then the locals who paint their houses bilious colours to attract tourists, then the *permanent* caravan set and finally the itinerant caravaners and mobile homers.'

'And each of them feels superior to all the others', Carole added. 'That's a very Irish trait. An Irishman never feels inferior to anyone.'

A few miles later we were caught in traffic congestion. In deepest rural Éire. A triathlon was taking place and stewards were gesticulating and shouting at drivers and each other. The aim appeared to be to create a free passage for the approaching runners. The effect was to render the N70 impassable, even to the skinniest triathlete. One particularly vocal steward brandished a shovel.

'Oh Jesus', Kieren exclaimed. We'd been gridlocked for ten minutes. 'Give an Irishman authority and a shovel and you've got trouble.'

Half an hour later we still hadn't moved. Carole said, 'They've too many stewards. That's also very Irish. If you don't know what you're doing, get as many people as you can on side to do it. So much organisation always turns to chaos.'

Kieren and Carole ran a restaurant and delicatessen in Cork. They worked ten hour days, six days a week.

'Where are you in the social hierarchy?' I asked.

'The Deep Shit Class.' Carole gave a snort of derision. 'Overdrawn and mortgaged to the eyebrows. We've a concrete holiday flat in Kenmare.'

'We're working harder and harder just to keep even. Ireland's tourist industry is fucked. Way over-priced. It's not value for money. You can pay less for better food and accommodation in Paris. Dublin's really a rip off. You add this to nine-eleven, foot and mouth, SARS, the Iraq war and we've got a crisis. Hotels are laying off staff and there's no jobs for young people.'

Carole pitied the young. They'd had a ten-year boom and grown used to spending €100 a week on mobile phones and getting legless. The downturn in the economy, she feared, would exacerbate their frustration into crime. 'People born in booms develop unrealistic expectations. Better to be brought up in hard times so you learn how to cope.'

Runners passed in dribs and drabs, knocking their hips on wing mirrors. Eventually the shovel waved us on. The road was narrow and snaked up to moorland. To reduce collisions, buses were forced to drive this eighty-mile circuit in one direction only, anti-clockwise, which made a long return journey when the farmer's wife wanted to go five miles to the nearest shop. Yet it seemed that most farmers here were tribunal lawyers and their wives could choose between the BMW or the Ranger Rover. It was all very prim and it didn't look real.

Things were different on Valentia Island. We crossed its bridge as a sightseeing detour. Its farms had tractors trashed with manure. Its fields weren't toys but large enough to grow things, seriously. They swept gently up to a hill line which gave no indication that it ended abruptly in ochrous cliffs. Also hidden was the famous slate quarry which sent its slabs to roof the most prestigious public buildings in London – the old House of Commons, the British Museum, The National Gallery – and floor the city's railway stations.

Valentia's greatest fame came in 1865 when the island was connected to Heart's Content in Newfoundland by the first transatlantic telegraph cable. This prodigious feat involved laying 2000 miles of cable over an ocean bed that dropped to depths exceeding 30,000 feet and a submerged mountain range 500 miles wide. When, in

1843, a doctor in the Indian Medical Service stumbled upon gutta percha, a highly durable rubber compound that could be melted and then moulded, the problem of insulating such a cable was solved. (Dr Mont's discovery also revolutionised golf, producing a ball that flew further and lasted longer). The original plan was for two ships to carry the cable, one laying until her supply was exhausted and the other taking over, the ends being spliced in mid-ocean. In 1857 the first attempt was made but after six days and 350 miles, the cable snapped as it dropped 12,000 feet off the Continental Shelf. A stronger cable was needed, and the engineers realised it would have to be laid in a single length. There was only one ship in the world capable of carrying such a weight and volume, and she was just about to be launched.

Isambard Brunel's intention was to design a ship large enough to steam to Australia and back without refuelling. He'd already successfully applied his bridge-building techniques to ship-building and produced the *Great Western* and the *Great Britain*. The *Great Eastern* would be something else: a steamer 692 feet long and 118 feet wide, with a displacement of 32,000 tons. She'd be driven by two mighty paddle-wheels with fifty-six-foot diameters, and be equipped to carry 4000 passengers. But things went badly from the start. She was built at Millwall where the Thames was too narrow for a conventional bow-first launch, so she had to be constructed parallel to the shore and launched sideways. Her journey to the water was an agony of inertia as she covered thirty-three feet six inches of slip in a fortnight. It took another two months of inching forward before the *Great Eastern* was afloat. By this time stress had caused Brunel's health to deteriorate. When six stokers were killed by a ruptured steam pipe on her first sea trials, the news proved too much and he died a few days later.

Unable to cover the increased costs of the delayed launch, the Eastern Steam Navigation Company was forced to sell. She was bought by the Great Ship Company to ply the transatlantic route. Her quota of passengers was never filled; she hit an uncharted rock in New York harbour and suffered severe damage in a storm. The repairs from these two accidents cost £130,000. She was put up for sale again and bought by three entrepreneurs who chartered her to the cable-layers, the Telegraph Construction Company. Her first attempt failed when once again the cable snapped, but the following year she succeeded. The first message transmitted read, 'Glory to God in the highest, on earth peace, goodwill to men'. This telegraphic link remained in use for a century, finally being declared redundant in 1965. The *Great Eastern* built on this achievement and went on to lay cables from France to America, Bombay to Aden and others in the Red Sea before being scrapped in 1888.

Thus it was that in 1865 the people of Valentia were the only people in the western world able to communicate directly with New York, even though it was impossible to put a call through to Dublin.

'The Irish' - Carole was casting pearls again - 'have always lived ironies. The absurd is often normal here. It's fed our happy-go-lucky nature and our sense of humour.'

'And who'd want to call Dublin anyway?' Kieran added.

John Scannel

John Scannell was three months short of his one hundredth birthday. He sat in a wheelchair in a nursing home at Camp, watching Tralee Bay shiver under a tease of whitecaps. He was a small man and wore a flat cap.

'And oi've never taken it off for a photograph', he said defiantly. It sat at a slight angle above a face with bushy eyebrows and a determined set. His mouth retained two teeth and the permanent foundations of a smile. His voice was strong and rose in animation to make a point or add weight to expletives that seemed unaccustomedly mild for a farmer. I kept on expecting him to excuse himself for the afternoon milking. He'd only recently retired, at ninety.

'Oi never spared myself. Oi worked and worked and worked. Oi ate everything that was put on the table. Smoked all my life. Then oi had me a heart attack in 1983 – but the mystery of it! – still here oi am! Oh my, oi don't know why.'

A priest passed and stopped to say goodbye. John heard the strange voice but couldn't place it. 'Oi don't know who you are', he said.

'I'm the priest. I've just taken mass.'

'Oh good God, Father', he exclaimed, whipping his cap off to reveal a bold growth of hair still holding grey, 'Oi didn't see you, it's my eyes, you know...' And he sat gripping his cap in both hands as if his soul depended on it until the priest had gone.

'Oi was born in 1903 on a farm below Beenoskee, near Lough Annascaul. Near Tom Crean's place. You heard of Tom Crean?'

'The Antarctic man?'

'Yes, oi knew Tom. A fine, quiet man. Well, oi was the youngest of seven children, four boys and three girls. We had to walk two miles to school and were only allowed to wear shoes in winter, though not everybody had them. In summer, if you arrived in shoes the teacher would send you back home again to leave them there and you'd to walk back barefoot.'

'Why?'

'Because the shoes, you see, had nails in them and they were after ripping up the school floor.'

'But you could have just left your shoes at the door.'

He smiled, as if no one had ever thought of that or it was a point not worth explaining. 'Oi started smoking then. On the way to school we passed by a railway station and we'd find all these butts and we'd pick them up and smoke them. Smoked all my life till I came here. Yes, Holy God, the sister found a packet of fags on me and said, 'You're not having any of these in here', and that put an end to it, but oi'm grateful to her. The farm we had was eighty-four acres, almost twice the size of many in the area, but some was coarse and twelve acres was bog. It'd been in our family eight generations. We kept sheep, pigs and cows, and grew some potatoes and turnips which always meant a lot of weeding. Neighbours all helped each other in those days but it was hard. The women worked the fields too. The First World War was good for farmers, good prices but after 1916 things got very bad. When Michael Collins was after getting shot people got mad at times. But it didn't matter what side people were on, they all got on working together. In the next war it didn't help us much. Prices stayed the same. Oi took over the farm in 1929, the year oi got married. My brothers didn't want it. The nearest market was Tralee, twenty miles away, it was. We took the pigs there for slaughter in a orse cart. Took six hours. They was fast orses in those days, strong orses, oh, a hundred times better than what you get today. Oi never bought a tractor. Oi ran two orses till 1978, till oi handed over to my son.'

'Did he keep them?'

His face furrowed. 'First thing he did was sell them. Oi can't blame him. Farming's gone. The change, oi can't understand it at all. Some had forty cows and they're all sold. My own son gets – wait till you're hearing this! – he gets two hundred euros a week pension! Oi never got a stump. When oi got married we couldn't afford a honeymoon. Oi had a man on the farm to help. You could hire a man easy then, for a day, week, month, whatever. There was lots of gypsies then too, you wouldn't see any now. Beggars, really. They was well-known in West Kerry. Some would help get the spuds in and they'd get spuds in return, no bother. You wouldn't give money, just a little bit food. They travelled about on foot.

We killed pigs and had bacon all year. Salted it and pressed it in cloth. Oh my! Spuds, bacon and cabbage made a rare meal! My wife was making eight to ten loaves on a Saturday so she wouldn't have to bake or cook on a Sunday. We cut turf for cooking and had paraffin for the lamps. Oh God, when oi was a young lad we had no light, only the lantern. When the gale winds came they knocked down the hay cocks - haggarts, we called them - the winds knocked them haggarts down and we had to put them back and oh my you got it in the ear if you didn't hold the lantern right. The mystery is, now there's light everywhere, but no haggarts to tie down.'

'When did electricity come?'

'In the sixties. We got the piped water in the fifties. And we got the gas in the sixties, gas in drums. Then we cooked on gas. Never had a fridge till recently. And never got a TV, oh my God oi couldn't face it. Just didn't fancy it' – he hesitated – 'except for the football, Kerry playing football. Oi'd not look at any other match. There's a set in my room here, never been switched on.'

'What did you do for entertainment?'

'We had the playing cards and there was a melodeon in every house. A melodeon cost ten shillings in those days. We'd meet in houses and have ceilidh dances. Everyone could do something. And oi read the papers. Never books but oi liked to get the paper every day. And later we got the radio.'

'Did you drink much'?

'Oi wasn't drinking as much as oi am now.' He winked. 'Couldn't afford to. Oi had The Guinness. We earned ten shillings a week in 1914. Oi remember it was tuppence ha'penny a pint before the war...'

'But you were only eleven!'

'Sure oi was only eleven, and working with it. Then Glory to God it was gone up penny by penny and it got to ninepence and then in 1918 *tenpence*, and there was war. You see if you had two pints, two times ninepence was eighteen which was one and six but two times tenpence was twenty which was one and eight and people didn't like that so there was war.'

Eighty-five years later the injustice still rankled. Then he asked, 'What's it now?'

'Three euros, forty cents.'

'Holy God.'

We sat in silence and I tried to grasp the span of events this man had lived through in the most momentous century the world had known. He had been around for World War One, the Civil War, World War Two, the regular succession of subsequent wars, The Troubles...it seemed unnecessary to seek his opinion on world peace, but did he think there would ever be a united Ireland?

'No, oi don't think so. There's a terrible hatred here, like Heaven and Hell. It's always in man's nature to fight. No, I don't think Ireland will ever be united.'

'Do you believe life is better now than in your youth?'

'Oi couldn't say, no, oi couldn't say. That's just the way things were then.'

I envied him his acceptance of things as they are, of living in the reality of the present and being tolerant of its positive and negative aspects. He wasn't out to gild the past. His life had been how it was in a world he couldn't change. He'd just got on with the job in hand, and had no regrets.

I wasn't used to meeting centenarians. I tried to extract one last superlative from a hundred orbits of the sun. What was the greatest sight he'd ever seen?

'Oh oi can tell you that. You see, oi've spent all my days here in West Kerry between Anascaul and Tralee. But once oi went to America. To visit family. Oi was seventy-five and it was the first time oi was in a plane. Oi took to it fine. You see, it was just like sitting in church, no different except when you came out you were some-where else. And oi was in California. Oi went for six weeks and, ach, after three oi was fed up with it but oi had to make the best of it. Sure oi had lots of friends and they carried me everywhere in cars. They had these roads, they were a wonder. They've four roads going and four roads coming, and you'll meet no one. Then they come on the daft side of the road! We went to Reno – oh God, what a mad spot – women putting dollars in machines and nothing coming of it. And oi'll tell you something oi saw, the ruin of the first Catholic church. It was made by the Mexicans and the bricks were made by the Indians with their own hands, that's what oi was told. And we went to Los Angeles, you know, and thirty miles south of it, oh my God, was the grandest thing oi ever saw. The Irvine Ranch. A hundred acres and my, yes, it's a sight to look at it, the oranges. Trees the size of this room, oi tell you, all covered in oranges. Oi'd never seen them growing till then. Yes, those oranges was the grandest thing oi ever saw in my life.'

Tom Crean

Open the cupboard door halfway along the wall on your left as you enter Anascaul's only pub. A panel of ice crystals is illuminated and a wind's taut moan is heard. Black and white photographs hang on the walls. They show a powerful man, head and shoulders above others, rugged and at his most handsome, strikingly so, when unshaven or fully bearded. For the most part the photographer has caught him in situations where a smile is inappropriate – about to embark on another suicidal mission, returned from finding Scott's body, watching *Endurance* disintegrate – and his face suits an expression of reflective alertness, a pipe permanently clamped between his lips. Above the pub's entrance a small plaque reads: 'Tom Crean, Antarctic Explorer, 1877-1938'.

Crean's serendipitous encounter with Scott's first expedition to the south was to lead to a record of endurance in Antarctica which equalled that of the most famous names in history in terms of miles travelled and time spent on the ice. He was one of a handful of men to serve under both Scott and Shackleton. He was awarded three polar medals and a clasp. Other awards are more enduring. In Victoria Land, Antarctica, Mount Crean rises to 8360 feet (2550 metres). On South Georgia the Crean Glacier flows four miles to the sea at Antarctic Bay. That his name is not more widely celebrated is largely due to the fact that he kept no journals, wrote few letters and sought no publicity for the exploits that made others famous.

He was born in a hamlet near Anascaul called Gurtuchrane. His parents were impoverished farmers who were scarcely able to feed their ten children. Tom was one of the younger ones. He learned to work hard at an early age, being forced to leave school at fourteen. His fiercely independent spirit erupted one day when it was discovered he'd accidentally allowed cattle access to a field and the family's potato crop was ruined. In an argument with his father the youngster vowed he'd go to sea and never return. He left home in a borrowed suit in July 1893 and enlisted in Queen Victoria's Royal Navy. He never saw his parents again.

In 1901 Crean found himself in New Zealand, assigned to HMS *Ringarooma*, a torpedo vessel serving in Britain's Pacific fleet, when Captain Robert Falcon Scott's *Discovery* put in for a refit. The navy had been ordered to render all assistance possible to Scott who was leading his first expedition to the Antarctic. Crean was part of the crew assigned to assist in repairing the rigging and tracing a leak. The day before Scott was due to sail one of his crew, Seaman Harry Baker, struck a Petty Officer and deserted. Scott asked for a naval replacement, cautioning enthusiasm among the young ranks by warning that this would be a two- or three-year commitment in severe conditions. The twenty-four-year old Crean volunteered, and was accepted.

Crean soon proved himself to be immensely strong in the punishing regime of man-hauling supplies. Soon he had joined Taff Evans, Ernest Joyce, Bill Lashly, Frank Wild and Thomas Williamson as the core of the 'other ranks' on whom the officers knew the success of the enterprise would largely depend. Among those officers was a fellow Irishman, Ernest Shackleton, born in County Kildare (but brought up in Yorkshire and London). Of the two of them Crean was first to make his mark by being in the support party that achieved a record Furthest South in 1902 while laying food depots ahead of the main expedition. He was also in that elite group who were the first humans to celebrate Christmas in a tent on Antarctica's 5,400,000 square miles of ice.

Scott, Wilson and Shackleton later reached within 480 miles of the Pole but almost died on the return journey. Man-hauling, inadequate provisions and scurvy weakened them almost to the point of defeat. By the time they stumbled back into the base Shackleton, who was suffering the worst, was being pulled on a sledge. Scott sent Shackleton home on the relief ship, a slight which wounded Shackleton deeply. He never served under Scott again and in 1909 success must have tasted all the sweeter when his own expedition smashed Scott's record and came within 100 miles of conquering the South Pole. He turned back, and only just made it, because he didn't want victory at the cost of lives, famously remarking to his wife, 'a live donkey is better than a dead lion'.

Crean meanwhile was paid £55 14s 11d (approximately £2,900 in buying terms today) for his two-and-a-half years' service with Scott and returned to the mundane life of the navy, promoted to Petty Officer, 1st Class. He was among the first to be recruited by Scott who petitioned the navy to release the Irishman for the 1912 expedition. Crean's love of animals made him the obvious choice as caretaker of the ponies. They were woefully inadequate for the environment and suffered terribly. Ponies and men hauled loads 400 miles to the base of the Beardmore Glacier, the ponies being killed when they became too weak to work. Scott was too squeamish for such work, so Crean elected to do it. His favourite, Bones, was among the last five to be shot at Shambles Camp.

With the benefit of hindsight it is clear that Scott made several fatal decisions. One of the most contentious was his selection of companions for the final 150-mile push to the pole. He had eight men with him. The final leg had been planned and provisioned for four. Astonishingly, Scott selected five. This meant the Polar party would be short rationed from the outset. His initial choice comprised himself, Wilson, Oates and Taffy Evans. (He was unaware that Taffy Evans was concealing a severe cut to his hand which he'd sustained a few days earlier. Evans would be the first to die). Now he added Birdy Bowers as the extra. Crean's biographer, Michael Smith, argues that the selection of Crean instead of Bowers (and certainly of Evans) might have made the difference between life and death for Scott and his companions. Crean was equal to any of them – and superior to most of them – in strength, stamina, fitness and attitude. He was, Smith asserts, the obvious choice.

The rejected trio of Crean, Lashly and Teddy Evans now embarked on the 750-mile journey back to base. It too became a gruelling race against death. At one stage, already weakening and their supplies running low, they realised they were miles off course and had missed the familiar descent to the Beardmore Glacier 2000 feet below. They were on the edge of the Shackleton Ice Falls and faced a three-day detour to regain the proper route. Evans proposed a desperate plan: they would simply jump on the sledge and ride over the edge into the unknown. Among ice cliffs and crevasses it was madness, and they knew it. When they pushed off, not one expected to survive. Evans later confessed it was the most terrifying experience of his life. He estimated the sledge reached a speed of 60mph as it leapt, bucked and careened downwards. Their legs dragged and hit obstructions until eventually the sledge rolled over and over and came to a halt a matter of yards from a crevasse that would have killed them. They'd lost some equipment, their trousers were shredded but they were alive.

Thirty-five miles from home they realised they weren't going to make it. Evans had succumbed to scurvy and was rapidly deteriorating. For the last four days Crean and Lashly had been hauling him on the sledge. It was decided that the strongest man, Crean, would travel on alone and try to reach Hut Point to raise the alarm. Fortified by only three biscuits and two chocolate sticks, Crean covered the distance in a remarkable eighteen hours. Lashly and Evans were rescued and this epic 1500-mile journey, in which the trio had manhauled their supplies and lived in tents without the means of washing or shaving for three-and-a-half months, ended without mishap.

One notable medical factor in this ordeal was the question of how Crean and Lashly managed to evade the debilitating ravage of scurvy suffered by Evans? They had shared the same diet and endured identical ordeals. Modern research shows that individual bodies can be markedly different in their ability to retain vitamin C, but also confirms that habitual smokers face a considerably reduced immunity to the disease. By this reckoning Crean should have been the first to suffer but once again, as often happened in his life, he enjoyed the proverbial luck of the Irish.

Eight months later Crean was with ten others searching for Scott when they spotted the black flag beside a snow-covered tent and discovered the grim fate of the expedition. The *Terra Nova* sailed back to England with the survivors and, after they had landed and told their story, an inexplicable entry was made in Crean's official military record. He was listed as having died in Antarctica on 17 February 1912, the very day his great friend Taff Evans died on the Beardmore Glacier. But Crean was very much alive, and willing. Despite having returned to Anascaul and bought a pub while on leave from the navy, Crean accepted at once when Shackleton invited him to join his latest, and most ambitious, expedition: an 1800-mile trek across the breadth of Antarctica.

The story has become a household legend. When the *Endurance* was finally crushed after drifting 1200 miles trapped in ice, Crean was put in charge of Tent Number Four. It was his responsibility to equip the sledges for the escape they would attempt to the nearest land, 364 miles away, when conditions allowed. He decided what was necessary and what was not. When Shackleton gave the order to march, any animal unable to contribute to the party's mobility was killed. Crean again undertook the wretched task, shooting three of the pups he'd cared for and the much-loved ship's cat, Mrs Chippy[1], which belonged to the ship's carpenter 'Chips' McNeish. When the party reached the end of the sea ice and launched their three boats, Crean was put in charge of the *Stancomb Wills* and guided it to Elephant Island. When Shackleton chose six men to accompany him on the desperate bid to cross 800 miles of the Southern Ocean in an open boat to reach help on South Georgia, Crean was one of them. And Crean was there in the final ordeal with Shackleton and Worsley when the three were forced to traverse South Georgia's murderous ice peaks. Starved, exhausted and wearing rags, they crossed a terrain that had never been conquered before and made their final descent though a waterfall before reaching a community of whalers at Stromness.

---

[1] Mrs Chippy has made a surprise comeback recently, made from the dyed fur of Chinese farmed rabbits, she has invaded boat chandlers and gift shops by the thousand.

Without the loss of a single life, Shackleton's men returned in early November 1916 to find Britain at war. Crean married the following year but continued to serve in the navy. The remaining war years were uneventful for him. His naval career of almost twenty-seven years came to an abrupt end in March 1920 following a fall down a hatch while his ship was docking at Rosyth. Crean's left arm remained paralysed for months and his vision was seriously impaired.

He returned to his wife, Nell, in Anascaul and for the next eighteen years ran the South Pole Inn. He never talked about his Antarctic experiences but shrugged them off and changed the subject. This was probably due partly to his natural reserve but also to the political situation. In the Civil War years and the lingering hatred of the British, particularly under the repressive acts committed by the Black and Tans, it was unwise to advertise an association with the former colonists, and all his adult life Crean had served with British forces or expeditions.

He kept a low profile. In *An Unsung Hero*, Michael Smith records the following anecdote about his later years. 'Two elderly residents of Anascaul recalled that as young girls they would sometimes accompany Crean on his daily walks into the nearby hills. On occasions he would take off his boots to dip his feet in the cool running water of the Owenascaul River. His feet, they remember, were black. But, typical of his modesty, Crean urged the young girls not to tell anyone his secret.'

Crean suffered appendicitis in July 1938. Medical treatment was delayed too long and the organ perforated. He died the week after his sixty-first birthday. In a gesture of reconciliation he'd built a tomb for his parents and family in the local cemetery. His remains were interred there. Around his neck remained the scapular – a benediction printed on cloth and worn on a leather cord – that had accompanied him on all his journeys.

Nell lived to be eighty-six and died in 1968. They had two daughters, Mary and Ellen, who married brothers called O'Brien. They ran their own building company and when they moved to Tralee, they built houses for themselves side by side, naming one *Terra Nova* and the other *Discovery*.

Fungie

The light was fading as *Ceana*, her sails goosewinged, surged towards the Dingle Peninsula. A short thunderstorm had left the sky a blue-black ink stain with feathered edges which draped the sea. The GPS promised we were heading for Dingle Bay but there was no sign of a gap in the hills ahead. Grey and two-dimensional they remained, and might have been retreating, when brightness broke through and made them glow gently as if lit from within. Restored in solidity and detail they suddenly appeared close, and an illusion of five miles became a reality of one. The parting of their edges was now obvious and I steered towards it as the waves adjusted for the shallows and increased their thrust. Once I was through, wind and sea instantly collapsed around me. Ceana rocked gently in the dying momentum and sails and sheets that had been taut for hours suddenly hung loose. I tidied them away and started the engine, vaguely wondering if Fungie might appear.

He came barrelling out of the water alongside as I motored to the marina, a burst of polished grey marble, his head twisting to affix me with one eye, his mouth hooked into a smile below his beak, a crescendoing appearance in a veil of spray. A dozen times he breached and dived, sometimes flashing white as he revolved underwater, crossing my bows and duelling with my keel in patterns of lunatic pleasure. Then he moved off to entertain other boats as he'd been doing for twenty years.

Throughout the centuries wild dolphins have adopted humans for company. The Greeks recorded instances of this bond. In New Zealand a Risso's dolphin nicknamed Pelorus Jack guided ships between Wellington and Nelson from 1888 to 1912 and, in the nineteen-seventies, a bottlenose took children for rides at Oponini. Fungie is Ireland's first recorded example, also a bottlenose, *Tursiops truncatus*, male, thirteen feet long and believed to be middle-aged. He was named after a young fisherman who was growing his first beard when he spotted him in 1984. Marine zoologists are at a loss to explain why a dolphin should forsake the company of its own kind and lead an anchoritic existence at the mouth of one particular bay. Fungie takes himself off to hunt but returns to his elected patch and role as escort. Given his estimated age, the tourist industry he supports hopes he'll be around for at least another twenty years.

Quite how anyone could gaze on these creatures and think of 'sea pigs' is hard to believe but *muca mara* is their Gaelic name on the Aran Islands. (The impression clearly has deeper roots as many dictionaries list 'sea-swine' as a synonym for porpoises). Intelligent and responsive to human engagement, dolphins were used by the US navy in the Gulf War to locate and identify mines with an eighty per cent success rate. They've been turned into media stars and are among the planet's best-loved creatures. Yet research among a population of wild dolphins off Scotland shows a more sinister side to their character.

In 1996 observers noticed a dolphin attacking its much smaller fellow species, a harbour porpoise (*Phocoena phocoena*) in the Moray Firth. The victim was butted and tossed into the air with such force that it turned somersaults. The porpoise was soon killed. At first this was regarded as aberrant behaviour by a rogue individual but subsequent evidence showed the practice to be far from infrequent. In 1994 the world's first recorded example of infanticide among cetaceans (whales, dolphins, porpoises) was observed in the same location. A dolphin known as ID192, of unknown sex but believed to be male, attacked a calf in the company of its presumed mother, ID22. ID22 remained passive throughout ID192's assault in which it repeatedly butted the calf out of the water and then caught it in its teeth. In 1998 five bottlenose dolphin calves were found dead with identical injuries to those of attacked porpoises.

One possible reason for this behaviour is sexual frustration among males. Females typically calve every two to four years and resist the advances of males while looking after their young. Within a few days of losing a calf, or after the calf is mature enough to be independent, females again become sexually responsive. Male dolphins are intelligent enough to work out that if they kill a cow's calf she will soon become interested in mating (but this behaviour would seem to go against the genetic imprinting for the species' survival). Could it be that the porpoises are being confused with young dolphins and are also killed out of misplaced sexual frustration? Or is this aggression a by-product of pollution or competition for food? No one knows, but it's a disturbing discovery.

Blaskets

The Blaskets are the most westerly group of islands in Europe. Slide them down their longitude of 10° 30'W until they are opposite Lisbon, and they'd be seventy-five miles from the Portuguese coast. Slide them upwards and they'd be the same distance from eastern Iceland. No other Irish islands have had so many books written about them and probably few in the world can match their ten square kilometres for the literary output of indigenous authors. Around forty books were written by Blasket men and women last century. At their peak in 1911 the population numbered 160 but this had dropped to fewer than fifty by 1953, the year their peat deposits were exhausted and they were evacuated at their own request. Today only one island is inhabited. Inishvikillane is an experimental home for re-introduced sea eagles, Irish red deer and Charles Haughey. It was while sailing from his holiday home on Inishvickillane to Dublin that Haughey had one of his frequent head-ons with Ireland, and the *Taurima* sank.

'In bad weather their appearance is utterly forbidding and they should be avoided.' *Irish Cruising Club Sailing Directions*, 1974.

Several of the Blaskets are rat-chewed mitres. Inishtooshert is a sleeping man. Inishtearaght is a sword-leafed plant on a pedestal pierced by a hole. They all look dangerous, as if at any moment they'll wake up and wreak havoc.

The inhabitants of Great Blasket grew oats and potatoes, and harvested dulse, carrageen and other nutritious sea vegetables. They kept sheep and a few hens and cows. They caught fish, rabbits, and seabirds and, each spring, lowered each other down cliffs on homespun ropes and stole eggs by the thousand. For fuel they burnt peat and gorse. Their boats were leather curraghs about nineteen feet long but of a sufficiently different design to merit their own name, *naomhog* (pl. *naomhoga*). They elected a King, one whose natural sense and leadership could be relied upon and whose final word always carried the day.

When the *Lusitania* sank in 1915 one lifeboat of survivors drifted to the Blaskets. On board was a black man, the first the islanders had ever encountered. He caused a storm of curiosity once the initial impression that he was a stoker still covered in soot proved false. Yet the Blasket islanders weren't always so white them-

selves. They lived in blackhouses. These were drystone construc-
tions roofed with thatch, usually with a central hole to allow the
smoke out. Soot soon blackened the interior, hence the name. Despite their poor reputation, blackhouses were much healthier than
many other forms of habitation, particularly when shared with a
cow. A weak inhalation of ammonia rose from the urine and proved
effective in preventing tuberculosis.

Life was never easy on the Blaskets and occasionally the islanders fell foul of laws they didn't understand. In his enchanting book
Some Lovely Islands (1968) Leslie Thomas records an incident
when some men were arrested for gathering puffins on a nearby
island. 'The puffins, it appeared, were private puffins belonging to a
lady landowner on the mainland.' The islanders went to court.

> ...they had a lawyer...and they stood dumbly and lis-
> tened as he spoke in their defence. ...The prosecution
> man was a clever bird from Dublin, who scorned the
> little man from Dingle championing the Blasket men. At
> one point, his voice booming in the cold courtroom, he
> asked: 'And has not my learned friend on the other
> side ever heard of the well-known principle of law, *mis-
> era est servitus ubi jus est aut incognitum aut vagum*?'
> The islandmen stood petrified at the sound of the
> words. But their man was good. 'On The Great
> Blasket', he replied quietly, 'the talk is of little else.'
>   The islanders won their case.

The first outsider to appreciate the strength of the Blasket culture was a Norwegian, Carl Marstrander. A lecturer at Dublin University, he inspired a young Cambridge student of classics to visit
the islands in August 1923. George Thomson was enraptured by
what he discovered. 'The conversation of those ragged peasants',
he wrote, 'as soon as I learnt to follow it, electrified me. It was as
though Homer had come alive. Its vitality was inexhaustible, yet it
was rhythmical, alliterative, formal, artificial, always on the point of
bursting into poetry.'

Thompson inspired several islanders to write down their stories.
Some had barely held a pen other than for the occasional necessity
of writing notes, and none had received a formal education beyond
the most basic level. But centuries of an oral traditional had made
them masterful story-tellers and their lives had been immersed in a
culture where eloquence and richness of vocabulary were valued
as much as life itself. They wrote in Gaelic but the translations of
their works managed to reproduce more than just a story, they cap-

tured the subtleties of wit, philosophy and tradition. These were mesmerising insights into minds scarcely moulded by modern times. Success inspired others to try their hand and many Blasket authors became household names. Among the best known were Thomas O'Crohan for *The Islandman,* Peig Sayers for *Peig* and *An Old Woman's Reflections*, Pádrig Tyers for *Blasket Memories* and Maurice O'Sullivan's *Twenty Years A-Growing*. In the latter account O'Sullivan, a boy at the time, recalls a thrush hunt.

> 'Now', said he [Pádrig Peg], 'this is Hallowe'en, and it is not known who will be living when it comes again, so I am going to propose another plan to make a night till morning of it. We will all go in twos and threes with lanterns through the Island hunting thrushes, and when we have made our round let everyone come back here. See you have a good fire down for us, Maura, and there is no fear but we'll have a roast for the night.'
>
> 'Very good', said one. 'A great thought', said another. Everyone agreed.
>
> 'You will come with me', said Pádrig Peg to Tomás and me...Off we went, the three of us with our lanterns, west to the Strand. It was a frosty night, the stars twinkling, the Milky Way stretched across the sky to the south and the Plough to the north, a light easterly breeze coming straight from Slea Head, gíog-gíog-gíog-gíog from peewits in the glen...
>
> Soon they were bagging their booty.
>
> 'We are doing well', said he, taking out his pipe again.
>
> 'Arra, man, we will soon have an ass's load if we go on like this', said Tomás.
>
> (Later) ... 'Were ye afraid at all?' said Pádrig.
>
> 'The devil a bit', said Tomás...
>
> 'How many have we now?' said Pádrig, getting up and turning towards us.
>
> 'Twenty-eight and the peewit.'
>
> 'Och, the devil, we have roast for the night, so.'
>
> Maurice O'Sullivan, *Twenty Years A-Growing* (1933)

Writing was the last industry. These authors were composing a swansong for the islands, and they knew it. Today, except for summer visitors, the Blaskets lie forsaken. For decades before the 1953 evacuation they had been emptying. The Blasket emigrants went to

Springfield, Massachusetts, to an area known as Hungry Hill.

*   *   *

Once out of the lee of the Blaskets I met open ocean again. I turned north-east towards the Shannon estuary and let the Atlantic rollers hoist me by the stern. To watch them approach was disquieting for they puffed themselves into tall pyramids and looked too fast and steep to be surmounted. This next one, for certain, would defy our buoyancy and pin us under. On and on they came, powering out of the crowd into individual magnificence.

As we neared each crest we began running away with a thrust of acceleration, a tremor as the boat struggled against the rudder's drag and a roar of surf at the bow. Then the wave would outpace us and we'd fall off its back with one of those heart-in-the-mouth gasps you emit when your car takes a bump in the road too fast.

The wind registered twenty-two knots, to which had to be added our eight through the water. Gradually my apprehension faded and for six hours I was immersed in exhilaration. The boat was built for this, her sails were balanced and tuned, the sea and wind were a matched dynamo. *Ceana* was at full stretch. A boat's happiness is palpable. She purred. I'd never had a sail like it. Somehow I'd stumbled upon a secret and experienced the supreme expression of the sport. It rained most of the day, at times torrentially. Yet these six hours were perfection and I knew it to my core.

I picked up a mooring at Carrigaholt as the weather deteriorated. The Atlantic tried to shove me one way while the Shannon shunted me the other. My log entry for that evening read:

> Wind now gusting to 35 knots from the north. It bellows. It strums the rigging and gnaws at boat, mooring and nerves. The dodgers flap, blocks rattle, water gurgles in the tank, under shifting tension the mooring rope creaks and groans, waves smash the hull and rush by with explosive haste, odd jars in lockers are pitched over and roll back and forth striking each other as they go. Without ear plugs, sleep will be impossible.

The following day I completed the forty-five miles to the Aran Islands under ideal conditions, putting the most exposed section of the entire coastline behind me. I felt a huge burden shift. A little over half of Ireland was now behind me. I'd been two months at sea and was beginning to like this life.

Aran Islands

'You're welcome here', said Joe.

'That's right', added John, 'welcome, you're very welcome.'

'Yes, welcome', Mike confirmed. He was slightly out of breath after dancing. 'Lord bless us, that's got the blood going. Haven't done that for years.'

'It shows. I've seen better coordination in a goat', John observed.

Inishmaan's pub had been deserted when I arrived so I sat outside and exercised my concertina. I was unaware of the trio's presence until Mike broke into some steps on the tarmac behind me. My hornpipe was erratic but so was his timing, though his limbs shed all heaviness and kept him airborne with a litheness that came from some youthful, unconscious reflex. He was a miner working in Montana. All three were born here, spoke Gaelic and on their regular home-coming holiday; Joe from London, John from Manchester.

'You'll take a drink', Joe suggested and, when I asked for a half of stout, 'You will not. You'll take a pint. God hates a coward.'

'I'm thinking that perhaps you're a fisherman', Mike remarked, 'your hands have the look of the sea about them. As honourable a profession as there is. And if so I'll warrant you're more successful than John here. He was a fisherman once, a more useless jigger who ever lowered a line would be hard to imagine.'

'And what would you know about fishing? The only thing you ever trawled was your balls.'

'Oh give up you two', Joe intervened, 'you'll make our friend here doubt there's a sparrow's worth of sense between the two of you and drive me to an early burial.'

Mike raised his rum and blackcurrant. 'Well, we're all right. We're flying. Winter is over.'

I was often to wonder at the abundance of strong characters among the Irish, more so, it seems, than in any other race. What gives them their self-assurance, what feeds their easy familiarity with strangers? They have the silver tongue, yes, but this is a manifestation of a deeper belief in their own worth. At its root, I believe, is the relative classlessness of Irish society. In ancient brehon law a maxim prevailed and was held dear: *is ferr fer a chiniud*, a man is better than his birth. Here you are assumed innocent of the crimes of your father and separated from the baggage of your background. Here conversation seems less an intellectual assessment, less a social probe, less a hierarchical challenge. It is simple and honest sociability. The speaking is valued above what is said. A contribution is recognised above all for its fellowship and this instils a sense of worth in everyone. I'm not claiming subtle inquisitions don't take place; it's just that they don't shape or define what in Ireland is still the art of conversation. The Irish remain a profoundly articulate and sociable race.

'I see the Gaelic school is on again', Joe whispered, as a group of young people in loud sweatshirts came in. Each summer intensive Gaelic courses ran on many west coast islands.

'It seems Gaelic is on a surer footing here than it is in Scotland', I remarked.

'Well it's a sorry state yours must be in', Joe countered, 'because here it's a dead buzzard.' The others nodded agreement. Joe was the eldest of ten children. He must have been in his late fifties. When he left home aged fifteen, he said, he went to Galway to look for work. 'They gave me a hard time, very hard for I had not a word of English whatsoever. I was made to feel stupid, like a country halfwit. That's changed now, bless the Lord. Now you're double the Irishman that can't speak it, but there's no use in it.'

'But look at all these people learning it. They're young. That's got to be a good sign.'

'Half of them will be Americans and the other half'll end up as librarians. There's no future to it.'

'They made it so everyone had to learn it', John explained. 'Now that was partly good and partly bad because when you have to do something you don't want to do it. To get into the university they made it that you had to pass an elementary Gaelic exam. Now some folk just don't have it where languages are concerned so they started giving out exemptions...'

'Praise us, that's a big word, Joe. I didn't think you had the likes in you.'

'There's a lot that would surprise you, Mike McGahern. And once they began with these exemptions then everyone wants one so no one takes Gaelic seriously any more.'

'Now I'll tell you a curious thing. When we were young here Gaelic was the only thing spoken. And it had been that way since the beginning. And people have surely been dying here for a long time, wouldn't you say? But you look in the cemetery and not one word of Gaelic will you see on a headstone. It's English they used. It's as if Gaelic wasn't good enough at the end, like it was the wrong stamp on your passport.'

'That's the truth, for sure. But there's some use for Gaelic now', John said. 'Now the likes of you, Alastair, if you took a fancy to living here, you couldn't buy a house unless you were versed in the Gaelic. That's policy here and in the Gaelic regions.'

'So Inishmaan's future is guaranteed. We'll end up with a population of Americans and librarians', Joe concluded.

I can't remember how many rounds later it was that someone suggested the melodeon. 'Give us a tune, Joe. Hey, Padraig, pass the box, no, not that one' – there were three on a shelf behind the barman – 'that's the one.'

The exiles had money to burn and there wasn't a sober soul in the place. Joe strapped himself into the instrument with such a fandangle of clumsiness that I wasn't hopeful of him being able to navigate the buttons. It took a while for him to register middle C, on which his bearings depended, then he took off and out the music poured. His fag drooped so low ash almost touched his chin, his mouth fixed a grimace and his eyes bored through the ceiling while his fingers fluttered. The more he drank the more complex the tunes became until suddenly the source was drained. A switch had been cast and he stopped mid-refrain. 'That's it, boys', he said. 'Me fingers are fucked.'

'We'll see you at the races', one of them said when I staggered to my feet. 'And don't forget the blessin o the ships. You'll need all the help you can get after here. That Connemara coastline's something else. A shoal of cunts, right enough.'

Shot in oblique light, the three Aran Islands – Inishmór, Inishmaan and Inisheer – are famous as aerial photographs. The camera usually captures the two-hundred foot cliffs as a black band in the foreground and includes tongues of surf rising from their base. Then it frames a panorama of details which momentarily baffle the eye. The land has been shattered, it seems, and the bits shoved back together. They are asymmetrical and multicoloured, these fragments, and their boundaries form a grey mesh. It is so unworldly that you stare at it for long enough to doubt your intelligence. Gradually comes the realisation that this is a landscape of walls. An estimated 1500 kilometres of them. Their purpose appears less to contain things, though they do (plots of potatoes, hay, sheep and cows) than to consume surface stone. Only this can justify subdivision upon subdivision until some enclosures are barely large enough for a cow to turn in, while others partition tables of rock on which nothing will grow except pokes of purple toadflax and mallow. 'Croggeries' are what the stony plots are termed, each accumulation leased by a tenant and embracing the good and the infertile.

The majority of productive land was created by hand. Generations hauled seaweed and layered their loads on the bare rock, and delved deep into fissures to scrape out any legacy of ready-made soil. Aran's colour came at great cost.

'Yes, we've got plenty stone here and the grass grows strong because of the limestone, you see.'

Peter Dirrane was a septuagenarian, returning home with his hayfork and collie when I met him.

'Unlike them.' He cast an arm towards the mainland. County Claire was all shale, he said, and Galway was granite. The Aran Islands were mainly limestone with intrusions of shale. 'That meant when the soil was made it was very rich. They sent cows over here from Connemara to winter. They came in the hookers. It's rare to see one now. Everything came and went by hooker. For the cows they mostly paid us in turf for we've no turf for the fires here. We sent them seaweed and potatoes and sally rods for creels, and gravestones.' He laughed through missing teeth. 'Yes, we cut nice big slabs for their graves. Plenty stone here.'

'Didn't the cows injure themselves?' I asked. You couldn't afford to look up from the ground the fields were so riddled with clefts.

'Oh yes there was always a few broken legs and they ended up in the pot, but the others learned.'

'Do you make much hay?' I nodded at his fork.

'Just a hobby really. There's not much agriculture goes on now.' He gazed round at the croggeries about us. All but one was a congestion of weeds. 'It's the tourism that keeps us going now.'

Four thousand tourists a day were said to descend on the islands in peak summer, mainly on Inishmór. Inishmaan was the forgotten island and only twelve stepped off the ferry, the *Happy Hooker*, that July morning. The four thousand come to see the walls and Dun Aengus, one of the prehistoric wonders of the Western World. They walk through its surrounding *chevaux de frise*, an array of lance-like rocks set against an enemy's approach, through its colossal walls forming three semicircles backed against a cliff whose edge is true and supports a visitor's chin while his gaze falls two hundred feet sheer to the surf below. They come to wonder why a fortress of such size was built when it lacked a source of fresh water and couldn't have endured a siege; who was the enemy and why were they so feared here that the Aran islanders built not just one fort of gargantuan proportions but no less than five spread across their small islands; whether perhaps these were not forts at all but temples to an unrecorded divinity. And the visitors come because of the works of J M Synge and Robert Flaherty.

Synge had yet to find himself when he first visited the islands in

1898 and was still seven years away from establishing himself as one of Ireland's finest playwrights. In Paris he met Yeats who mentioned the Aran Islands as having a way of life that deserved recording. Synge was twenty-seven at the time and had already undergone surgery for Hodgkin's disease, a cancer of the lymphocytes which would recur and claim his life at the age of thirty-eight, when he made the first of five annual trips to Inishmaan. Here he lodged with a family for a few weeks at a time and observed the life around him, collecting stories that would inspire his plays, most famously, *The Playboy of the Western World* (1907).

The Playboy was intended to shock through its strong language and sexual imagery, and shock it did, causing riots on its opening night but running on to great success.

Synge's book *The Aran Islands* was also published in 1907, the year that marked the height of his triumph. It is short, personal and in many ways restrained, as if the task of 'expressing a life that has never found expression' exhausted him and he was only able to snatch a few scenes and patch them together as extended notes. Yet his ear and eye are keen, and the book is a delightful insight into a lost world.

> The general knowledge of time on the island depends, curiously enough, on the direction of the wind. Nearly all the cottages are built, like this one, with two doors opposite each other, the more sheltered of which lies open all day to give light to the interior. If the wind is northerly the south door is opened, and the shadow of the door-post moving across the kitchen floor indicates the hour; as soon, however, as the wind changes to the south the other door is opened, and the people, who never think of putting up a primitive dial, are at a loss.
>
> In my cottage I've never heard a word of English from the women except when they were speaking to the pigs or to the dogs...
>
> 'A man who is not afraid of the sea will soon be drownded', he said, 'for he will be going out on a day he shouldn't. But we do be afraid of the sea, and we do only be drownded now and again.'
>
> J M Synge *The Aran Islands*

Far more influential in bringing the Aran Islands to public attention was Robert J Flaherty, the 'father' of the drama-documentary. In 1923 his classic 'Nanook of the North' was first screened to much acclaim, depicting the harsh existence of the Eskimos of the Belcher Islands in eastern Hudson Bay. Flaherty was sent a copy of Synge's book and decided to make the Aran Islands the next subject of his continuing theme, Man's Struggle Against Nature.

Flaherty later admitted he 'should have been shot' for the risks he asked the islanders to take for the scenes of curraghs being rowed in mountainous seas. Much of the film is taken up with these frail craft negotiating waves that derive none of their terror from special effects. At its heart the story is of the daily lives of the archetypal family. 'Tiger' King was persuaded to portray the strapping young father who breaks rocks to create a potato plot and hunts basking sharks. He wears the standard homespuns, the man's bobble beret and pampooties, moccasins of untanned leather. Maggie Dirrane played the mother, hauling seaweed on her back and leaping into the sea to help with his curragh. In commercial terms the film brought reasonable returns but the shark hunt, which was presented as a documentary of contemporary life, provoked widespread controversy.

The islanders had last hunted sharks a generation before and the knowledge of how to go about it had faded into uncertainty. A dying centenarian from County Galway was found who had hunted sharks and could describe the process, but knowing and doing proved two different things. Time after time, when a shark was located and the camera was running, Tiger found the creature's hide impenetrable and his harpoons bent. It took a second season before the sequence was obtained, and only after a shark was secured with a harpoon gun from a larger boat. The shark was exhausted and close to death when the line was transferred to Tiger in his curragh and the camera captured him finishing it off.

How fitting it was, therefore, that when the film was being promoted in the Gaumont-British Film Company's London office, on Wardour Street, the stuffed shark sent there for display proved too large for the window. A centre cut was removed and a modicum of consistency was thus maintained in the unreliability of art.

* * *

curragh *Ireland, W & NW:* Hide- and now cloth-covered boat that works from the coastal beaches;... Other recorded names:...**cor(r)ach, corragh, courache, curac(h), curachán (dim).** Note also; **Achill Island curragh, Aran Islands canoe, Boyne currach, Donegal curragh, namóg**
A Dictionary of the World's Watercraft

Half a dozen curraghs lay upside-down by the harbour. About twenty feet long by five wide, they were a lath of hazel or willow covered in canvas and heavily tarred. They were ideally suited to this coast. Three men would carry an upside-down curragh on their shoulders, their upper bodies hidden inside the hull, and like a beetle on its own legs the curragh would walk to the sea. Their lightness made them simple to launch and highly responsive to the oar, while their up-turned prow glanced over surf. They were cheap to make and simple to patch. An old flour bag, some twine and a daub of tar did the trick. Occasionally still used as work boats but maintained mostly for the summer races, curraghs had become scarcer over the years and now were found only in parts of the west.

The exiles never made it to Inishmaan's races but Peter Dirrane was there.

'Are you related to Maggie Dirrane who was in The Film?' I asked.

'Well, a cousin of sorts.' He waved the subject aside. 'Well, it would be a fine day if it weren't for the fog.'

Out of this yoghurt of obscurity a blur sharpened into two curraghs with four men apiece bent over their oars. They were bow and bow with nothing to choose between them. Spray burst from their oars and the craft surged towards the finishing line amidst shouts of support and abuse from the crowd.

'We're not calling them oars here', Peter said, 'we're calling them paddles.'

They were remarkably slender, the blade barely wider than the loom.

'You see their hands, how the paddles are long and overlap and one hand must go under the other. In a calm like this it makes no odds which, but in a sea if the wind comes from the right then the right hand must be on top. That's because the left will be the leeward side which is lower in the water so the leeward oar needs to rise higher between strokes to clear the waves, so the left hand must have the space below it.' He worked an imaginary pair of oars to demonstrate the point. 'Ah, I wish I was out there myself.' He could contain himself no longer and ran down to steady the boat as the competitors disembarked and the next crew took their places.

Six tractors arrived, each stacked with a family, to start the children's races in the adjacent field. A small box of plastic trophies followed in the ten-ton bucket of a digger. Picnickers set out their rugs among rabbit holes and the odd dog gatecrashed an event and saw off the more timid competition while adults rushed in to restore order and lavish consolation. Halfway through the final of the sack race, jumped in BLACK DIAMOND POLISH COAL bags, I realised time had run away with me and I was about to miss the Blessing of the Boats at Kilronan on Inishmór.

I arrived too late for *Ceana* to take part and was only able to follow the proceedings through binoculars. Blessing ceremonies have been revived in many ports around Ireland. Their origin lies far back in time though they gradually slipped into disuse last century along with other customs such as the dipping of sails on passing islands connected with St Macdara and St Gregory. Kilronan's Blessing ceremony was revived fourteen years ago and, although some cynics decried it as a tourist gimmick, there wasn't a single local boat that was game to miss it.

They were clad from end to end in bunting, eight large fishing boats and a host of smaller craft. A priest was assisted onto the lifeboat (appropriately enough) which led the flotilla to the entrance of the bay. Here he arose and stood at the bow, a striking figure in white robes but a poor example, I felt, for flouting the use of a life-jacket. As each boat passed he made the sign of the cross, sprinkled water and blessed her by name. Klaxons and hooters sounded as the vessels returned to the pier for mass. Awards followed, each winner being presented with a trophy which appeared to be sized in inverse proportion to the skill it represented; best net-mender, splicer, deckhand, mate, skipper, decorated boat, single catch, season catch...until they had run out of bests and almost everyone had their careers justified. The women cheered, the men blushed, holding their crystal decanters as disinterestedly as they would under-sized haddocks.

'Is it possible', I asked the priest, 'for you to bless, long-distance, a boat that missed the ceremony?'

He was young and bearded. 'It is within the Church's power to do anything in the name of God. All you have to do is to anoint your boat with holy water, available free from the bucket at my feet. You'll need a bottle.'

I saw I would also need to be quick as a crowd had descended on the bucket. I sized up their containers and realised it would be touch and go.

In a bin I found an empty coke bottle, small. I squandered precious time rinsing it as I couldn't be sure any remnants wouldn't contaminate the blessing. The priest didn't flinch when he saw it. He was just replenishing the well from a hose, adding some concentrate from his bottle and intoning words I couldn't hear.

'Good luck', he added.

I completed the ceremony that evening and *Ceana* was blessed. It was to last until I reached Lough Foyle.

Sailors' Beliefs and Customs

The practice of men in western cultures wearing earrings is widespread today but formerly it was uncommon except among sailors. It was their fear of being washed up and left exposed to carrion-eaters that prompted them to adopt the custom. By piercing their ears with an investment of gold sailors hoped that in the event of being washed overboard, they would always have on their person sufficient funds for a decent burial.

'That's let the cat out of the bag!' The expression holds good to this day for a revelation that will result in retribution. The cat was the cat o' nine tails, nine leather thongs with knots at their end which would first bruise the skin, then mulch it. Blood was usually drawn after the fifth lash. Twenty-five lashes was the prescription for being drunk on duty. Sentences of over a hundred lashes were not uncommon; on occasions two hundred were ordered, an ordeal few survived. The cat was handled by the boson's mate. In order to diminish his enthusiasm for the task, many sailors had a crucifixion scene tattooed over the full extent of their back. Not only did they hope that the image of Christ would induce the mate to soften his blows, but a conviction grew that the saviour's power could actually repel the descent of the lash.

Keelhauling was reserved for the most serious of offences. A rope was passed under the ship and the victim tied by wrists and ankles to each end. The rope was then pulled round one circuit of the hull. Today all boats use antifouling, a toxic paint designed to erode as it poisons the razor-edged shells that colonise hulls. In past centuries these scarifying crusts could be six inches deep. Keelhauling, almost without exception, was a death sentence. The majority of victims had their heads ripped off, the others either drowned or never recovered from the loss of blood and flesh. Hanging was a far more merciful alternative.

Among men under constant threat from the weather a wide spectrum of superstitions developed in the hope of attracting good fortune or to give warning of impending bad fortune. Petrels and seagulls were believed to be reincarnations of dead sailors. To meet them in the middle of an ocean was a sure sign of an approaching storm. However the bird which commanded the greatest awe, as Coleridge famously depicted, was the 'eagle' of the Southern Ocean, the albatross. It also heralded an approaching storm (not surprisingly, as they frequent the region of storms) and to kill one brought everlasting bad luck. A loaf of bread, a hatch cover or any other object that normally rests a specific way up on a ship was never left inverted or that would invoke the same action to befall the vessel. A suitcase was considered a Jonah on a fishing vessel in the Newfoundland Banks and bad luck was brought by using a shoehorn, wearing grey mittens (instead of white) or long boots cut down into 'stag boots'. The same was true of anyone who spat into the hold or turned a dory anti-clockwise or against the sun.

In the 1980s I worked on a Faroese prawn fishing boat off the coast of Greenland. I remember the harsh rebuke I received for whistling while waiting for the trawl to end. To whistle at sea is to whistle up a storm. Certain creatures are still unmentionable in boats as they too are harbingers of bad luck. Mariners the world over refrain from uttering the words 'salmon' (the code 'silver ones' is used instead), 'rabbits' ('furry ones') or 'pig' ('hog', 'curly tail', 'Dennis', 'Mr Dennis', 'Grecian' or 'Jack'). Some captains never allowed pork or bacon to be carried on a ship's maiden voyage.

If a wife wished to prevent her husband's ship from putting to sea she would put a black cat under a basket. Women were traditionally regarded as ill-portents on fishing boats (perhaps because jealousies invariably arose among the crew) and ministers or priests were complete pests both on land and water. If a man of the cloth was seen by a fisherman on his way to board a vessel the fisherman had to return home and set out as many times as it took to complete the journey without sighting such a doom-laden spectre. Faroese whalers believe their quarry will elude them if a pastor in a boat passes between them and the shore.

Boatmen on Ireland's west coast used to remove white stones from their ballast because of a traditional link with death. In the rest of Ireland today it is rare to find a vessel that does not have a phial of holy water secured in its bow. And in Britain a coin is still always secreted in a new ship when the keel is laid.

The British Admiralty continues to pay homage to superstition when it comes to the naming of ships. Reptiles are no longer chosen after the Navy tallied up its losses over the centuries: four *Vipers*, four *Serpents*, three *Lizards*, two *Dragons*, two *Snakes*, a *Cobra*, an *Adder*, an *Alligator* and a *Crocodile*. Tradition also held that it was unlucky to change the name of a ship. The *Vulture*, launched as the *Lairdstock*, finally ran out of luck in 1942 and foundered on Rathlin Island as the *Lochgarry*. The *Mary Celeste* was previously the *Amazon*.

Galway Races

Galway was Ireland's boomtown. It wore its credentials as the fastest-growing metropolis in cranes, mushrooming suburbs and virgin bypasses. A sense of shock pervaded the air at the injustice of rush-hours and parking charges, as if the ancestral right to shop by tractor was being violated and politicians ought to do something about it. Not only that but the character of the place had been hijacked by trendies and turned into brasserieville. A coterie of streets was now an al fresco café-bar where, whether you bought a beer or latté or not, you'd be lucky to escape having someone else's spilt over you. If the sun shone the cobbles were covered in tables, stalls and buskers. So many outlets sold ferry trips to the Aran Islands that you felt you'd be pitched into jail if a policeman stopped you and you were unable to produce your ticket. Galway was humming, alive from its suburbs to its hooker harbour and along its seaside promenade. At the end of July, during the week of its greatest event of the year, Galway Races, it was brimming fit to burst.

The track was a short bus ride from the centre. 'Here's a programme fer ye, boy', said my neighbour, a man in a flat cap. He looked only a few years older than me. 'It's a spare. And I'd be recommending The Gamekeeper in the big one.' A wink tipped his ruddy face.

We walked across a mile of fields filling with cars, and an underpass took us below the hallowed turf ('soft going') to the main concourse. Suspended television screens beamed in races from Folkstone and Bloemfontein. 'Bets taken in euros or sterling', 'Minimum bet €10', read signs around a square of bookies. They stood on boxes above the crowd, each with their spotters alongside. They wore suits, gabardines and the serious expressions of raptors. Umbrellas were rigged to hold loud colours against the likelihood of rain. Some spots were already falling. There must have been over fifty bookies. A few had blackboards and chalk dust on their cuffs; the majority sported electronic screens operated by a lackey at a laptop. Binoculars were raised to scrutinise the changing odds of rivals, words were whispered, signals semaphored and then cuffs rubbed, chalk scribbled and luminous digits blinked. The Flatcap perused the odds. The Gamekeeper was 8:1, second to the favourite, Crimson Flower at 6:1. The Flatcap spotted a bookie a fraction behind the times and handed over a fifty-euro note, securing 10:1.

'Gamekeeper won in 2000 and 2001', he beamed. 'Flunked last year but he's definitely on form. And likes it soft, too.'

I put €5 on him at the Tote, baffled by the jargon of each ways, places and all the rest. The Flatcap was affronted by my caution. 'Ye'll regret such a fishbone, boy. Ye'll kick yerself when he wins. That orse'll rip the arse out o' the jockey to be first, oi tell you, no word o' a lie.' His glee at his impending windfall was barely containable. 'Oh come on. Let's be getting a pie while we wait.'

The eatery covered an acre. Circular chest-high tables perched on columns. No chairs. 'Don't let go yer plate or ye'll lose it.' Teenagers in blue cruised continuously and snatched up dishes at the merest hint of neglect. Such was their fervour they might have been on piece rates. It all seemed very American in efficiency but without the banal pleasantries. Through a window we could see a steady traffic of helicopters.

'Ye haven't seen the half of it, boy', The Flatcap remarked, a moustache of grease appearing above his mouth. 'If yer anybody ye got to arrive by helicopter. All the society knobs come like that. Ten-thousand-euro bets are nothing here, God's my witness. And these knobs take the same hotel rooms every year and play poker all night. The races are pigeon feed. The real money happens at night. And the politicians flock in too. Fianna Fáil are here – it's them that's in power, unfortunately – and they got a hospitality tent where all the party faithful *have* to show up and make a donation.'

'Is it all done openly?'

'Used to be.' He laughed. 'They try to be discreet now but there's a lot of dirty laundry and lubricating done here, I'm telling you.'

The helicopters continued to jostle for position in the upper panes of the eatery. Their passengers wouldn't be joining us here. This was the average man's social club. I looked around at an overwhelming predominance of old and middle-aged men. Granted, race tracks were a traditional preserve of men, but it looked an unnatural bias. As unnatural as the composition of rural pubs where the single man drowning his loneliness was as archetypally Ireland as accent and charm. My companion read my thoughts.

'Are ye married?'

'Yes. And you?'

'No.' Wistfulness frosted his eyes. 'Not much chance of that where I came from.'

I didn't pursue it. I thought I knew what he meant.

It was a legacy of The Famine again. One of its many repercussions was to make farmers and labourers in particular more fearful of having large families. The risk of further suffering increased with more dependents and the division of farms among more heirs exacerbated the likelihood of future impoverishment. The patriarch now held onto the farm for longer before allowing his heir to take over the land that brought with it both the means and the right to marry. But even that right was qualified. It was deemed unacceptable for the heir, usually the eldest son, to introduce a wife to the family home until all his siblings had left to establish homes of their own. Thus in rural communities a convention of later marriage, or no marriage at all, developed. By 1900 around thirty per cent of men and twenty-five per cent of women in Ireland never married, when ten per cent was the norm for both sexes in the rest of Europe. A survey in 1926 produced even more alarming figures for rural workers: forty-one per cent of farm labourers never married while as many as eighty-four per cent of farmers' younger sons and daughters, classified as 'relatives assisting on farms', went through life unwed.

Women have always emigrated in much greater numbers from the countryside than men. 'So by the time the unwed heir came to look for a spouse', wrote John Ardagh in *Ireland and the Irish* (1994), 'there was not much choice locally. Still emotionally tied to his parents, and sexually innocent, if not repressed, he was often ill-equipped for seeking or finding a girl, so he never married. ... As it was mostly the men who married so late, a woman frequently had a much older husband who had spent his life under the influence of his mother and was still emotionally tied to her; so brides had classic mother-in-law problems, more than in most countries. ...and when an Irishman gets drunk, it's said, it is about his mother that he sings.'

In 1973 the social anthropologist Hugh Brody published his research into rural life on Ireland's western seaboard as a portrait of a typical, but mythical, community called Inishkillane. 'Out of 436 people living in Inishkillane, therefore, a total of 131 people can be said to be chronically sexually isolated; none of these people has a sexual partner in the house or the neighbourhood, and none can realistically expect to find one. ... The middle-aged and the elderly have possession of over half the houses in the parish. In none of these houses is there any real possibility of a younger generation emerging. ... Families tend to expect that at least one son will remain at home to keep the farm going ...therefore, one son in each family is faced with a choice between staying celibate at home and emigrating with the chance of marriage.' [*Inishkillane*].

Daughters had it no better and the Church contributed to their internal conflict, as Brody continues: 'It is the position of the woman and the prolongation of virginity – the two most striking weaknesses in post-famine tradition – which the Church has most dignified. The two qualities are secured with the single myth of the Virgin. Mary was the first to consecrate her virginity to God. In this way she led to God all who instated her virginity.' It was to escape this grip of both Church and patriarchy, and their obsessive vigilance over the virtue of their daughters, that many women left. Even in the cities there were restraints; until 1977 a woman was forced to resign from a civil service post on marriage. Civil divorce was allowed for the first time in the Republic in 1995.

Tolerance of contraceptives is also an exceptionally recent development. The Pope reaffirmed condemnation of their use in 1967 and their sale remained illegal until 1993. In the late eighties, in defiance of the law, Richard Branson allowed the Irish Family Planning Association to open a condom stall in his Virgin Megastore in Dublin. The stall did a good trade but, shortly before the anachronistic law was changed, Virgin was fined £500 for selling illegal merchandise. The fine was paid by the rock group U2. Abortions remain illegal to this day. Under an 1861 law introduced by the British and maintained by the Irish, homosexuality was a criminal offence until 1993. Lesbians have never suffered any legal prohibition under the Victorian pretence that they do not exist.

Boyhoods lasting forty years, sexuality denied, the enforced inferiority of women, despondency, abuse; blame The Famine, blame the Church. Yet the accusations do not wholly rest comfortably. The Famine happened a long time ago, the Church is losing its sway over minds and habits and, in 2002, Ireland had the youngest population of any country in Europe with 37.4% of its people under the age of twenty-five. Yet the Irish crude marriage rate per thousand of population remains one of the lowest in the world at 5.1, compared with 12 in the USA and 9 in France. Undoubtedly a major factor now is the lower value placed on marriage by the young in preference to the relatively new freedom of cohabiting, but there still exists that lost generation or two for whom marriage was always out of reach. They are, of course, represented in public, by men. 'Today you can still see them', John Ardagh concluded, 'propping up the bars of village pubs, these "mountainy men" in their later years, often leading very isolated lives. Many are clinically depressed, suffering from "the nerves" as it is called, but few take their own lives.' Instead, it seemed, many take their lives to join the rich and influential at Galway Races.

'We'd better get going', The Flatcap said. 'They'll be in the showing area soon.'

The concourse had filled in our absence. We jostled our way through a throng of smart but not outrageous fashions and a troop of boys in gold braid blowing into brass. The Gamekeeper was being walked round the arena when we arrived. My companion studied his musculature, the evenness of his gait. He nodded. 'Good. A bit on edge but that's no bad thing. Keenness, confidence, nervousness' – he held out a hand and made it flutter like a hovering hawk – 'they can go either way out there. Yes, boy, I'd say yer five euros are safe.'

Crimson Flower shook her head and peeled her lips as she worried at the bit. Peace In Ireland snorted and kept crabbing sideways, eyes wide in agitation. Pakiefromathleague had strings of saliva round his nose. The jockeys all looked emaciated. They might have been children wearing adults' faces. Their vests shocked.

Twenty minutes later the start was called. It looked very casual to me, the boxes being dispensed with and the horses drawn up in a ragged line. The Gamekeeper got off to a flier.

'There he goes now keep him steady don't lose yer head tuck in there and go easy plenty of time yes nice nice second place doesn't he move well let the others tire themselves yes yes…'

Half the crowd seemed to have lost interest after the first furlong. The favourite, Crimson Flower, was trailing and never mentioned in the torrent of commentary from a thousand loudspeakers. Decent Pilot led bravely but soon faded and Dark Trojan took over. The Gamekeeper was, apparently, running a tactically brilliant race by cruising along in second.

'God bless him. It'll be a famous day.' The Flatcap smiled, his €500 as good as in his hand.

Excitement revived in the last furlong. The shouts from those left with a chance were deafening. 'Begod move it!' 'Go Pakie go!' 'Shift ya bastard!' 'Yeeeeeees!' The jockeys were all standing in frenzies of whip-thrashing.

Suddenly the unforgivable happened. The Gamekeeper valiantly maintained his speed. But everyone else increased theirs. Rapid Deployment appeared from obscurity and recorded the biggest win of his career. Raise A Storm came second and Pakiefromathleague crossed a nose or two behind.

The crowd's noise switched to a low murmur. There was a crackle as Mr Flatcap's note crumpled before dropping to the ground to join a covering of others. Crumpled hopes - everywhere. He smiled.

'Rock of Cashel, that's the one to go for next, boy.'

Viewpoints

I hitched to Roundstone with an Israeli couple on holiday. Connemara's bogs went on for so long they were a subcontinent in themselves. The Israelis exclaimed in excited tones. Every so often it became too much, we sheered into a lay-by and they excused themselves to take photographs. I tried to gauge the aim of their lenses and identify the source of their wonder, finally concluding they had to be botanists.

'Is the flowers you like so much?' I ventured.

'No. The water.'

Roundstone Buses

SERVICES FROM ROUNDSTONE TO CLIFDEN

MONDAY – SATURDAY

11.34 (Thursdays only)

19.44 (Wednesdays only)   PLEASE NOTE: All times are approxi

19.49 (Fridays only)   mate.

Sea Serpents

The sun is out, the odd tic from Neptune wrinkles the sea but otherwise it is a Monetesque reflection of the sky in greysilver. A distant Connemara cuts thinly through the middle and the Twelve Pins undulate in the haze. In nautical terms *Ceana* is under way but not making way. She's detached and floundering, her sails are limp. Occasionally some unseen motion from the deep makes her rock and she gathers a sailful of air as she flops to one side, flipping the boom noisily over as she does so. Then she repeats the performance from side to side in the diminishing momentum of a pendulum. It's an irksome ritual that just adds wear and tear to boat and owner. You feel each jar as acutely as a chandler's invoice. Then peace. I could roll away the sails and motor but today I'm not in a hurry, not intimidated by the forecast. I'm content to be an impressionist splodge in a picture.

I'm not aware of having heard it recently but 'The Fields of Anthenry' enters my head and irritatingly commandeers the spaces between thoughts. I can't shake it off. Some dolphins pass but find me no sport and disappear. They bring a breeze in their wake and suddenly I'm making way, dispensing an arabesque trail of eddies from my stern. My position is 53° 20.5 N, 10° 05.5 W as I move from 2003 in the water to 1959 on the chart. For some reason this chart of Wallace's has no longitude or latitude so I have nothing to relate my GPS readings to; I must rely on compass bearings taken on landmarks to fix my position. In weather like this, it's no hardship. Connemara looks benign, as if she's gathered in all her stray rocks in praise of the day. But they're out there.

I dip my hat to St Macdara's Island. That's the tradition. Or maybe it should be the sails, but I can't be bothered. A short time later the island, my key landmark, promptly disappears. The mist rolls on and in no time Connemara is consumed. I automatically turn to my GPS before realising it is useless. All is not lost though for I can see both Skird and Mile Rocks. I just have to steer between them and I can plot a safe course to avoid Boot and Toole Rocks, followed closely by Sunk Bellows and Wild Bellows. Soon it's raining. The Israelis, I reflect, will be ecstatic.

The breeze is now a good blow of twenty knots. Within half an hour not enough wind has become too much. Monet has pushed off, dissolved into a particularly violent Turner. I reach the key mark and swing round to pass between Skird and Mile. It doesn't feel right. I check my bearings. If I'm where I think I am then it's right. I continue. Doubts gnaw at me. This doesn't feel right, THIS DOES-N'T FEEL RIGHT. I swing the rudder round and bail out. The sails whiplash until I can get them under control again. I can't justify what I've just done except on intuition. I can't place the danger but I can feel it. Retreating is the only safe thing to do. Now I'm going in the opposite direction to my destination but with the benefit of added distance, everything suddenly snaps into sense. What I thought were Mile Rocks is in fact the outer fringe of Skird Rocks. I'd con-fused my distances and turned too soon. My heart races at the sim-plicity and potential disaster of my mistake. I was heading into the heart of the reef.

An hour later the barometer and fog are both rising. I pass Slyne Head as a new high threatens to dump me in doldrums once more. I'm safe now. There's only Least Shoals to worry about. 'Great rip-pling over these shoals', states the chart in what sounds like mas-terful understatement. But there's no rippling. I've a clear passage to Inishbofin. The Anthenry Fields have vanished. A hooker with claret sails overhauls me, more successfully capturing what I now like to think of, over a can of beer, as the dregs of the Skird Squall. That's one of the beauties of sailing. If you survive a near-disaster, it is so readily convertible to adventure.

Basking in surrealism again, I look for sea serpents. It looks just the weather for them.

I spent most of my early life an hour's drive from Loch Ness and became obsessed by the mysterious 'monsters'. (I learned early on that there couldn't possibly be just one). As a volunteer with the Loch Ness Investigation Bureau I spent weeks sitting on the roof of a Bedford van scanning the loch, camera at the ready. Devouring every book I could on the subject I came across one that continues to enthral me: Bernard Heuvelmans's *In the Wake of Sea Serpents.*

Heuvelmans's work is a collection of eye-witness accounts with a critical analysis of their details in an attempt to support or discredit their veracity. His premise is that all reported sightings of strange phenomena must be treated with scepticism because cases of mis-taken identity are common and, it seems, hoaxes are endemic, par-ticularly in Ireland. Among sightings reported here between 1850 and 1890 Heuvelmans uncovered numerous fictitious accounts of sea serpents which he hypothesised might be journalists trying to ridicule the Royal Navy in the campaign for Home Rule.

But the one that appeared off Kilkee in County Clare in 1871 was very different and could not be easily dismissed. 'According to the *Limerick Chronicle* it had an enormous head, shaped somewhat like that of a horse and "a huge mane of seaweed-looking hair, which rose and fell with the motion of the water". It had glassy eyes and much alarmed the witnesses, so that one lady "nearly fainted at the sight", not perhaps unnaturally'. On this occasion the witnesses were named and included a 'well-known clergyman in the north of Ireland'.

Around 1908 a distinguished observer joined the ranks of believers. Vice-Admiral Robert H Anstruther, RN was in command of HMS *Caesar* on passage between Ireland and the Isle of Man when he chanced upon a huge 'chameleon-like' creature'.

> In the first dog-watch I was standing on the bridge, when suddenly something shot out of the water right in front of me, about half a ship's length off, straight up into the air about the height of the foremast head, about fifty feet. I, of course, had my galilee-glass handy, and quickly fixed them on the quadruped – for a four-footed or, at any rate, a four-legged, beast it proved to be. With outstretched neck and legs it fell, or rather dived, into the sea again. I had never seen such a creature before in all my long experience at sea, so I hastily called the navigating officer, who was at the standard compass, to come to my end of the bridge, in case the reptile, or whatever one may call it, should show itself again. No sooner had he got to my side than up it shot again, and I had another good look at it, and this time the navigating officer, Lieutenant-Commander (now Captain) H.J.L.W.K. Wilcox saw it as well. It did not appear to have scales, but rather the shiny skin of a reptile. We waited and waited, but it never rose again.

Early in July 1910 a Captain Jorgenson of the Norwegian three-master *Felix* en route to Canada reported a sighting of a sea serpent off Rathlin Island. It was a brief encounter and the part of body visible was estimated at about fourteen feet long but its writhing on the surface made such a forceful impression that he was in no doubt it was an exceptionally large and unusual animal.

But the one I reckoned I had the best chance of seeing was the creature spotted – albeit almost a century earlier one summer's day in 1910 – not far from my current location in Kilkerrin Bay (marked Kilkieran on my chart). It was a classic 'swan-neck' sighting made by Howard St George, an English gentleman, and his son on a holiday fishing trip. He sought no publicity for his story which was not published until 1932 when it appeared as a modest, almost embarrassed, inclusion in an anthology with an unfortunate title for a memoir of such a sensitive nature.

> I was about eighty yards away. The animal was partly submerged. It looked about the size of a large farm cart, a large hairy body with serpent's head and neck held erect, about six feet long. It was calmly floating towards the Atlantic on the ebb tide in the wild surroundings of Kilkerrin Bay, Connemara, fifteen miles from Screebe. My son and I were returning home in a small naphta launch which was fairly silent. The thing we saw was very similar to a picture which appeared in the *Daily Mail* of what another man saw at about the same time. I personally have never published anything of what we saw.
>
> G Cornwallis-West *Edwardians go Fishing*

In a subsequent interview years later Howard St George recalled a few more details. As well as being big and hairy the body was brown and the head at the end of its long neck was 'swaying from side to side as though looking for something'.

Sea serpents in modern times appear to be much shyer but are still occasionally spotted. John Ridgway recorded an alarming encounter with one in 1966 while rowing the Atlantic with Chay Blyth.

I see no reason why these creatures should not be out there, not 'monsters' or 'serpents' of the mind but new species of flesh and blood yet to be substantiated with a name. Species intelligent enough to give man a wide berth. I looked for them in vain and respected them no less for it.

Inishbofin

Nautical-speak today conforms to the cold edge of precision. Charts, pilots, weather adopt the language of control, the fickleness of nature bridled by Admiralty standards and categorised into rankings. The wind's philanderings are broken down into bites of speed from Light Air (Force 1, Velocity 1-3 knots, Wave Height 0m, Ripples formed, no foam crests, direction shown by smoke but not by wind vanes) right up to Hurricane (Force 12, Velocity 64 kn+, Wave Height 14m) when no description is necessary because most of the world is airborne. Charts and pilots adopt the same approach with 'slights', 'moderates', 'severes' and 'extremes'. It's understandable. A uniform glossary of comparatives is useful, albeit dull. It was not always thus. In the past dangers were represented with style and even panache. The 1848-9 chart of Inishbofin marks a hazard at the northwest point of the island, the western extremity of North Beach Bay, with the words, 'Holes communicating with Sea'.

But there was no communication on this particular afternoon. I lined up the leading towers of Inishbofin's harbour and held my breath. The rock face was only a boat-length away. So clear was the water I might have been hovering, looking down on gangs of sea urchins loitering among leathery belts of weed. Sea pinks passed at head height and their pollen sugared the staleness of stranded bladderwort. Once through the narrow passage I executed a sharp turn into a haven defended on all sides from the wind. To my right the rock face melded into a ruined castle, half in the water and half on a low headland.

The turn was necessary to avoid Bishop Rock and I imagined the unfortunate man spread-eagled over its crust of barnacles. In Cromwellian times a bishop was said to have been tied to this rock below high water level and allowed to drown. The small island of Inishbofin remained the last outpost of resistance to Cromwell's conquest of Ireland. When it fell the castle was used as a prison for Catholic priests. Under a 1585 statute these were guilty of treason and fifty were rounded up and held here prior to being shipped to the West Indies.

On such a perfect summer's day any act of violence seemed unbelievable. Even sheep were in breech of decency by masticating the landscape. I could hear their chewing and indigestion, mingled with the sounds of children warring over sandcastles while their parents sunbathed. I felt as if I'd stumbled upon an outreach of Turkey as the anchor chain rattled through the stemhead and signalled that I was now off-duty. The sea was too blue, the sun too hot, the beaches too bright for old Ireland. Yet she betrayed herself in a straggle of bungalows occupying high ground to my left where, as part of Ireland's greening of all things red in Britain (green telephone kiosks, green letterboxes, Green Nose Day), a green post van began a slanting descent through fields, stamping *An Post* on the scene.

Visiting yachts had become scarce now. Dingle was the cut-off point for most cruisers, the expanse of exposed coast to the north acting as a deterrent. The huddle of boats resting in the bay were mainly foreigners flying the limp colours of France, Germany and Holland, joined by a Norwegian and an American. We exchanged waves when our eyes met but perhaps we were too inured to the isolation of long distances to consider the possibility of conversing over twenty yards or of broaching a cell of privacy. Owning a boat involved the same pretence of invisibility that all neighbours divided by low walls must adopt.

I walked Inishbofin's three miles of length. *I could happily live here,* I thought. With a mile of width and an irregularity of bays it had enough space and variety to stretch both legs and mind. The islanders clearly thought expansively too. There were only 180 of them but they had as many districts as downtown New York; West Quarter, Fawnmore, Middle Quarter, Cloonamore and East End. Each had its limits defined by carved signs. I walked through a palate of irises, buttercups, montbretia, lupins, daisies and a host of other flowers I should know but have never bothered to identify. Oystercatchers and curlews piped in the distance while pipits and larks pulled parachute stunts overhead. I watched a farmer cover more ground than his dog in an effort to gather his sheep. By the time I reached him, and added to the confusion, he'd given up and conceded a win to the flock. It was their third victory that week, he explained. 'But truth to tell it's not that important anyway.'

Nothing seemed that important. Doors lay open as if the same clock once used on the Aran Islands was still in service here. I could hear snatches of conversation and scoldings as I passed, and tea was being taken outside on kitchen chairs facing the sun. East Village owned the best beach and the best views, looking over to the mainland's layers of mountains dominated by the perfect cone of Croagh Patrick. I walked to Ooghdoty Cove on the strength of its name alone and passed Inishbofin's twenty-odd schoolchildren having swimming lessons in the sea. Like a harem of seals they were clad in black wetsuits.

'You're welcome', said the barman at the Dolphin Bar that evening.

'So you are' echoed Robert, an Irishman sailing with his family on their annual holiday. He'd been coming to Inishbofin for over twenty years.

'We saw you arrive. This island's God's trailer for heaven, isn't it Mary?'

Mary smiled over her lager and blew a spout of cigarette smoke towards God. Their sixteen-year-old daughter looked as though she'd rather be in Dublin's Temple Bar. 'Filthy habit', Robert confided. 'More women smoke in Ireland as a percentage of the population than anywhere else in the world. That's a fact. Heard it on the radio today.'

'Robert's a surveyor', Mary explained, tiredly, as if she longed for some fulfilment that might be served by other professions: say, bakers, plumbers or shepherds. 'He collects statistics.'

'We're from Ballinasloe', Robert continued. 'You heard of Ballinasloe? Country town east of Galway. Famous for its horse fair in October. You heard of the Ballinasloe Horse Fair? No? Jesus! Don't they educate you in Scotland? Well let me tell you it's the biggest horse market in the country and it was once the biggest in Europe. In 1856 they sold ninety-nine thousand six hundred and eighty sheep and twenty thousand cattle there.'

'But they're not horses', I pointed out.

'I know. I can't remember how many horses they sold but it was a lot. What I can tell you is that they were the best cavalry horses in the world. Ballinasloe was only rivalled by the fair at Nijni Nogorod in Russia. In fact, when the Russian commander General Platov came to the Congress of Vienna in 1815 he said' – he paused to deepen and pinch his voice while Mary stared at him and silently shook her head – "I know nothink about England or Ireland, apart from the fair at Ballinasloe". How's that then for fame?'

'Very impressive. What sort of surveying do you do?'

'New roads, old buildings, women. Actually not so much of the latter now. Some years ago I was sent to Inishkea South. Now there's a place you should go to. Beautiful! I had to survey the evacuated village. What knocked me over was the alignment of the main street. You'd think they'd just knocked up these villages but they were *planned.* They built to a design but you'd never know to look at them. That's what's so clever. The spacing was irregular but the alignment was perfect.'

'Why was the island evacuated?'

'They lost half the young men in a fishing disaster. Caught in a storm. In October 1927, it was. Killed thirteen here fishing out of

Bofin. It's a common story on the west.'

Yet Bofin had survived. Its fishing industry had faded only recently. It was probably the least-visited of all the inhabited islands, along with nearby Inishturk, and yet somehow they'd struggled by on a low budget of tourism and the employment of vital services. Perversely the isolation that had killed off so many communities was now the prime selling point of these two. They had no famous sights and no unique culture. In a region where Gaelic was a prevalent and proud heritage, they were exceptions and had adopted English. Theirs was the honeypot of nothingness.

Musicians drifted in with tattered boxes. Fiddles appeared, a button box, flute, bohran and finally a set of silver tubes was slotted into the shape of uillean pipes. They differed from Highland pipes in every aspect and demanded considerably more technical ability to play. Fingers, wrists and elbows all worked away to produce two octaves and harmonizing chords.

No one can be sure where bagpipes first originated. Some say Turkey, others Greece. A sculpture of around AD51 in Rome depicts a piper resembling the conventional Highlander of today. When Gerald of Wales, a well-travelled Anglo-Norman chronicler at large around 1180, visited Ireland he does not list bagpipes in his detailed account of the country, but he does record them in Wales.

Quite when they entered Ireland, were rotated from the vertical to the horizontal and fitted with all the extras; none of these are known. All that can be said for certain is that by 1367 they were a prevalent source of torment to the English. In that year the Statues of Kilkenny were promulgated and pipers were banned from entering the Pale. It became a crime for anyone to give them food or shelter. In Elizabethan times many were hanged. According to one historian, Francis O'Neill, as late as the nineteenth century pipers were 'jailed as assiduously as they have been inconsiderately discountenanced and suppressed by the clergy'. Fortunately they survived. The uillean pipes, to my mind, come closest to expressing the voice of the human soul. In the dinginess of a corner something in me bled.

An eighty-three year old woman sang a ballad. An Israeli backpacker won equal applause for a mouthorgan tune desecrated by nerves and malfunctions, and a spoons player with the vibrato of a pneumatic drill gave me an elementary lesson on instrument preparation. On a beer mat he drew:

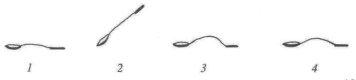

1   *2*   *3*   *4*

A matching pair of spoons was apparently the way to go, and best if they had a spatula-style bulge at the handle. The basic spoon (1) should first be straightened (2) to get rid of the manufacturer's preference for an eating bend rather than a playing one, and then shaped into a generous bow. 3 is excessive, 4 is just right. Finally wrap cotton elastoplast round the handles to create a non-slip surface to butt into your palm...

'And away you go, loike dis.' The spoons blurred as they travelled between his forearm and thigh, changed pitch on reaching his hand which swivelled to provide either a hard or hollow resonance and trilled back and forwards over his fingers. His face hardened in concentration as he subtitled *The Kesh.*

'You know, it's not quite what it seems here', Robert began as the musicians recharged their glasses. Drink had sapped his former fizz. 'Living here would be very different. It's a very divided community. Take the ferries for example. Two boats owned by different people run identical schedules. They depart and arrive within minutes of each other. It's cut-throat competition and splits people into two rival camps determined by whose service they use.'

'Is it serious, this division?'

'Oh people get on but there's a definite edge to it. Each camp takes pains to avoid the other. There's active feuds here.'

I left early, tired after a long day. The sun had long since set but a rosy patch of brightness remained and backlit a cross protruding above the graveyard wall. As a circle it was irregular yet in effect it provided the authentic symbol of a Celtic cross. The illusion dissolved as I watched. Nothing was quite as it seemed, not even here on my idealised island. As I walked back to my boat I caught a familiar fragrance - acrid, sweet, cosy. The burning of 'turf'. And I knew that despite the charging of €9 for mineral waters, the jollification of villages for the tour buses, the force-feeding of 'Traditional Music Sessions' by cash-hardened trios wired to mikes and the general homogenisation by European regulations, not all of Ireland's former charm had been sacrificed. Bofin was different. The cutting of turf remained a communal task. Its five quarters were a statement of pride. It nurtured spontaneous music and active feuds. The more honest, meaningful measures of cultural vitality were in place. On Bofin there was something worth getting upset about, and the spirit to care.

O'

≈

O'Leary, O'Donovan, O'Driscoll...the 'o' in Irish names is not a contraction of 'of' but an Anglicisation of 'ua' meaning 'grandson'.

Lynne Truss *Eats, Shoots & Leaves*

Grace O'Malley

When Wallace Clark's galley, *Aileach*, was launched below Rockfleet Castle in Clew Bay, her square sail carried the emblem of a virago. Red-robed and wielding a sword, the figure represented Granuaile, or Grace O'Malley, one of the most remarkable personalities of the sixteenth century, or any century for that matter. For most of her life this self-styled warrior queen was the most powerful naval commander in all Ireland and the scourge of the Elizabethans. The tall spare tower at Rockfleet was where she died but her strongholds were many. Inishbofin was the home port for her fleet and she strung a chain from her keep across the harbour entrance to dissuade intruders. But her favourite repose, not that she rested much, was in the castle before me on Clare Island, a rather modest edifice for a pirate of her means, quaint with its machicolations.

It was with difficulty that I found a spare visitors' mooring. Most were taken up with the local fishermen's *potaí stóir*, the largely submerged keep-cages for accumulating catches of lobsters and crabs. Such abuse was a particularly O'Malley sort of thing to do.

Grace O'Malley is largely absent from the annals of Irish history. The country had little interest in maritime matters, never being a formidable sea power and, during the one epoch when Grace provided the exception, it was embarrassing to be shown up by a woman. But she features prominently in the Elizabethan State Papers and in 1585 is described as 'for forty years the nurse of all rebellions in the west'. Unique as a woman warrior she also enjoyed the rare distinction in her profession of dying peacefully in bed.

Her destiny was not inevitable but it helped that she was born, in 1530, into the family whose lineage had provided the chiefs of the Connacht O'Malleys for 200 years. Along with her milk Grania (Irish for Grace) would have ingested the family motto: 'Invincible on land and sea'. Her father is said to have taken her as a child on trading ventures to Spain, crossing the Bay of Biscay in an open boat. On one trip Grace cut her hair in order to look more like a boy and was called Grania *moile*, bald Grania, later corrupted to Granuaile.

At the age of sixteen she married Donald O'Flaherty, the son of a neighbouring chief whose business was to terrorise the port of Galway and plunder its shipping. Never one to stay at home Grace joined her husband and for the next twenty years she led expeditions with him and on her own and was seldom without either a helm or a sword in her hand. Donald was killed in 1566 and Grace brought what was now her fleet, and the most powerful naval force in Ireland, back to her family castle on Clare Island. The same year she married again, this time a man of Norman extraction, Richard Burke, known as 'Iron Dick'. He brought into her ownership ports to the north useful for attacking the merchant shipping of Sligo, the land around Rockfleet and its castle, at that time called Carrigahowley. Shortly before she deemed the marriage 'no longer convenient' and ended it, a son was born. Legend has it that the delivery was complicated by Turkish pirates. They were attacking Grace's galley at the time (though historically there is no evidence of Turkish ships off western Ireland before the 17th century) and had the upper hand until Grace appeared wrapped in a blanket. She shot the Turkish captain, rallied her men, repulsed the attackers and within an hour of the delivery had added another ship to her collection.

Grace's golden period of dominion was coming to an end. The Tudors were determined to crush the rebels of Connacht and Mayo. A Royal Navy pinnace, the oddly-named *Handmaid*, was sent to patrol the coast. The gunfire of even the smallest warship could destroy any number of galleys. Grace abandoned Clare Island and retreated to Carrigahowley where the shallows of Clew Bay afforded her some protection. She was unable to the throw the habit of piracy, and it was still good business, but her fleet was decimated in a storm in 1586, two years before the one which destroyed the Spanish armada. By 1593 the cunning and cruel governor, Bingham, had reduced her to poverty. Her cattle were seized, her movements restricted and her unpaid rent left her deep in debt.

Facing certain imprisonment she did what any self-respecting heroine would do: she wrote to Queen Elizabeth suggesting they talk things over. Surprisingly, Elizabeth agreed. That July Grace sailed her own ship to London and tied up at Royal Quay, Greenwich. Sadly the conversation between Elizabeth and Grace O'Malley is unrecorded; a loss to historians equal to Elizabeth's undisclosed confrontation with her ill-fated cousin, Mary Queen of Scots. Despite having nothing left to bargain with Grace emerged from the meeting with a pardon and the offer of being made a countess. She refused on the grounds that as she was already the Queen of Connacht becoming a countess was a move in the wrong direction.

She was by then 63 years old and under promise of good behaviour. To the English, maybe, but not to anyone else. In 1596 she personally led a raiding feud against the MacNeils of Barra.

Grace died in 1603, peacefully, at home. Irrepressible in death as in life, she somehow inveigled her remains to be buried, so it's said, with Cistercian rites in the now-ruined Clare Island Abbey.

Reek Sunday

The notice at the foot of the mountain read:

> Croaghpatrick PILGRIMAGE
> Every Pilgrim who ascends the mountain on St Patrick's Day or within the octave or any time during the months of June, July, August & September, & PRAYS IN OR NEAR THE CHAPEL for the intentions of our Holy Father the Pope may gain a plenary indulgence on condition of going to Confession and Holy Communion on the summit or within the week.
> THE TRADITIONAL STATIONS.
> There are three 'stations'...
> 1st Station - LEACHT BENAIN
> The pilgrim walks seven times round the mound of stones saying seven Our Fathers, seven Hail Marys and one Creed...

I camped in a field near the start of the climb. At 2am I heard the first vehicles arrive and excited voices splitting the night with jokes. By 5am the traffic had become continuous and was closing in on my tent. By the time I'd finished breakfast the most profitable cash-crop the farmers of Murrisk produce was growing nicely. Cars covered their fields at €3 a plot and ranks of all-night buses from as far afield as Derry, Dublin and Kilkenny added special dividends along the edges. Already the zigzag line of figures wending up the mountain formed a solid line of colour. Alive and intense against the lower greenery but thinning to a motionless strand where the high scree met the mist, it was reminiscent of a scene from the Klondike Gold Rush.

Campbell's pub was open and enjoying its privileged position at the gateway to the Reek. From all directions people were converging on the lane which led uphill. Vendors and their stalls further impeded their progress. 'Sticks for the Reek, €1' read signs beside half a dozen men with piles of neatly trimmed willows, though one entrepreneur had set himself higher up the slope and optimistically offered: '€1 rent, €2 buy'. With food, drink and Mary and Jesus trinkets in abundance, there was no excuse for pilgrims to be poorly equipped for their ordeal. I did, however, question the sense of a group of benevolents handing out free Bibles to people about to climb a 765-metre mountain.

Nowhere was the going easy. Millions of feet had cut a winding trail which climbed relentlessly. Where it wasn't flowing ball-bearings of grit, it was bog or restless bits of rubble. Where it wasn't any of these, for its top third, it was a vast slope of scree, immaculately engineered for twisting ankles, steep enough for the use of all fours and constantly shifting so that any progress up was halved by the mountain coming down. Rock missiles clattered past from the feet ahead and it was easy to imagine some pilgrims might be delivering their Our Fathers face to face.

But the views made the penance easier. Clew Bay is said to have 365 islands and we pilgrims could see them all. Spread out below us was Granuaile's kingdom, her islands, the haphazard dumpings of geological wheelbarrows shaped liked brush marks, hats and a crushed alphabet; her seaway and labyrinthine channels turning sepia in their shallows; her coastline torn between earth and water and left a ragged indecision of spits, bars, bays and isthmuses; possibly her verdancy where cattle grazed until herd by herd they were removed by Bingham; but not her hills, a sequence of russet steps to the horizon, for she was not to be drawn far from the security of her galleys; and not her bungalows.

The Reek, or Croagh Patrick, is the holiest mountain in Ireland. Mount Brandon, near Dingle, runs it a close second, and Slieve League also has its shrines, but it was The Reek that St Patrick deigned to make famous and from here that he evicted Ireland's snakes. Today's pilgrimage is a shadow of what repenters did in the past. Not only did it include a circuit of holy islands but the route up Croagh Patrick started further away, added on a few more foothills and covered twenty-five miles. They walked it barefoot. The practice has not entirely died out.

He was choosing his steps carefully, leaning on his stick, occasionally grimacing but covering the ground at much the same speed as those wearing boots. Mud had oozed between his toes and dried. Cuts bled along the sides of each foot.

'Is it as painful as it looks?'

'It's OK now. It was a bit bad to begin with but you'd be surprised how many flat rocks you can find when you have to. Tis the third time I've done it barefoot.'

'How long will it take you?'

'One and a half up, two and a half down.'

That was about the time I thought it would take me. He was middle-aged and looked as fit as a professional darts player. 'Have you been practising and hardening your feet.'

He seemed shocked. 'I think that would be cheating'. And he hobbled on.

I overtook people, others overtook me. Through the upwards migration came the counterflow of the Blessed. Greater than the natural hazards was now the constant danger of being either tripped or disembowelled by a stave. They were prodded in front of your legs, idly swung at groin height in moments of distraction, flailed as their owners struggled for balance and occasionally thrown as balance was lost.

'Sorry.' 'Beg yer pardon.' 'Are ya'll right?' 'Would you mind your own business there!' 'Lord has it not got a life of its own.'

Halfway up I overtook a priest. His collar was visible above his North Face Gore-Tex. He looked barely a decade out of the seminary and hadn't spent a euro on a stick.

'Could you explain what a plenary indulgence is?' I asked, and apologised for having been brought up a Protestant.

His smile carried the relief of a breather rather than the joy of meeting me. 'Plenary means full or complete. A plenary indulgence is the complete remission of all temporal sins you have confessed and for which you have asked forgiveness.' He paused to catch his breath. 'I'm sure you'll agree, that's quite a big thing.'

I agreed. 'In Western Scotland the Catholics of Barra go to church on Sunday morning and play football in the afternoon. In Lewis the Protestants go to church as well but padlock the childrens' swings for the day. That distinction has always struck me very forcibly.'

'Confession is intended to free the repentant to enjoy a life that is good in God's eyes. There seems little point in burdening someone who is genuinely repentant with eternal guilt. If you like, I'll hear your confession at the top.'

If it were a jibe, it was concealed. 'Thanks. I'll have to think about that. Are you on your way to work, then?'

'Yes, there's a roster of priests running mass every thirty minutes at the top from eight to three in the afternoon.'

'How many people make the climb?'

'Two years ago there were thirty thousand. Last year twenty-five. Now if you'll excuse me, I must keep going.' Then he yielded to his own curiosity. 'How's it walking in a kilt?'

'Fine. As long as the wind doesn't get up.'

By the time I reached the summit I'd counted fourteen other barefooteds, one a woman. There were people in plimsolls and even low heels. Jeans, T-shirts and light frocks were common. In the mist a light drizzle fell and a chilly breeze ravaged the edge of the crowd. Inside the huddle a surprising warmth emerged. The drizzle turned to rain. T-shirts turned to clingfilm. Faces looked miserable but eyes were fixed on the glass booth attached to a white chapel, in which a priest in full vestments was holding up a vessel and delivering mass through a system of loudspeakers. A candle flamed on either side of him. The cosiness inside cut a cruel comparison with conditions outside but elevated the priest's position to one of useful superiority. 'Donations for oratory' stated a notice outside the booth, and a note was pinned alongside: 'No litter'. It defied belief. That someone could have endured the punishing climb, have recited so many blessings and been on the brink of achieving their plenary indulgence, only to blow it by popping a sweetie paper in the box. However, it takes all sorts and we were certainly all there. Old and young – and an astonishing number of teenagers – skinny and obese, the fit and the chain-smokers, the odd ethnic minority and, I was told though I never spotted any, always a strong representation of gypsies.

The queue for the confessional was long. Besides, I didn't know where to begin.

The descent was worse than the climb. At one point I met two young women on all fours going down *backwards*. One kept glancing round to check their route but the other never lifted her eyes from the rocks below her hands. She moaned continuously, occasionally crying out, placing each foot a few inches lower in a process of obvious pain. I had heard that some people put dried peas in their shoes to increase their suffering and assumed she was enduring some similar self-infliction. When I couldn't bear her distress any more and asked if I could help, her friend explained they'd be fine. They couldn't stand heights. Her friend was too terrified to turn round. They'd take it slowly. They'd been to the top. They'd made it to the chapel, so they'd be fine.

It was impossible not to meet people. If they didn't break the ice by tripping you with their stick, or you them, then you'd be brought into intimacy on a moving carpet of rubble. Soon I collided with a fatalist.

'Have you come over from Germany specially for the climb?' I asked.

'I've lived here for twenty years', Helmut replied. 'What brings you to Ireland?'

I explained.

'That must be nice, just sailing every day.'

'It's getting better. But it's hard work, and often I've been pretty scared.'

'What's there to be scared about?'

'Weather. Rocks. Waves.'

'You might as well be scared about birds and trees.' He shrugged. 'OK, so what's the worst thing that could happen to you?'

'I could drown.'

'And why's that bad?' He then explained his views on reincarnation, how this life was followed by others, endlessly, in different bodies. 'It's just like changing cars', he concluded.

Near the bottom the jubilation of those gaining ground on their pint at Campbell's could be heard.

'I feel great! All the better for coming back with a clean sheet!'

'That's the last time we're doing this for the crack!'

'There used to be sixty tousand would do it in the old days', said a man, approaching seventy, leaning against a rock, enviously watching the continuous flow of new arrivals. 'Oi must have done it forty times meeself and oi'd be up there today if oi didn't have the angina. It was better in the old days. People had time to talk. No one's got time to talk any more, only at funerals and here on the Reek.' He lent forward conspiratorially. 'We've become very *Americanized*, you know.' It was a distasteful word and he pulled a face. 'The Reek's a miracle of a place, oi can tell you. Now one year oi had a special climb, Jesus, brings tears to me eyes it does even now tinking about it…'

He'd met a Polish man. This man had spent the war in a concentration camp and every day he prayed to be spared his hell on earth. One night he had a vision in which God spoke to him, saying he'd be spared but he would have to give thanks on a holy mountain in the West. It took him thirty years to find Croagh Patrick and then he knew he'd found the right place.

'That was his first visit and oi offered to take him up. Oh Sweet Mother, he cried the whole way and out came some of the tings he'd seen and it was like his heart was bleedin those things he'd held all those years and couldn't let go and here they were just pourin out and it got me goin and oi cried too, from start to finish this stranger and me cried all the way and he says it was the greatest thing he'd done in his life, and when oi look back on it, you know, it was mine too.' Tears wetted his cheeks. 'Well, good luck boy, nice talkin to you.'

The final two hundred yards had filled with pamphleteers. Paper was being thrust at me from all directions by blowsy men and women with do-gooder expressions and armfuls of religious tracts. I stopped to read one, *The Way of the Cross.*

> In the pioneer days in America the new settlers were
> surrounded by tribes of savage Indians. The words,

'RUNNING THE GAUNTLET' were enough to make any man whiten at the lips, and shudder at the heart. When the Indians had taken a white man captive and were in a mood to play with him, he'd be given a chance to live by running the gauntlet. This was composed of two lines of Indian warriors with a path between. They were armed with clubs, tomahawks, and knives. Each warrior did his best to strike down and kill the man who was running for his life between the painted savages. Usually the captive was killed.

Satan has a gauntlet through which every young person must pass, which is more dreadful and dangerous than any Indian gauntlet ever was...

The distributors of this imaginative scaremongery must have felt slightly uneasy to find that, a two-minute walk from them, outside Campbell's pub, two red Indians had moved in and were busking before a packed roadside of bystanders. They were dressed in full beads and feathers, had painted faces and were playing a variety of instruments and singing in time with recorded sound effects. Their boxes of tapes and CDs were disappearing as fast as their helper could unpack them. When each song ended the applause endured until the next one began. The gauntlet, it seemed, had come full circle to a happy conclusion.

'Satan will try to corrupt your mind...tempt you to make a god of Pleasure...to live for the Theatre, the Concert and the Ballroom...' the pamphlet continued.

At the foot of a mountain where coincidence is accorded no credibility, it was hard not to imagine St Patrick striding past with a grin, his €1 stick and a couple of CDs in his pocket.

The papers the next day reported that 22,000 people reached the summit and the only casualty was a South African woman in her thirties who died tragically – or, depending on your point of view, changed cars unexpectedly – as a result of a heart attack on the descent.

The transformative power of Croagh Patrick on Reek Sunday is undeniable. You can take or leave the ecclesiolatry and the well-intentioned handouts of outmoded metaphor but only the insensate can fail to be invigorated by the energy that carries twenty thousand non-outdoorsy people up a mountain. To be among them is in itself a fellowship, a communion. Whatever makes two girls measure, in inches, their terror of a 2,500-foot descent, an act of courage rendered inconspicuous by its apparent ordinariness, is what carries us forwards as individuals, nations and a species.

Holes Communicating With Sea

ingernail clippings of mist were scattered over Croagh Patrick as I left Clew Bay. From the sea the mountain appeared to have shrunk overnight. Its gruff scree had hardened into a smooth surface with the pleasing curves of thrown clay. Its ribbon of colour had gone. It was ordinary again.

I splashed my way across a furrowed sea, genoa bent against the starboard rail, sheet tight and emitting a muscular grunt whenever the wind pounced with extra force. Abeam lay Claire Island's Great Wall, seven feet tall and seven miles long, built at a cost of £1500 in the 1880s as a relief project by the Congested Districts Board. It cut the land as cleanly as an appendectomy scar. What once divided grazing from tillage now obstructed a sheep's right of innocent passage between grazings. Then Clare Island conveniently stepped aside and allowed me to make passage for Achill Head.

The West Atlantic Roll suddenly met me. Dark waves galloped in, bludgeoning their way with leaded momentum. Even their droplets carried the sting of shotgun pellets. The crests rose and narrowed, rose again and reached the critical point of imbalance, swithered a moment and retreated, tortoise-like, into their bodies.

In *Passage to Juneau*, Jonathan Raban breaks down the movements of a ship into components which he calls the 'six degrees of freedom – pitch, roll, sway, heave, surge and yaw'. *Ceana* was improvising with a few more. She was crabbing, sashaying and goose-stepping. Every so often she was slugged on the nose. Stunned, she crept forwards, managed a few yaws and surges then – *WHAM*! – stalled again. The mainsail luffed an oath. She suffered the blows with resignation until Achill Head appeared at 388° and I was able to abandon tacking and lay a direct course.

Sullied clouds formed a convention in the east. They spelt trouble and I immediately became conscious of my finger, the Larne finger. The tip was still numb. It felt frozen and my thumb, acting on its own, seemed to take grotesque pleasure in prodding it, unable to understand, constantly trying to communicate with the stranger in the pack. Still, it worked fine and registered the genoa sheet slipping by onto a reach as wood feels under sandpaper. We were now into the sway, heave, rock and roll cycle, and thankful to have lost pitch and yaw. In my tea mug the ocean's surface found a replica.

I turned on the radio. Against a fitting background of crackle and hiss Joanne Byrne was being interviewed. She spoke on behalf of the couple, the static spoke on behalf of the nation. The subject, that had gripped the nation since its announcement and then turned into a sour grape, was being touted as the country's 'glitziest wedding reception ever'. Taoiseach Bertie Ahern's daughter, Georgina, was marrying pop-idol Nicky Byrne of Westlife. We heard that Georgina's hair would be done by 'Irish celebrity crimper' Gary Kavanagh and her make-up by Abby Ireland of Laura Mercier. Her dress was slipping out of a unique mould by Limerick's Synan O'Mahony. We were not told who was doing the groom's make-up or hair but judging from a photograph I saw of him later, I suspect the hair was by Bostick. He would be wearing a Tyrell and Brennan suit. The crackles crackled and hisses hissed. The reason for the nation's outrage was that the reception of the prime minister's daughter would not be taking place in Ballyhaunis or Belturbet but in France. Not only would Ireland be denied the boost to its economy by 400 filthy-rich superstar guests but the Irish would be denied all sight and sound of the spectacle. This was, the people felt, an infringement of their rights. By paying their taxes they had bought the franchise to manage their prime minister's affairs, both public and private. They afforded his lifestyle; they had to be included in it. They were his extended family. It was easy to see where both sides were at fault.

'Georgina and Nicky are very upset about the insinuations of disloyalty', protested Joanne Byrne, the wedding co-ordinator. 'They are a private couple just like anyone else and are entitled to have the day they've always dreamed of.' It was she who had negotiated a deal 'in the region of €850,000' (£570,000) with *Hello!* magazine for exclusive media coverage, a sum estimated to cover the cost of hors d'oeuvres at the sixteenth-century Chateau d'Ésclimont. The guests would not be allowed to take in cameras or picture-messaging phones, she added, and security would be 'tighter than a pair of Joe Dolan trousers'.

I'd never heard of Joe Dolan, Tyrell or Brennan, and was heading for my own pair of tight trousers. According to the Pilot, Carrickbeg was right at the crotch.

> Achill Head may be rounded inshore of Carrickakin if
> conditions allow; be careful to avoid Carrickbeg, half a
> cable south of the head, which covers at half-tide…
> Achill Head is a most spectacular promontory, the cliffs

on its north side being the highest in Ireland... The views enjoyed rounding it amply compensate for the rough sea to which a yacht is subjected in any but the lightest wind.

There was by now what can only be called 'a great rippling in the area'. One moment a lobster boat ahead was halfway up my mast, the next it disappeared for an improbable length of time. I changed course to 317°, disconnected Fleming and felt the tiller wriggle unhappily as we heaved and corkscrewed towards the narrows. The flood tide was already stampeding into a dangerously slender gap. A shag in the posture of crucifixion occupied Carrickakin. I glanced at the chart and checked my line of approach. Six knots. If we hit Carrickbeg at this speed we'd cartwheel over it.

Achill Head's colonnades extended underwater and restricted my passage to fifty yards. There was no turning back. I could hear the suck of the ocean and see mouths of whirlpools gaping beyond Carrickakin. Waves shunted *Ceana* towards the reef. The shag fled. I was twenty yards away. Mustard-yellow fronds broiled around the rock and glinted in the sun. Salt sparkled in the air. Life thrilled in me as we passed through, clean as a billiard shot. I won leeway to my left and Achill Head was retreating, turning as it did so to present its most striking profile. It had been sledge-hammered into a balancing act of boulders. A gust might bring the whole lot down. As a scene of demolition it was magnificent.

The land now fell away into the mouth of Blacksod Bay and abandoned me to mid-ocean. At least that's how it felt with the known world receding to a sandwich filling between sea and cloud. From the chart I identified a trio of bumps as Nephin Beg, Maumykelly and Knocklettercuss. I added them to my collection. Ireland, I think, surely has to have the most inventive names in Anglo-Gaeldom. Certainly Scotland and Wales have come up with pretty mundane hybrids by comparison.

Andrew Phelan, another sailor enamoured by the titles of the rocks he might hit, points out in *Ireland From the Sea* that 'the long names of rocks are Gaelic words run together; eg Mullanncarrickscolta may be *mullach an carraig scoilte*, "the top of the broken rock"'. For the most part, as Tororragaum ('the head of the pollock') illustrates, they are best left untranslated.

My name collection covered almost two sides of A4 and included the Aughcooshneil shallows, Aillyhaloo Point, Claddaghatootee Beach, Ardgappary hill, Ballyvoddy township, Emlaghnabehy Lough and rocks Fenewanabullock and Mweeleenareeava. As I perused my list, a short story suggested itself:

'If you Knockamaphatroon and do not Lacknassaggart you Cancapple your Ballyvoddy in Ballynahoonagh', says I.

'Carrickculloo!' says he, 'if I Knocknalarabana and Struffaunloughawee I trust you won't be Gumpaunatooreen if I Gooreenatinny and Claddaghatootee?'

'If a Carrigeenfaddy takes you', says I, 'for a Crocknasmug or a Bunacurry, then Scoltdoo but it's Ballyhoorisky. Mind your Emlaghnabehy and don't go Owenboliska.'

'Fenewanabullocks!' he cries, Coolcross-ly. 'Stop your Crockacooan, you Carrrickmoylenacurhoga...'

'Mweeleenareeava!' I retort, but feel Tracabad and Rinnafreese mid-sentence. 'Aghaweel', I Carrickadda, Tanderagee-ly. 'It's all Bullighonawaush to me.'

Black Rock was now visible on my left, a miniature Skellig Michael with a lighthouse on top. Against the horizon it looked too low, a gift to storms. A shiver ran down my spine as I thought of what it would be like in winter; the tip of a periscope inched above a knocknalarabana of waves. Soon I was navigating round Rusheen Island where machinery rusted above some ruins. It was a low island the size of a football pitch. Rusheen was the baby, Inishkea South the mother. Between them was a semi-circle of white sand and a lagoon where ripples had been banned. As I dropped anchor the clouds dissolved. Sunlight turned the beach into a hurtful glare. I changed from oilskins to T-shirt, adventure to holiday. My skin began to burn. Inishkea's hill shrank in the haze and trembled. The ghost town at its foot grew ghostlier still.

I rowed my inflatable to the far end of the beach and crossed a rasping tongue of the Atlantic to the neighbouring island of Inishkea North. At its peak around eighty people lived here, compared to the South's two hundred. The North was smaller, flatter and susceptible to droughts in summer but was blessed with the remains of one of the earliest Christian chapels in the country. The South had the best harbour and two inexhaustible springs. Despite the eighty-yard gap between them, the islands had a history of feuds. They tended their animals and lazy-beds separately and used the mainland as their first call for assistance.

I landed on a shore of jumbled boulders and walked over a treeless landscape of what in the Hebrides is called machair; close-cropped grass almost of fairway quality which feels like a carpet underfoot and is a calcium-rich bed of crushed shells. The North's two lines of houses bordered the sea, almost all roofless, their walls crumbling and those closest to the shore filling with sand. Rabbits by the hundred alternately froze and darted, startling some cattle, sheep and a proprietorial board of donkeys. The largest building was intact and locked. 'Inishkea North National School 1894' read a plaque above the door. Another was clearly in service as a refuge for shepherds. Their last bottle of Chardonnay, *Hair of the Dingo,* stood empty in the window alongside a bowl of corks.

The chapel was on top of a hillock like an upturned bucket of sand. It was a depression, adequate for one large hermit or two small intimate ones, into which soil and slabs had collapsed. Some slabs were incised with a simple cross while the largest bore a whorl whose intricacy was partly obscured by orange discs of lichen. I might have been the first to stumble across this holy site. Its raw state lent it an air of enduring potency. A round boulder with miraculous powers called the Godstone was said to be hidden here. It had never been located. Scattered about lay the graves of islanders, not a named one among them, their small crosses chiselled from thin slabs and all askew.

A sudden splash. It came from the bay. A fishing boat was there. A gangplank had been erected over one side. For a while I couldn't understand what was happening. On board men were waving their arms. Then a cow appeared over the gunwales and mounted the gangplank. Her dive was spectacular. With front legs doubled back under her stomach, rear legs held stiffly in the posture of walking and nose high in the air she fell in the trajectory of a slightly rounded plummet. The splash engulfed both cow and fishing boat. The spray settled on an empty patch of water. For a worrying second it remained empty, then there was an eruption and a head appeared, water flowing from her ears. She swam for shore, sedately and with the aura of one who habitually takes a dip, yet at a deceptively brisk pace. I have always found a source of fascination in cows, in their bulk and casual power, curiosity and fretfulness, the menace implicit in their horns, their sloppy bone structure reminiscent of a badly erected tent. But a cow out of context is doubly arresting. Once aground she never faltered and took off into the machair without a backward glance. Altogether six cows walked the plank for the start of their summer grazing.

Inishkea South was occupied when I returned. A family had arrived by speedboat and were having a barbecue. It was odd smelling roasting meat floating through the decaying ruins. By the harbour I came to the memorial bearing the names of the twelve fishermen who drowned in the storm of 28 October 1927. I worked my way along the main street barging into private homes and snooping on the lives of those who once lived there.

The wind had been a problem. It had blown driftwood far inland. All the houses stood with their backs to the west. Their fireplaces were tiny, indicating that fuel was precious and probably hauled from the mainland. Close to each fireplace was a recess in the wall and I wondered what they kept there? An oil lamp? But there was no trace of soot. Matches...flints...keepsakes...a Madonna? And I wondered who occupied the three largest houses which were the only ones to have an upper storey.

'The school would have been one but I don't know about the others. The priest and the doctor, probably', Joe Campion suggested. Steaks and sausages hissed to his prod. He'd been coming here since he was a child and loved the place. 'If they had a doctor and priest. Here, have a bite to eat and some poteen.' He winked. 'The real McCoy!' Then a finger crossed his lips. 'Made it myself!'

'How do you make it?'

'I'll give you the recipe.' He added soda water. 'Slainte!'

It was clear and smelt like turpentine. It blocked my lungs. I choked, then felt lava burning a trail through my chest. 'Terrific', I said. 'I'd better get back from the fire till I've practised a bit.'

'You soon get used to it.'

'Do you sell it?'

'Only the excess. I get eighty-five euros a gallon. That's exactly half the price of shop whiskey.'

'Do many people make it?'

'Not now. I know a few others but the risk of getting caught is too high. The danger is the smell and neighbours snaking on you.'

'Have you ever been caught?'

His wife had been studiously ignoring the subject till then, but she looked up. He caught her glance and smiled. 'A few close shaves but I've still a clean record. But let's change the subject. Do you know about the whaling? They whaled here, you know, the Norwegians.'

Later we walked along a spit to Rusheen which at low water ceased to be an island.

'The whales must have been plentiful here in the past because there were three stations. One here, one near Achill and another at Ardelly in Blacksod Bay. Now it's curious that the Norwegians came here, wouldn't you say? You'd think with that big coast of theirs they'd have whales enough of their own but they built this station here in 1917 and ran it for four years. I don't know why they gave up so soon. No whales, I imagine.'

We strolled among fragments of oversized engines. A camshaft protruded from a bank of shingle and a litter of unrecognisable pieces led past tangled hawsers, rusted to the feebleness of pastry, to the huge boiler which had outlived the building around it.

'They caught some minke and fin whales, but it was mainly basking sharks they went for. Some years ago...oh, nineteen-eighty it must have been, some Mayo fishermen tried to revive the sharking but they gave up. Too few sharks.'

I thought of Tomás O'Crohan who wrote in *The Islandman* that in his eighty years on the Blasket Islands he recalled only one basking shark ever being caught there. It got accidentally fouled in fishing nets. The oil from its liver kept a population of around 150 in lamplight for five years.

'You know, the records for all the whales landed here are still in existence.'

Later I found them. Between 1917 and 1921 Rusheen's whaling station landed an average of sixty basking sharks each year, yielding 4000 barrels of oil. The industry was already in decline by the time the Norwegians arrived. At its peak a decade earlier the 'fishing' in the Achill area had secured 1080 sharks in a single season. Little wonder they were a scarce species now.

We surveyed the relics of butchery. They held both revulsion and intrigue in that such an industry could have flourished here.

Joe pulled a face. 'It's not my game.'

'Nor mine.'

We returned to a more cheerful subject.

'Slainte' said Joe.

'Slainte' said Colette.

'Slainte' said the teenagers.

'Slainte.'

Poteen Recipe

Preparation Time: about 19 days.

Serves: about 10 at a quarter gallon each.

Ingredients: rye, sugar, treacle, baker's yeast, water.

Take 1 stone of rye and steep in bath, just enough water to soak. It swells.

After about 5 days take grain out. Leave in a warm place, turning it frequently until the shoots start to appear.

In a wooden barrel of hot water stir 4 stone of sugar until it dissolves, then add 1 gallon of treacle and 2 pounds of baker's yeast which has been broken fine. Stir well and add grain. Add water to cover. Always keep water at blood temperature.

Put cover over barrel and check to see if sizzling (after 2 days).

The longer it works the better, 6 days is good. If not working, add a bucket or two of warm water. Let it sit 10 days in all (last 4 it's not really working). The bitterer it is the better. If sweet, not gone so well. Drain and save the liquid.

Apply heat and distil. Ensure no airlock in worm by filling with water.

Catch only the result that will burn, which it should at first. It gets weaker as you go. Test frequently with a lit piece of paper.

Pan Pan

There is no *red port left* in the cellar.

I still had to run through this elementary *aide-mémoire* to remind me which was port (red light, left). There was no handy jingle for starboard so rudimentary sailors served their apprenticeships in a world of left and not-left. On my immediate not-left was Eagle Island, the corner to the vast bite that is Donegal Bay. Its lighthouse formed a Prussian spike on a helmet of charcoal.

The light appears to be accident prone. In August 1940 it got strafed by a German fighter's machine gun during an attack on a ship. The sea regularly smashes its panes. Eagle Island and its neighbour, Blackrock, fifteen nautical miles to the southwest, have been referred to as Ireland's 'Cape Horns'. These two outposts are the closest parts of Ireland to the edge of the Continental Shelf which ends just twenty miles away. Here the seabed suddenly drops to 100 fathoms. Coming from the other direction, the east-bound storm water hits the shallows and the energy that was contained within the ocean depths must find release upwards. This patch of the Atlantic is a nursery for freak waves.

One of Ireland's legendary sailors met some here in the 1920s. Conor O'Brian was not a man to exaggerate. He thrived on danger. In his books, *From Three Yachts* and *Across Three Oceans,* he dismisses most Southern Ocean storms in a paragraph. The sea he encountered off Eagle Island merits a whole page.

'It is difficult to estimate the height of a sea, but if this was not the biggest I ever met it must have been mighty near it. The spray of the breakers was going over Eagle Island, and that is 160 feet high. Three years later I saw in the South Indian Ocean a sea which I classed as phenomenal, and my impression was that it would have looked big among the common stuff that was going this day, but nothing bigger than the one phenomenal sea of this day. I think they both exceeded 30 feet, but only momentarily; since, being caused by the superimposition of two sets of waves, they were quite unstable. It felt for all the world like being kicked down several flights of stairs. She [his yacht *Kelpie]* got out of it with about six feet of her bulwarks burst out and, as I discovered when later on I had an opportunity of investigating the bad leak which plagued us henceforth, as much of her garboard strake started from the keel.'

The Spanish Armada found it no easier here. In July 1588 the grand fleet had left Spain to invade England with 130 ships carrying 29,453 men. In scale and logistics this was a massive undertaking. Half of the vessels were in excess of 700 tons. Things went badly from the start. Defeated by Drake and then scattered north by an exceptional run of summer storms, the fleet was driven up to Shetland. For lack of a trustworthy chronometer, no ship at this time could ascertain its longitude. Latitude, however, could be calculated with an astrolabe or cross-staff, given a glimpse of the sun or stars. Once round Shetland the order was given to turn at latitude 61.5°N and 'run WSW until you are in the latitude of 58 degrees and then SW to Cape Finisterre.'

Their charts were unreliable. In the early days Spain was believed to be much closer to Ireland than it is. An early chart labelled the township of Carrigaholt at the mouth of the Shannon as 'Carrigaholt-next-Spain'. The fleet's intention to keep far out to sea was thwarted by the weather. Unable to beat sufficiently to windward, and without auxiliary power, the Spaniards fell foul of hazard after hazard. Twenty-five ships were lost on the Irish coast. Nine of them failed to weather Eagle Island. The power of that storm can be deduced from anchors uncovered by divers; despite their immense size and strength, one anchor's ring had been snapped and a fluke from another had been ripped off. Other relics tell a more personal story, such as the ring found with an engraving of hands holding a heart and a buckle above the inscription, *No tengo mas que dar te* – I have nothing more to give you. Most of those aboard drowned. The survivors who made it ashore had to evade the Elizabethan forces hunting them down on the mainland. Captain Cuellar of the *Labia* spent nine months as a fugitive in Connacht and Ulster before escaping to Scotland, and eventually home to Spain. Two-thirds of his colleagues had perished in the enterprise. Of the Great Armada only fifty-seven vessels and between nine and ten thousand men made it back.

But this August, off contemporary Ireland in The Year of Bertie Ahern's Daughter's Wedding, my waves arrived with business-like bustle and a whiskery lather on top and I rounded Cape Horn on one of her off-days. With the wind astern I was now on a run. I loosened the kicking strap, let out the mainsail until it filled like a fat chef's apron, poled out the genoa on the opposite side and felt *Ceana* steady as the wind gripped her on both sides. A quiver of excitement ran down her decks each time she accelerated into a trough on bolsters of surf. Fleming happily twitched his cogs and tweaked the tiller. At his feet some law of dynamics formed a rope of bubbles just below the surface and it twisted and wove patterns far behind us. We scattered a cluster of puffins and they took to the air with their usual bumbling incompetence. Legs stuck out straight behind and splayed feet angled to serve as ailerons they bounced on several wave crests before gaining clearance. I felt a special affinity with them. Because of their red knees they are still known as Albannaghs (Scotsmen) in Donegal.

'PAN PAN, PAN PAN, PAN PAN.'

The radio burst into life. I grabbed my log and pencil in preparation for recording the message which would follow. Pan Pan was the second category of distress signal. The first was a mayday (French: *m'aidez*) when a vessel or person was 'in grave and imminent danger'. A mayday rallied all rescue forces for an immediate call-out. Any vessel in the vicinity was obliged to interrupt its passage and render assistance. A radio silence was imposed on all other maritime traffic. Pan Pan (French again: *en pain*, in difficulty) was the call used to advise the world that a vessel was damaged or disabled in some critical way but the situation was not yet life-threatening. It put the rescue forces on standby and established communications to monitor the vessel's progress.

'All ships, all ships, all ships, this is Malin Head Radio, Malin Head Radio. The following emergency issued at 0900 hours. An aircraft with 365 souls on board has declared an emergency with fumes in the flight cabin. This is a twin-engined aircraft at 28,000 feet. All ships to keep a look out and inform Malin Head Radio. The aircraft's position is fifty-three degrees thirty north, seventeen degrees zero zero west and is expected to coast over Clew Bay in fifteen minutes. Sligo helicopter and Ballyglass lifeboat are on standby. Malin Head Radio, out.'

I didn't like the use of the word 'souls'. It seemed a pessimistic choice. Clew Bay was a little to the south of me but I scanned the skies, hoping to see nothing and wondering how I'd cope with 365 people swimming towards me for salvation. Did those 'souls' know there was an emergency? How often does this happen? How often when we sit eating our plastic-borne meals and thinking everything is normal have yachts, ships, lifeboats and helicopters been put on standby and eyes turned towards us? I suddenly felt very afraid for those passengers, and thankful to be where I was, steering my own vessel, facing my own hazards on the sea.

'ALL SHIPS, ALL SHIPS, ALL SHIPS. This is Malin Head Radio, Malin Head Radio. Airbus 330 is now over land. Pan Pan cancelled at zero nine two five hours. Malin Head Radio, out.'

The plane was now over land. The buck had passed to the garda and fire services. The following day I read the papers. There was no mention of a disaster. Airbus 330 must have made it home.

Sea Birds

It was turning cold. The late August mornings cut with an autumnal chill. As always, the birds went about their business with complete indifference to the weather.

Unlike humans who can withstand a relatively wide range of body temperature variations, birds have to maintain a higher temperature within a very narrow band of tolerance. In cold climates their main concern is to reduce heat loss to the ground, water and air, and to produce sufficient metabolic heat from food or fat reserves. Here they are at a disadvantage because they can produce only white fat which is much less efficient than the 'heat pad' effect of brown fat, a mitochondria-rich tissue which forms around the vital organs of mammals as diverse as voles and bears. Even an increase in body weight as considerable as fourteen percent typically allows a bird only an extra twenty-four hours without food, enough to carry it through a cold night-time fast.

Insulation is the key. Feathers are superbly bad conductors. In winter feather weight may increase by up to 70%. For land birds the down feathers which trap air under the outer contour feathers make the vital difference. At night they can be fluffed up to increase their thermal value. For sea dwellers such as the auks, feathers must be kept waterproof by smearing a secretion from a gland under the tail. An extra thick layer of fat further reduces heat loss.

When a bird is miserably cold, it shivers. Small smooth muscles which are attached to feathers quiver in a process of heat generation called thermogenesis. The feathers become more erect (as with hair on humans) and this causes the skin to become distorted into what we call goose flesh or pimples. By standing still and shivering birds can reduce their heat loss by between twenty and fifty percent. Huddling together is the next best thing. Members of the tree creeper family can be found packed together by the dozen. Few seabirds do this except the Emperor penguin, the bird which endures the lowest temperatures of all.

The internal organs of birds are more efficient than ours. The hearts of the smallest species are proportionately twice the size of the human heart. Like ours they are four-chambered but more powerful and pump blood at higher pressure. The constant activity of the heart, supported by other muscles, is the major generator of heat in a bird's body. Next come the secretory glands, especially the restless liver, and the brain also acts as a thermal booster. Its working temperature is hotter than arterial blood.

The lungs lose more heat than they create but are supreme in their primary purpose of taking in oxygen and venting waste gases. A bird's respiratory system consists of lungs and airsacs. Air passes through them in two stages so that two breaths, in and out, are required to complete one cycle. Air breathed in is drawn through the lungs to air sacs in the abdomen. As the bird breathes out this air returns to the lungs where it remains until driven into another set of sacs by the new intake of air. On the next out-breath it is this 'old' air that is exhaled. Thus the lungs are constantly flushed with air which passes through their dense concentration of capillaries *twice*. They move very little as they are essentially a corridor between expanding and contracting air sacs. Most birds have nine air sacs but shore and aquatic species have twelve, and the volumes of their abdominal and post-thoracic air sacs are much larger. These can retain air and provide additional buoyancy when desired or be emptied for swimming underwater. Inflated air sacs also act as cushions to protect the viscera on impact with the water when landing and diving. This is what enables a gannet to survive the collision with the surface when it plummets from those awesome heights.

The circulatory system has also had to evolve differently from most vertebrates to enable the distinctive avian lifestyle to continue. One example is the cross-connection of the two jugular veins of the head so that blood can drain unimpeded when the head is severely twisted and one vein may be strangled. Another is the ingenious treatment of the legs. Legs are the Achilles' heels of birds. Skin, lungs, urine and faeces all siphon away warmth but legs are potentially lethal appendages in this respect. Long, thin and unprotected, they constantly bleed precious heat to the environment. Birds get round the problem in two ways. Firstly they let their legs go cold, as low as a degree above freezing point, so that they have little heat to lose. Superficial veins contract in low temperatures shutting off the supply of blood. But leg tissues still need oxygen, so some blood must be allowed to circulate through deeper veins. How to deal with this super-cooled blood returning to the body is a problem. Its solution lies in a second ingenious anatomical feature. Veins carry chilled blood from the legs back into the torso through a sheath of arteries which act as a heat exchanger, warming the cold venal blood before it reaches the heart. The arterial blood on its way to the legs is cooled before it reaches these arteries: it is oxygen, not heat, that is required there. Thus blood circulates but heat is retained in a shorter loop within the torso. (Such counter-current blood flows are also found in some mammals, for example timber wolves, but are prevalent in all cold climate birds).

In case you've ever wondered about the heron stalking the winter shore or the duck standing on ice, their bodies are warm inside but their legs are indeed bloody nearly freezing.

Sligo Coroner

I rounded the corner of Benwee Head and entered the great bite out of northwest Ireland that is Donegal Bay. A watery sun seeped through a collusion of cloud and haze. The Atlantic couldn't decide on a suitable colour for the day. Ahead it experimented with eggshell blue which currents had already defaced with scribblings; on either side it had slicked up an oily sheen where rainbow tints flashed momentarily among ripples, while behind lay a horizon in the full awfulness of a bruised and hung-over pallor.

The surface heaved a little in an attempt to justify being an ocean, a land breeze filled the sails for a while but soon it all became too much and it lapsed into lethargy. I started the engine, cooked porridge and ate it at the bow looking down on the blurred outlines of jellyfish, thousands of them, ranging in size from hamburgers to standard lampshades.

It was going to be a long day. I'd got up at 4.30am and left in the dark, shining a spotlight ahead to pick out my route through Broadhaven Bay's tangle of lobster buoys. I was hoping to cover the sixty miles to Raghly Point in good time to meet the coroner of Sligo and attend a Classic Boat gathering he'd advised me not to miss. I turned on the radio to see what was on the nation's mind this August morning.

The news from the south was not good. Ballybunion's website had been stolen by an American porn outfit. Ballybunion was a small town and popular seaside resort at the mouth of the Shannon. According to my guidebook its chief claim to fame was that in June 1834 an ancient feud between two families erupted into a punch-up on the beach involving 3000 people. Bill Clinton had visited Ballybunion and it had a golf course. 'However', the guidebook added, 'from October to April the town is completely lifeless and you'll be lucky to find a place to stay let alone anywhere to eat.' The Ballybunioners had decided to do something about this. Six years ago, the news said, the Ballybunion Marketing Group had developed a website, www.ballybunion.org, to promote their town. Unfortunately the hosting company sent its renewal invoice to a discontinued email address, the bill went unpaid, the web domain name was put on the market and sold within four minutes for €4 to a porn merchant in Rhode Island. Quite why ballybunion.org was considered a scoop for selling internet pornography was not clear to me but it had caused considerable distress and embarrassment to the community. Said chairman of the Marketing Group, Con McCarthy, 'To see this guy coming along and doing this to our website is just heartbreaking. There's a few avenues we can explore and hopefully something will come of one of them.'

'You're late', were the coroner's first words.

I'd reached Raghly Point early in the evening. No other boat was in the bay. The coroner sailed in twenty minutes later.

'Where are all the classic boats?'

'I got the wrong day. We're off to a barbecue. I've got you a mooring. Follow me.'

Apart from a floppy white sun hat Desmond might have just stepped out of his office, standing at the tiller as he was in a tweed jacket and flannel trousers. He was about sixty, I guessed, a small jocular man who spoke neatly dissected sentences in a smooth Irish syrup. A week earlier I'd chanced upon him at Little Killary with a gathering of friends who dealt in adventure and coconut-cracking handshakes. There was a man who'd been aboard the *Tom Crean* when it had to be abandoned in a force ten during its attempt to replicate Shackleton's voyage from Elephant Island to South Georgia; a man who'd canoed round Cape Horn and another who'd led a joint Russian-Irish expedition to paddle round Novaya Zemlya but was beaten by the ice. The coroner appeared to be a father-figure among them but was in his element, playing the *seanchaí* (storyteller) to perfection, adding wit and erudition to any place, event or topic that was thrown up.

We caught our moorings just as the tide's retreat from Sligo, five miles away, turned the channel into a floodgate. It began ducking buoys and threatened to pitchpole our dingy until Desmond turned the nose downstream, his tweed jacket drenched, and we joined driftwood and plastic containers accelerating towards the luxurious dwellings of Rosses Point.

'I once gave an after-dinner speech at a convention of coroners', Desmond said, an hour later with a piece of steak between his hands, 'and as a little novelty for the occasion I brought along a human leg bone with a bullet hole through it. Now what was interesting was that I'd found this bone on an island and it was about three centuries old. The trajectory of the bullet was such that it must have been fired from high above the victim and as this island was flat, that could only mean it was fired from a ship, and only the English owned ships of that size then. It was considered very ungentlemanly in those days to shoot people from the rigging of a ship. So, this was my point. From a little piece of evidence it was possible to deduce a dastardly deed, how it was done and who did it. What I learned that evening was never to trust a convention of coroners. My bone was passed around and stolen.'

'Do you still hold resentment against the English?'

'No, not a bit. This wallowing in the past is just a popularist thing to do, an excuse to blame our failings on others and not take responsibility for them. I was the coroner in 1979 when the IRA blew up Mountbatten in his yacht near here. That was a terrible thing to do. He lived in Classiebawn Castle, just down the road. He was a popular man. He wasn't responsible for the troubles in any way. We're all planters here. The pre-Celts were planters. We all once came from somewhere else. In Ireland today we've got to learn to accept everyone. It's said here that the IRA are seventy per cent nationalism and thirty hooliganism, while the Unionists are seventy per cent hooliganism and thirty nationalism.' He paused to tear a mouthful of meat. 'In the republic we've got to embrace the Twelfth of July, you know, the Battle of the Boyne celebrations equally with St Patrick's Day. Only then can we heal. One day we'll be united. There's an annual Orange Parade at Rossnowlagh in County Donegal and there's never any trouble there.'

'The republic should celebrate the defeat that deprived them of three hundred years of independence? Is that what you're saying? I thought you'd be lynched for suggesting that.'

'Lynched. Now that's an interesting word. Do you know where it came from? It came from a mayor of Galway town called James Lynch Fitzpatrick who strung up his own son from his bedroom window in 1493. The lad had murdered a Spanish guest who'd taken a fancy to his girlfriend. There you go! But enough of politics! I think there are two things you should do while you're here. You should see the cursing stones of Inishmurray and find yourself a miracle at Knock.'

The following day we sailed to Inishmurray.

'You ever read any Joyce?' Desmond asked. 'Difficult man. I once went to a talk by a brilliant professor. Liam Connor, I think it was. Superb man. He was able to isolate Joyce's genius and convey it in simple terms. The only problem was, there was a bit of drink involved and I can't remember what he said.'

He was back in tweed jacket and immersed in anecdotes as he let the sails flap and steered us off course.

'You heard of the Siege of Sligo? No? Well you wouldn't have missed it if you'd been here in 1691. It was the talk of the place then. Anyway the town had its big "Sligo 750" celebrations in 1995 and I got involved in the re-enactment of the battle as a project for the long-term unemployed. Oh my God, never again! They were hell to work with, never turned up on time, always fooled around. But that changed when I told them we were going to get a real canon and use real gunpowder. I can tell you, Health and Safety took a bit of persuading! It went right to the top. If it hadn't been for the ninety-four ceasefire in the North, we'd never have got permission. Anyway...'

I nudged the tiller over until Inishmurray's thin greenness appeared over the bow.

'...I put the word out for old cannons and a relative in Nottingham rang me one day to say there was one for sale near him. So I went over with a couple of friends and one of them happened to be a priest. Well, can you believe it; we found that the cannon was for sale in the house next door to Kenneth Clarke! Imagine it! Three Irishmen purchasing a cannon just over the hedge from the Chancellor of the Exchequer! Of course then we wondered how the hell we were going to smuggle this thing back into Ireland. It was technically a weapon and that was illegal. So we threw a tarpaulin over it and put it in the boot. The priest was in the rear and when we got to customs this officer put his head through the window and asked if we'd anything to declare. "Nothing at all, sir," says I, "except an old canon in the back." So the man looks to the rear and sees the priest sitting there in his collar. Then he erupts in laughter. "That's very good, on you go", says he.'

We nosed into a cove. An orange buoy occupied the centre of a circle barely large enough to allow *Ceana* to turn.

'That's a good mooring', Desmond announced. 'A friend laid it and he's got a twenty-eight ton boat.'

We tied up and rowed ashore. Inishmurray's two hundred acres were filled with rank grass and networked by rabbit highways. Ragwort's yellow dusters and nettles brushed our knees as we ploughed a path past ruined houses to the cashel at the centre of the island. (From afar it resembled a conning tower and lent Inishmurray the profile of a submarine. The Royal Navy was fooled one night in 1916 and torpedoed the island). So flat was the going that at times the sea was hidden and it looked as if Donegal's mountains, five miles away, might be connected to this illusion of the great plains. Heckling gulls rose into an enormous sky. In 1880 a population of 102 lived here in fifteen houses. When the island was evacuated in 1948, there were forty-six left.

'Inishmurray was the last Irish soil Columba touched before going into exile. He founded the monastery but it was his friend, St Molaise, who ran it. It became one of the penitential islands on the great tour for pilgrims but this didn't stop the locals brewing poteen.

Old Ireland it was called and the most famous illicit drop in the country. There was a smoke signal system from the mainland. One sign heralded the arrival of pilgrims, another, the priest, and a third, most importantly, the excisemen.'

Within the cashel's low wall were the remains of sixth century buildings. Fifteen hundred years of erosion and at least two Viking attacks had done remarkably little damage to a beehive school, sweathouse, three drystone chapels, graves and incised standing stones. A semblance of glory seeped through its neglect. I hesitated before entering, an uneasiness descending as it always did on highly-charged spiritual ground. I felt an intruder. I had no knowledge of the customs and rituals that separate the sacred from the profane. At such moments our denial of divinity and myth seems among mankind's greatest losses. I paused and tried to make my peace. Then I crawled into the beehive cell and shone a torch round the perfection of the dome. A claustrophobic shiver tightened over my skull. I felt buried in a rock-fall and I scuttled out, panting deeply. When I found Desmond, he was embracing a standing stone and gripping it through two thumbholes perforating its edges.

'The birthing stone.'

'Really? In a monastery?'

'It's a more modern superstition. Women didn't actually give birth here but came to offer supplications to cure infertility.' He stood there as if trapped in stocks. 'I love this place. I've visited many times but it always excites me.'

Almost skipping, he led me through a doorway bearded with lichen.

'The chapels here were for men only, and only men were buried in this graveyard. Women had their own chapel and later a nunnery outside the complex. The islanders too were buried in segregated cemeteries. They said that on the few occasions a woman insisted on being buried next to her husband, the following morning her coffin would be found unearthed and lying on the surface. The graveyard just wouldn't accept it. So they said.'

'Was that the practice elsewhere in Ireland?'

'Not as far as I know. Now, we're standing in St Molaise's chapel. There used to be a wooden statue of him here but the National Museum in Dublin took it. You had to reverse out of the chapel so you never turned your back on the saint.' He carefully went through the procedure as if St Molaise were there to catch him out. I did the same.

'But this is what we've come to see. Clocha Breaca, the cursing stones. They're the only ones in Ireland. You can count them three times and you'll always get a different number.'

'I can count anything three times and get a different number.'

I counted fifty-two the first time and settled for that. They were sandstone balls standing on a square altar about the size of a dinner table for eight. Some were almost perfect spheres but the majority were oval or flattened like curling stones. They ranged in size from oranges to water melons and were packed closely together. Most appeared to have been sculpted by the sea. Two of the largest were different: they were hollow and fitted with stoppers. One was unique for being rectangular.

'How did they work?'

'I don't know. I think you had to go round the island's Stations of the Cross in reverse and turn a stone each time you passed. The way you turned the stones was vital in placing a curse on someone.'

'What sort of curses?'

'Oh the usual, I imagine. Death, heartbreak, illness, infirmity, infertility, destitution, fire, cows kicking the bucket...'

'Isn't that a risky thing to be doing?' I interrupted. Desmond had removed a stopper and was twiddling it this way and that. 'I mean, it could be a sort of Pandora's Box and you're letting everything out.'

'Yes, you could be right.' He slapped the stopper back. 'I imagine it's what you're thinking at the time that counts. And I believe you can use the stones for blessings too. Curses one way, blessings the other. Do you care to try one?'

'Thanks, but no.'

Oystercatchers scuttled about, flashing a white cross on their backs when they took to flight.

'The cross of St Brigid', Desmond explained.

Everything here seemed imbued with Christianity. I read symbols in lichens and felt the supplicant's breath in the wind. Even the rabbits displayed sanctimony in their right to remain undisturbed.

When we returned to the boat, the view was slightly out of joint. Something had shifted and it could only have been the boat. I felt something give as I hauled on the mooring rope. I carried on pulling and seconds later a twist of metal broke the surface, a crude hook of wire the thickness of half-a-dozen coat-hangers.

I thought: *Twenty-eight tons? Fenewanabullocks!* I turned to Desmond but said nothing.

Stones, bless him.

Knock

Today the gable of the old church is coated in a creamy-chocolate froth of pebbledash. Inlaid angels hover in semi-relief. The angels look fine but the pebbledash jars; apparently it was all they could do to stop pilgrims making off with bits of mortar and masonry. Around this Wimpy-coated shrine has been built an empire of basilica, Calvary, churches, chapels, confessionals, vocational and reconciliation centres, hotels, hostels and a religious retail park.

Against all odds Monsignor Horan succeeded in financing and building an international airport in this backwater of Mayo. It was ridiculed as a white elephant in the press and in song and has never known stacking in its airspace, but it remains viable. The 747s follow the flight path of angels. Knock attracts one and half million visitors each year and, along with Lourdes and Fatima, ranks among Europe's three foremost places of pilgrimage.

At around 8pm on the evening of 21 August 1879 two young women were hurrying home in torrential rain when they noticed something strange happening below the south wall of the village church. Mary Beirne and Mary McLoughlin saw three figures dressed in white standing there 'glowing in heavenly light' and untouched by the downpour. In the middle was a woman wearing a brilliant crown with a golden rose at its base. Her hands were raised in prayer. On each side of her stood a man, one turned to her in an attitude of respect, the other appeared to be preaching. He wore a small mitre and held an open book. Behind him a lamb stood on an altar and angels hovered above.

Mary Beirne ran to tell her relations. They rushed to the church and saw the vision too. Over a two-hour period twenty-two people aged between six and seventy-five witnessed the apparitions who were identified as the Virgin Mary, St Joseph and St John the Evangelist. Some witnesses lent forward and touched the illuminated ground and found it dry. One old woman suffered a heart attack on her way to the scene and the others left to assist her. When they returned, the figures had gone. Many others claimed to have seen the radiance from a distance.

What remains unusual about this vision is that no word was spoken by the apparitions and that there were three of them. Most 'commonly' Our Lady appears on her own and addresses those present, as happened thirty-eight years later in 1917 at Fatima.

The Knock vision was also unusual for the large number of witnesses. The Catholic Church is notoriously sceptical of any claimed miracle or vision and it was particularly reluctant to treat this case seriously. After centuries of suppression, in which the faith had been driven underground and was practised in private houses, the Church felt it had lost too much authority. Anything that empowered a belief in direct communication with God further undermined the Church's control.

In addition, the Land League had been formed that same year (in Irishtown, also in County Mayo) and the bishop of the diocese in which Knock happened to be was a landowner. A vision in a poor village was the last thing the authorities wanted.

Ten days after the event a woman brought her deaf daughter to the site, prised out a piece of mortar with a pin and pushed the fragment into one of the child's ears. She was cured. As more and more claims of cures were made the local priest began recording them. By October they totalled 637.

Soon Father Cavanagh was receiving around eighty letters a day requesting information on how to effect a cure at the shrine. The Church could no longer ignore what was happening, so a team of investigators was sent to Knock. Fifteen witnesses wrote testimonials. The investigation concluded that the evidence appeared sound and reliable. The Church took no further action until it instigated a second Enquiry in 1936. By then only three witnesses were still alive, one of them being Mary Beirne who died two weeks after its conclusion. The Holy See ratified the apparition the same year.

'What I can't understand', I said to a receptionist standing under a crown of thorns, 'is how the witnesses *knew* they were looking at St Joseph and St John?'

'All of them immediately recognised Our Lady and St Joseph but only one recognised St John. Apparently that person had seen a statue of the saint in Galway.'

'But we have no idea what these saints looked like. History left no likenesses of them. These statues are works of art.'

'We're talking miracles here.'

In a gift shop two women faced the same dilemma.

Woman 1 (*picking up statue*): 'Who's this?'

Woman 2: 'It could be her.'

Woman shopkeeper (*sweetly*): 'That's Saint Philomena.'

Woman 1: 'Are you sure?'

Shopkeeper: 'Absolutely.'

Woman 2: 'She doesn't look quite right.'

Shopkeeper: 'Which saint are you after?'
Woman 2: 'Saint Philomena.'
Woman 1: 'It's for a friend you see and it has to be Saint Philomena.'
Shopkeeper (*brusquely*): 'Anyone who knows anything about her will immediately recognise that as Saint Philomena, I can assure you.'
The women still hesitate. Shopkeeper sighs, reaches under counter, withdraws fat catalogue and flicks through it.
Shopkeeper (*pointing triumphantly*): 'There. Quite clearly, Saint Philomena.'
Woman 1: 'Lovely, I'll take one.'

I glanced through the catalogue. Saint Philomena was a fourteen year old martyr, it said, the patron saint of 'bodily ills, desperate causes, forgotten causes, impossible causes, lost causes, sick people, sickness'. Her website was www.philomena.it. There were hundreds upon hundreds of statues of all the saints in various poses and outfits, each photographed and with its order number. They were all made in Italy with the exception of the Portuguese franchise on the Fatima icons. And many of them could be found on the shelves around me, suffocating in the eternal refrains of 'Sweet Molly Malone' emanating from hidden speakers. You could buy saints as moving holograms, key-rings, beads, wallets, candles, biros, balloons and statues ranging in size from miniatures to sitting wolfhounds. Their colours wounded the eye. Mother Theresa had made it but the transmogrification into plastic had not been kind and she looked simian, almost Neanderthal. I paused before a three-foot-six-inch Madonna in a cloak of glitter with two doves on her feet and a '€300' tag hanging from her ear. Beside her was a rack of cards, one a caricature of a screaming woman: 'IF YOU TELL ME IT'S PMS ONE MORE TIME, I'LL STAPLE YOUR BALLS TO THE FLOOR'.

I strolled Knock's acres of tarmac. It was a quiet day but there were around thirty buses parked and more drifting in all the time. The devotees were mainly elderly women. I watched them filling containers with holy water from eighteen pushbutton taps and wondered how such a flow was consecrated. The modern basilica appeared almost empty yet there must have been 400 communicants receiving mass from eight priests. According to my brochure there was room inside for another 11,600 souls. The building was of an outlandish design. Substitute crescents for its crosses, add the muezzin's call to the tower and the effect of its flat roof and walls shaped like a blunt-ended star would make it indistinguishable from a mosque. This struck me as an additional achievement.

It was too easy to mock. Too easy to be misled by a shallow interpretation of tack and commercialism. When Desmond's son visited Knock, aged eight and already exercising his love of words, he remarked: 'It's a geriatric playground, isn't it?'

That was my initial impression, but the faces of those in the basilica read otherwise. Perhaps it was the low light or my imagination but there seemed an uncommon degree of engagement, of connection. Knock satisfied a need. Good work was done here. Inishmurray did it for me, Knock didn't. That was as much as I could say. It was an irritatingly humbling experience.

Cures for Seasickness ('Mal de mer')

That seasickness continues to inflict misery and debilitate many is largely because scientists still don't understand the human body's defensive response to a boat's motion. One theory advocates that the brain registers the 'off-balance' signals it receives as food poisoning and activates the emergency process for ejecting toxins and conserving energy. Whatever the causes here are some remedies, traditional and modern:

- Nantucket whalers tied a length of string to a piece of pork fat. The sufferer was forced to swallow the fat, whereupon the string was pulled to induce vomiting. The process was repeated whenever the symptoms reappeared.

- Royal Made Ping an Dan (Chinese herbal remedy, extremely rare).

- Ginger (*zingiber officinale*), Ginger Nut biscuits, ginger and brandy, ginger and anything.

- Apple cider vinegar.

- Saltwater.

- Soda crackers, Coca-cola, bitters (either Italian Fernet Branca or Angostura).

- Fresh air, staying warm on deck, focusing on the horizon, having a distraction (such as taking the helm).

- Time – usually three days.

- Acupuncture, wristbands.

- The Transderm-Scop patch (scopolamine - a derivative of belladonna poison, also used in a 'truth serum').

- Stugeron and other pharmaceutical pills.

- Suppositories (an alternative to pills which can be ejected by vomiting).

- Oral sprays.

- A prayer to the patron saint of the malady, Saint Erasmus, also known as Elmo (unfortunately no website).

'There's only one sure way to cure sea sickness', said Desmond. 'Sit under a tree.'

Killybegs

A couple of trawlers steamed into Killybegs, the country's premium fishing port. Behind them drifted a squabble of gulls like scraps of airborne litter, avid eyes on lazy wings. They were the only signs of activity. The port seemed dead, the fleet dormant. Seven super-trawlers were tied up in a line awaiting the calendar's next allocation of work days. And there beyond them, dwarfing even their breathtaking dimensions, was Ireland's disgrace, *Atlantic Dawn*. At 144 metres long 'the largest and potentially most destructive fishing machine in the world', as conservationists dubbed her, was the size of a passenger liner. In one day she could net what ten traditional fishing boats caught in a year. Her hull was painted black.

Ireland's fishing fleet was already thirty per cent over capacity and in contravention of EU regulations when the *Atlantic Dawn* was privately built for an Irish businessman in 2001. She was constructed in Norway at a cost of £50 million. The taoiseach and government ministers attended her arrival in Dublin, joined by 100,000 people who caused fifteen-mile traffic jams. Her purse seine is reputed to be 3,600 feet in diameter and 550 feet deep, the equivalent of throwing two Millennium domes around a shoal of fish. On board is a factory capable of packing and freezing 300 tonnes daily, and a full hold of 7000 tonnes is worth around £1.4 million each trip. Her crew of 100 comes mainly from Estonia where wages are fifty per cent lower than those in Ireland.

Everything about her is controversial. She was built as the MFV *Atlantic Dawn* - Motor Fishing Vessel - and yet she is registered as MV, a merchant vessel. Through this classification she does not have to comply with the EU's strict fishing regulations. In legal terms she is not part of Ireland's official fishing fleet and she is not allowed to fish in Irish waters. Instead she is a distant-water fisher; she plunders the stocks of the developing world. She is reputed to have negotiated a deal with the government of Mauritania through the Dutch Pelagic Fishing Company by exploiting legal loopholes and operating through a tangle of confidential arrangements.

The species caught is sardinelle, a small fish which migrates in large shoals between Morocco and the southern shores of West Africa. Sardinelle are a staple food in Senegal, and other countries.

Salt and Emerald

In the 1990s the assessed catch off Africa was an annual 300,000 tonnes. This has risen to 500,000 tonnes each year and the Dutch Pelagic Fishing Company hopes to increase it to 800,000 tonnes. It is estimated that the effective fishing capacity of the modern breed of super-trawlers is five times greater than that of the pelagic trawlers of a decade ago. *Atlantic Dawn* is in a class apart, a mega-catcher capable of decimating the sardinelle all on her own.

Should the Irish government and the European Union tolerate, and even subsidise, the construction and operation of such vessels whose sole aim is to profit through the exploitation of the poorest nations on earth – at the same time as defying both United Nations fishing policy and the logic of conservation?

God's Tear

The barometer was falling. *Ceana* tugged at her anchor and bucked with all the friskiness of a rodeo. The wind was blowing into Church Pool from the one chink in its protection. The view though the port window was filled with a cemetery where cows were ripping up grass and rasping their ribs on gravestones. I'd rowed ashore the previous night and found an uncommon number of Scotts recumbent there. Now I'd missed the first weather forecast and the second mentioned only a Small Craft Warning before asking me to retune to Channel 02 where nothing appeared. I had to choose between staying put, taking an eight-mile direct route to Aranmore with tricky navigation or a safer more exposed alternative twice as long. The thought of a day spent beside a collection of dead Scotts was too depressing. With visibility down to half a mile, I put a couple of reefs in the main and took the long way round.

'Hallo yacht! Is there enough wind for you?' The radio voice then laughed. I looked about and saw nothing at first but then a small fishing boat rose momentarily from one trough and disappeared into the next on the edge of the mist.

'I'd manage fine on less. How's it for you?'

'Sure it's grand but it puts the speed on me for it's going to get worse. And the hurrier I go the behinder I get.'

I saw him wave on his next appearance then I saw him no more.

'Are you all right?' I called. No reply.

'Fishing boat are you there, are you all right?'

'Sure I'm here. I'm raising me pot.'

I felt great warmth for this voice, this stranger with whom I shared a mist-enveloped pocket of the Atlantic. Our exchange brought a sense of fellowship out of all proportion to its brevity. I was on a beam reach under three reefs, driving through spindrift at bursts of eight knots. Aranmore's dark cliffs formed a wall on my right. I knew this delicate state of harmony could end in an instant with the failure of a single shackle pin. As the wind crept up, gusting now to thirty knots, and the sea turned whiter, I couldn't help wondering if I too would find that the hurrier I went the behinder I'd get.

By the time I secured a mooring in a bay off Aranmore Sound, a gale was pummelling Ireland. Unable to launch my inflatable I was marooned, happily, and settled down with John McGahern's *That*

They May Face the Rising Sun. My bunk see-sawed, jars slid and rattled on shelves and the portholes gave an impression of life inside a laundrette.

'So you made it!' Dermot McVeigh was in the pub that evening when he introduced himself to me. A ruddy-faced man with a wave of fair hair, he was already a couple of sheets to the wind.

I nodded. He held the advantage in our encounter. Everyone on the island knew I was the stranger off the yacht.

He winked. 'And was there enough wind for you out there?'

'So it was you! Thanks for that call. It cheered me up to know you were out there too. How was the fishing?'

An accordion player started up joined by a man on a banjo.

'Poor, very poor. Out of a hundred pots I take twelve lobsters on average. Five years ago it was three times that. And I do the gillnetting, you know, for salmon. But that's poor too. It's the seals I blame. You're not Greenpeace, are you? Well I don't care if you are. It's the seals that's the problem. Twenty-five years ago we got a bounty for a seal head. Two punts fifty for each one. Now they're protected unless we catch them in our nets. Well, they'd change their tune if it was *their* nets with just fish heads in them. And Owey Island, that's north of here, and no word of a lie there's seals there that know how to unlatch a pot and get the lobster inside.'

It was hard to find some cheer. The weather, seals, lobsters and fishing were out. Trust and honesty were out: the islanders' sense of security had just been rocked by the first serious theft in living memory. The previous day the cooperative store which sold ironmongery and farming goods had been robbed of €100,000. 'The key had been hidden in the usual safe place', Dermot explained, 'but some bastard helped himself. Six weeks' takings, forty grand in cash. I suppose we'll have to lock our houses now.' We sat in silence. Then Dermot found something uplifting.

'Begod! She comes well-equipped!'

Some dancers had taken to the floor and he was staring at one particular woman. 'Tis the Ballinascarty Half Set they're doing, and doesn't it show them off to perfection?'

The men looked rough, like fishermen still in their work boots but they knew the steps as well as their partners. The dance appeared to be in three parts with a polka followed by a jig and hornpipe but all involved foot-stabbing, heeling and back-kicking even as they helicoptered. This they did in a wrestling grip with hands forming interlocking hooks. So fast did they spin that at times each woman was airborne. It was a riveting display of renaissance delicacy and Fingalian violence, and it lasted twenty minutes.

'Do you often have dances like this?'

'Not often enough with the likes of her around.'

The storm continued. I watched the ferry come and go. It was the *Rhum*, a former Caledonian-MacBrayne ferry which had served the Small Isles in the Hebrides. A lot of Scotland's leftovers seemed to end up in Ireland. *Rhum*'s sister ship, *Canna*, worked out of Rathlin Island. Aranmore's lifeboat had a more emotional link with my homeland. Based at Longhope on the Orcadian island of Hoy in 1969 she capsized during a rescue with the loss of all eight crew.

She looked invincible next to my mooring. I always found the presence of these muscular orange craft reassuring. The organisation responsible for them had its origins in the depressingly-named 'Liverpool Institution for Recovering Drowned Persons', founded in 1771. Sir William Hillary, a veteran of the Napoleonic Wars, had reorganised it into the more upbeat 'National Institution for the Preservation of Life from Shipwreck' (simplified to the 'Shipwreck Institution') by 1824, the year its operations were extended to Ireland. Seven Irish lifeboat stations were built, then two more in 1825.

Lack of funds and the famine halted further growth but several independent posts were created. These were incorporated into the Royal National Lifeboat Institution, as it became in 1861, and gradually cover was extended to the entire Irish coastline. Today the RNLI runs 203 lifeboat stations in Britain and Ireland. Since 1824 has saved 135,000 lives.

The lifeboat cavorted at her mooring. Wind shook Aranmore's grass making it quiver like horseflesh. Cottongrass danced in bogs. Sheep gave up the nomadic life and settled in the lee of collapsed dykes. I walked the island in a day on a circle of fresh tarmac.

East side: houses, pubs, shop, cashless cooperative, beach where rowdies raced All Terrain Vehicles each evening, fine views to mainland. South: houses, fierce sheep dogs, paddling beach, fine views to islands. West: cliffs, lighthouse, fine views to Canada. North: fields. Centre: bogs, hill, lough, rubbish dump.

I reached the cliffs I'd passed two days earlier and looked down into Binn na d'Truideog, the central segment in a shamrock of coves. A chute of rubble offered a frightening scramble as the only way up or down this amphitheatre of crags. The swell was racing in and being shredded on Sharp Rock, Spire Rocks and a dozen others. The scene was a churning commotion of spray. I imagined myself in a boat amongst it, and shuddered. Then I thought no more about it until Charlie Boyle stopped to offer me a lift. I was approaching the lighthouse at the time.

'I saw you looking into Binn na d'Truideog', he said. 'Well I'll tell you a story about that. It was the twentieth of March 1983, I'll never forget the date. I was the attendant at the light. It was automated in '76 but I had to check it regularly. On that day I was doing something I'd never done before. I'd made a model sailing boat, ach, I suppose it was a foot or fourteen inches long and I'd taken my grandson along to sail it on Lough a' Chomhanaigh. There'd been pretty stormy weather and the wind was still strong and it wouldn't sail properly. "Come on," I said, "we'll go down to the lighthouse and get a little bit of lead for the ballast for that's what's needed." I knew there was some scraps there. Well, when we got close I saw a man walking about. "I wonder who that can be?" says I. "He's looking a bit washed up." And to be sure he was all wet but wearing one of these wetsuit things. He looked that pleased to see me. "My name's Wayne Dickinson," he says, "and I've just crossed the Atlantic from Boston." Well, I thought he was some nutcase so I said, "Oh yes?" not believing a word of it. But it was true. He'd just taken 142 days to cross in a boat only eight times bigger than my little model. *God's Tear* it was called, eight foot nine inches long, the smallest boat to cross the Atlantic.'[1]

He paused and pointed to Binn na d'Thruideog. 'That's where he landed. His boat was destroyed. "She told me to jump, to leave her," he said. He crawled up the crags on his hands and knees with just what he was wearing. He thought he'd reached an uninhabited Scottish island, then he found an old shoe and that gave him hope that someone might be living here. Then we came along. He was exhausted. He asked me to help him out of his suit and he was wet inside, so I took him home and gave him a hot bath and dry clothes. He was a week with us because of the bad weather. Over the next few days people salvaged bits of wreckage from his boat and brought them to him but he didn't like it. "Put it back," he would say, "let her be".'

'Why had he set out in winter?'

'I thought that curious too, so I asked him. He said he hoped to get westerlies to carry him across. And you know, every year after that his mother wrote to us, saying how grateful she was for what we'd done. But, ach, I'm not much of a writer myself and this year we never heard from her so perhaps she's died. But I still can't get over it. Crossing the Atlantic in a slip of a boat like that.'

---

[1] Wayne's record did not last long. The same year, 1983, Tom Maclean duplicated the west-east crossing in his 7' 11" *Giltspur* (having cut her down from 9' 9" after a record-breaking crossing the previous year). Yet at the same time Eric Peters was completing an east-west crossing in the 5' 8" *Toniky Nou*. In 1993 Hugo Vihlen crossed in *Father's Day*, 5'4". In 1998 Tom McNally completed half a crossing, from Tangiers to Gran Canaria in *Vera Hugh II,* only 3' 11" in length.

Light Dues

...flash, flash, flash...

Each year it costs an average of £70 million to keep those flashes going around the coasts of Britain and Ireland. So I discovered when I looked into it, having wondered for years who paid for Muckle Flugga, Eddystone, the Tuskar, Hook, Fastnet and all the rest of them, and how the dues were calculated. The matter is one of general confusion and misconception. I'd lost count of the times former lighthouse-keepers had told me that if a ship came within the dipping distance of a light, a charge was levied and repeated for the number of lights passed, that a tonnage charge per light was applied and that it was a fixed charge regardless of how many lights might have been of assistance. Not even the individual Lighthouse Boards fully understood the system. They referred me to Customs and Excise who passed me on to the Department for Transport, Ports Division.

The confusion is understandable because no international agreement exists. Every country makes up its own rules. The Netherlands make no charge for their lights. Britain and Ireland charge quite heavily but, as a DfT official told me: 'Marking the extremities of our land is a nightmare as we have a long and very complex coastline, and we stand right in the way of all passing traffic seeking entry to North European ports'. Accordingly, the British Isles and Ireland pool their resources for the benefit of the General Lighthouse Authorities (GLA), which comprises Trinity House (England and Wales), the Northern Lighthouse Board (Scotland) and the Commissioners of Irish Lights.

Who pays? Perhaps it's more interesting to start with who doesn't. Any ship used by Her Majesty is exempt. So are naval ships and those involved in pollution control, harbour maintenance, government business and sewage transportation. Sail-training and historic sailing ships go free, as do all vessels under twenty tons (except fishing boats), which includes the majority of pleasure yachts. Finally, no dues are paid by 'dumb barges' and any other vessels built without a means of propulsion.

The bottom line is that commercial freighters and some fishing vessels foot the bill. In Ireland all fishing boats are exempt but in

Britain only those under ten metres are excused and all others are charged on their length. A twenty-metre trawler currently pays £390 annually. All other ships are charged on their net tonnage, at thirty-five pence per ton. The maximum charge is £13,650 for a ship of 35,000 tons or over. This is a fixed fee irrespective of how many lights the ship passes and it is levied for *each voyage*, no matter how long or short, when a British or Irish port is entered. From Bristol to Liverpool is the same cost as from Australia to Liverpool. After seven visits to any of our ports within a year, the ship is exonerated from further light dues for that period. The only exception to these conditions is if the ship puts into port 'from stress of weather', for repairs, stores, crew changes or medical emergencies; under these circumstances the visit is free.

A key point in this system, which one official described as 'a bag of anomalies', is that only ships docking in our waters pay dues. A freighter travelling from Halifax, Nova Scotia, to Hamburg and using every light on the west coast of Ireland and the south coast of England en route, pays dues only to Germany and no other country gets a share of them. This has important ramifications for trade. If that ship has cargo for Cork it may prefer to avoid stopping at Cork because of the light dues, preferring instead to continue to Rotterdam (no light dues) and tranship its cargo to a smaller vessel which will do the run to Cork and incur greatly reduced costs. Thus Cork misses out on the lion's share of other revenues.

Running a ship is not for the shallow of purse. The costing of the most economical voyage occupies the minds of the best accountants. In our ports a ship not only pays light dues but also stevedore (cargo handling), harbour and pilotage charges and possibly deep-sea pilotage fees as well. The Netherlands may not exact light dues but they impose a 'fairway' charge for using their marked channels, and their pilotage fees are considerably higher than Britain's. It becomes a complex matrix.

In Ireland light dues are collected by Irish Customs whereas in Britain a ship's broker performs the task. As ships put into port, their brokers settle all bills and invoice their clients. A check is maintained by harbour authorities who monitor shipping movements and pass the details on to the relevant lighthouse board which issues an invoice for any omitted payments. Light dues are always paid because the authorities have the power to detain any ship which owes money, a recourse every ship owner is keen to avoid as each day spent in port brings wildly escalating additional charges.

The money from British and Irish light dues is kept separate from the Exchequer and goes into a central pot called the General Lighthouse Fund (GLF), administered by the Department for Transport. This year the fund expects to receive £71 million, a profit of one million. This is inadequate for the proposed new capital outlays but the GLF has a reserve fund for extraordinary payments. The GLF sanctions the costs of the three boards. Revenues from Irish lights and a small annual grant from the Irish government, currently cover thirty-five per cent of the costs of the Commissioners of Irish Lights – a figure the GLF considers far too low and which it is endeavouring to have increased. The UK government pays no subsidy towards the upkeep of lights. The dues were last increased in 1993. Since then they have actually been reduced four times, reflecting economies in operation through automation and a downscaling of the administrative fleet and depots.

All is far from plain sailing in the business. The largest vessel owners have organised themselves into a lobby group to press for the abolition of light dues. Their premise is that in this day of e-navigation (dGPS, Loran, etc) ships no longer use lighthouses so it is anachronistic to have to pay for them. The Independent Light Dues Forum expresses its dissent through MPs and Brussels but its members stop short of direct action through fear of having their vessels impounded. In its defence, the General Lighthouse Authority has been admirably proactive in its campaign to be indispensable. It has always had the fallback argument of asking how ships will navigate our tricky waters if the GPS system collapses or their on-board electricity supply fails.

These are not hypothetical situations but cases which occur with alarming frequency. In one recent instance a tanker's GPS suffered a blip and gave its position as being off Torquay when in fact it was in the Bristol Channel. The GLA has now become an e-navigation server itself. Realising that traditional aids (lights and audible fog signals) account for 95% of their maintenance expenditure but are of use to about 5% of their clients, the GLA has been equipping many of its lighthouses with the latest electronic technology. Not only does the modern lighthouse flash, moan and send out an ID letter which lights up on a ship's radar, but an increasing number also transmit the latest position-pinpointing signals generated by differential GPS (a GPS fix which has been received, checked and corrected), Loran C and the Automatic Identification System.

Bloody Foreland

The aftermath of the storm left an out-of-sorts, sloppy sea. Owey Island appeared to have broken loose and was bobbing about like a larger version of its light-fingered seals. Buoyant and careless they dozed with their snouts pointing heaven-wards and squeezed into a snorkel which never seemed to get swamped. Salmon, lobster and a siesta seemed stylish living compared to mine. I opened a can of tuna and plotted waypoints.

I was anticipating Bloody Foreland. In my mind I'd elevated it to the status of some Lorelei or Cape Despair, a point of no return where ships perished in a roiling sea. It sounded evil. The weather suddenly thickened. Soon my mast was stirring a ceiling of fog. I reached for my fog horn and blew a note whose reverberation hurt my ears. I repeated this every minute and listened for any answer. I felt very small, very vulnerable in that whiteout. Every half-identified sound became a freighter about to run me down. After twenty minutes my eyes deceived me with a flashing pinprick of white light. I thought I'd imagined it at first but then it came again, three flashes this time. Three white flashes: the warning of an East Cardinal buoy, placed to the east of a dangerous rock or wreck. I rushed below to consult the chart. It showed no danger. But it was out of date. Back at the tiller I peered into the fog to fix the direction of the lights. 048° and now four flashes. That was a mystery. Back to the chart. A long search. Then I found it. Tory Island lighthouse! Four flashes every thirty seconds! Ten miles away! A matter of minutes later the fog thinned and I broke out into a sharp-edged world of distance and colour.

Bloody Foreland remained elusive but I could see the conical mass of Errigal Mountain posing like a diminutive Fujiama. Below it spread the Rosses, a low treeless region of fields, bogs, islands and promontories, distinguished for their beaches and the memory of one of Ireland's most benevolent landlords. Lord George Hill, the fifth son of the Marquis of Downshire, is widely regarded as a rare example of the noble and good. He bought a small estate around Gweedore and Bunbeg in 1834 and by the time of his death in 1879 had amassed 24,000 acres. In his book, *Facts from Gweedore* (published in 1845) he described the poverty he encountered. In a parish with a population of 4000, thirty had a mattress for their bed (twenty-eight of chaff and two of feather), one person owned a cart and one a plough. The region's poultry stock amounted to twenty-seven geese and three turkeys. No vegetables were grown except potatoes and cabbage. When fish were abundant the cost of salt soared and they were unable to preserve them. Even the Irish passion for a decent burial was hard to fulfil but those who could paid annual 'retaining fees' of sheaves of corn to the carpenter as deposits on their coffin.

Lord Hill built roads and bridges and 'improved' the land by doing away with the archaic Rundale system of agriculture in which tenants were allocated an equal mixture of the best and worst land on an annual rotation. The system was fair but inefficient in terms of travelling time and wasted land between plots. He 'squared off' the land into larger, permanent holdings for his tenants and constructed a 'model farm'. His shop supplied every item imaginable. He built a mill and set up an agency for supplying wool and processing equipment to encourage a home knitting industry. He gave annual prizes for the best-kept cottage, best vegetables, butter and livestock. When the Famine came he was among the first to sell corn at a price below cost and by acting promptly and using his mill to capacity, he was able to avert some of the extremes of deprivation. He even learnt Irish, it is said, to better engage with his tenantry.

Yet he suffered the common dilemma of the landlords of Ireland. One observer, Robert Lynd, noted in 1909 that although they were 'one of the most worthless aristocracies in history, they too had their tragedy. They could not be altogether English, and would not be altogether Irish.' Hill's tenants never accepted him and saw his changes as autocratic foibles imposed on them without regard for their opinions or customs.

Lord Hill was unquestionably an enterprising landlord outwith the conventional mould, but it appears that he did little unless it would enhance his profit or reputation, and he was nothing if not a good self-publicist. *Facts from Gweedore* was designed not only to advertise the success of his model farm but to attract visitors to a hotel he built adjacent to it. By abolishing the Rundale system he also removed his tenants' rights to subdivide their holdings or build additional dwellings on them to accommodate their sons. His rents were considered high and any threat to his monopoly of trading on the estate brought immediate retribution. A woman who set up a bakery in opposition to his own was evicted. The knitting enterprise proved very profitable to him. His disparaging view of life on the estate before his arrival and the glowing account his book gave of it after his improvements displayed such a bias that the local, long-incumbent priest, Father McFadden, referred to the work as *Fictions From*

Gweedore. As for the magnanimous gesture of supplying cheap corn during the Famine, Father McFadden pointed out that Lord Hill had received £700 from the government to provide relief aid and he did so simply to keep his tenantry in work and not reduced to indolence in the poorhouse.

The Rosses fizzled out along with the substance of philanthropy, and I realised Bloody Foreland had gone too. All fang and raised hackle in name but the reality was a sprawl of bungalow blight running upfield to a patch of bald, mildly ruddy rock. Full wheelchair access and a vague bend in the coast. That was it!

Then Tory Island was before me. Ireland's remotest inhabited island: the only one to have a reigning King, an anachronistic naming system, the originator of the contemptuous term 'a Tory' and the rocks on which HMS *Wasp* perished under mysterious circumstances.

At first it appeared to be four islands but they gradually merged into one. My pilot described the place as 'a slab of granite two-and-a-half miles long upended at the north and sloping down to the sea in the south'. Sparse as it was, it was a perfect summary of what lay ahead.

The distance that had appeared generous for reflection shortened rapidly and suddenly I was into the frantic preparations for arrival: fenders out; warps attached and coiled ready for a flawless despatch into the hands of some innocent strolling the harbour; reducing sail; chart consultation; depth monitoring and, not least of it, trying to find a gap in what appeared to be a solid harbour wall. Then I caught sight of the transit posts or, to be more accurate, one transit post. The other was missing and one transit post on its own is as good as no transit post. I took a guess and homed in only to find the bottom rushing up to meet me. I altered course for a crab pot and this seemed a better line. Soon I was inside a snug harbour, almost new, throwing a line which fell short in a dozen tangles to a fisherman who didn't even bother to remove his hands from his pockets.

'Not easy getting in here', I remarked, when I was safely strung up against the quay.

'Oh aye, the transit post's away.' He made it sound like a holiday. 'A tractor flattened it a fortnight back. No, I tell a lie. It must be near a month ago, I'd say. Maybe three weeks.'

Two, three, four weeks, whatever. Time enough to have fixed the principal navigation aid for entering a port, I thought, and knew at once I was going to like Tory.

Tory

Tory's houses were more run-down than those of other islands. They rambled along the southern shore and gathered in huddles in a couple of places where they complained about their gout and rickets and shivered in inadequate clothing. Their mortar was loose, their gutters leaked and their paint flaked. There were few gardens. Grass was preserved for grazing and a semi-desert of granite grit and heather held the high ground.

These houses were engaged in a constant stand-off against their environment. Wind rippled lines of washing strung out before them, and I could imagine it doing the same to their walls in winter. A sense of lassitude prevailed and overcame even the orange and blue home that spoke most violently against it.

Just as in the Scottish Highlands where the pin-neat house is the holiday home or that of the more affluent incomer and the decrepit steading with its wrecked machinery lying about is the abode of the deeply-rooted 'local', so Tory's apparent neglect spoke to me of something old and genuine. There was a shortage of work, youth and money here. Tory was as it had to be because the clinical homogenisation that affluence brings had yet to arrive.

The islanders were once infamous as cattle robbers. They went on raiding parties to the mainland and became so successful and despised that the word 'Tory' entered the language as a synonym for 'thief'. By the late 17th century it was sufficiently well-established for the Whigs to select it as the most abusive name they could find for their political opponents. The name stuck and endured officially until 1833 when the Tories became the Conservatives. That such a small and insignificant island should lend its image to a Westminster party was a considerable achievement, and it should have been a warning to the Government not to underestimate the real Tories. But it wasn't. When the islanders refused to pay their rent in 1884, a gunboat with soldiers and police was despatched to collect the dues. The islanders watched it approach and cursed it. Some say a cursing stone was used and later lost when a storm ravaged the graveyard in which it was kept. HMS *Wasp* never arrived. She foundered on the western reefs with the loss of all but six lives. The rent was never recovered and to this day the islanders remain exempt from rates. It's a salutary lesson in civil disobedience.

Their graves lay below the lighthouse within a small walled cemetery barely distinguishable from the surrounding barrens. Of the nine nameless headstones, eight were marked 'HMS Wasp, 22 Sept 1884', and one belonged to a seamen washed up in 1940. Like the migrating birds which island-hopped between Greenland and the south and included Tory as a stopover, so the wind and currents acted as a conveyor belt on the same route and deposited the victims of the North Atlantic convoys along the western seaboards of Scotland and Ireland.

From the Butt of Lewis to the Blaskets there were lonely cemeteries like this one with the anonymous on their own or gathered together under the names of their ships. And above both them and their transience pass the replenishing cycles of Arctic terns, black-headed gulls and, most prevalent of all, fulmars effortlessly floating on starched wings.

I left the cemetery and followed the birds sporting on the up-draughts. Such was the sparse growth and desolation I might have been 3000 feet up on the Cairngorm plateau. I came to a school desk complete with inkwell and attached seat alone in the nowhere. No other rubbish. No other explanation: it had to be art. Art was thick here. On the edge of cliffs I came to a tiny building, newly roofed and with windows on all sides. There was no road to it. A vase of flowers stood on a sill and inside hung a gallery of paintings. It was locked.

Beyond, cliffs rose towards the peak of the Tory wedge. By the east end it was a precipice in flamingo pink. So uniform was the gradient of the land that when darkness fell the light from the lighthouse, one of the most powerful in the country, must have raked the bedrooms of almost every one of the 240 who lived here. *Flash, flash, flash, flash,* every thirty seconds. A recipe for epilepsy.

The King of Tory was standing below the island's landmark tower when I met him. He took his duties seriously and had just been down to the harbour to cast an eye over the trickle of visitors disembarking from the first ferry of the day. With twenty-four hours on the island I was already old news and on nodding terms. We nodded and I studied the tower, a curiosity resembling the base of a factory chimney about twenty feet high. It was ruined and made of granite.

'It's the only one on an Irish island', he offered, 'and they say it was used as a refuge against the Vikings.'

'It looks much older.'

'It is. Older than the Celts. It was built by the Fomorians, I'm told, and they were early sea-traders. I like the history myself. It tells us who we are. And have you seen the cross, the tau-cross?'

He led me a short distance to a T-shaped stone beside the harbour. I put the King at about five foot seven inches and the cross was taller. Had it been twenty yards closer to *Ceana* it would have made a convenient bollard for mooring warps.

'Tau is the nineteenth letter of the Greek alphabet so that's how it gets its name. This is the oldest thing on the island. They reckon it goes back to a thousand years BC and was cut in Egypt.'

I ran a hand over its surface which the wind had sandpapered smooth. Egypt and Tory seemed an unlikely partnership but, on reflection, was no stranger than Crete and Rathlin. Rathlin had axes but Tory looked weak on trading potential with only granite.

'Make sure you're tied up tight tonight, there's rough weather coming in.' He studied my boat. 'My oath! Yous must have fairly well settled your account with the Man Above to be travelling about in that.' He turned and smiled. 'I'm Patsy Dan Mac Rúarí Rodgers.'

'And you're the King of Tory?'

'I am.'

He was a wiry man with a sharp face and pointed chin. A gold ring pierced his right ear and he had a close-cropped sandy moustache. In his blue jacket and blue peaked cap with a circle of braid, he looked vaguely ex-navy gone hip.

'What exactly do you do as the King?'

'Being *Rí Thóraigh* is like being a mayor. I see myself as a goodwill merchant, a promoter of Tory. I love people and boats and this island. All I want to do is good for people and good for Tory.'

'How did the role come about?'

'It stems from the old days when not everyone could read or write. They'd come to someone who could for help with letters and filling out forms and so this person would become a helper and advisor. It was always someone trusted and respected and so the title of King was given to them.'

'Is it hereditary?'

'Usually, but sometimes a person doesn't want it or is not up to it. The son and the daughter of the last King didn't want it and they had the right to confer it on someone else, so they gave it to me. In 1993.'

Later when I mentioned the King I felt locals regarded the role as a straight-faced joke. Nothing was said but the tongue appeared firmly in the cheek. Yet there was no doubting the king's enthusiasm for his adopted role. 'We've a lot to cherish here. We're unique in all Ireland for our system of names. Och, it's not so strong now but it's still a tradition that a child is given Christian names which trace its ancestry back two or three generations on both sides of the family. I'm just Patsy Dan for short.' He grinned, and surveyed his kingdom.

'We were pretty washed-up as a community in the seventies but things are good now. They've just spent seven million on harbour improvements. We've got two wind generators and young families for our school.'

'And you've got your paintings.'

'Yes, it was Derek Hill who got us going. An Englishman. He used to come here every summer and he got us going. Maybe you've seen the memorial to him on the cliffs? That used to be his studio. We've just finished renovating it. There used to be eight of us but there's only four left now.'

Hill, the last of the 'Gentleman Painters', was already a well-known portrait and landscape painter when he began visiting Tory. An islander called James Dixon was so unimpressed by the artist's work that he told Hill he himself could do better. Hill supplied him with paper, paints and brushes. Dixon discarded the brushes, made his own from the tail hairs of a donkey and set to work. Hill was struck by the originality of Dixon's style. Dixon was in his sixties and without any artistic training. He had never left the island nor had any exposure to the world of art. Hill encouraged him and soon others were having a shot themselves. Under Hill's patronage Tory's School of Primitive Painting achieved wider sales and recognition.

'You're one of them?'

'I am. I can hardly keep up with the demand. I paint at night from eleven to five or six in the morning. So I use my cat's eyes.' He raised a hand to his cap. 'Now, if you'll excuse me I want to go and warn a family camping about the gales tonight. Enjoy your stay on Tory. You're most welcome.'

Inside the gallery of Rory Rogers I gazed at pictures in primal colours with wonky perspective. Ships lay flat on the sea and Tory Island had shrunk to the size of a raft barely able to contain the figures walking on it. The prices for the smaller ones were €350. Then a wooden pulley lying on a table caught my eye. Beside it stood a shiny steel thermos jug. I wondered if it contained coffee for visitors and asked the young woman attendant.

'That's from *Cabin Fever*', she replied. 'You know. The reality TV boat that hit the rocks here?'

'Oh yes, I remember.' I'd read about the accident. We'd passed each other the week before she foundered. At the time I was passing through Donaghadee Sound. She'd looked like a pirate ship. Radio Telefís Éireann, the national television network, had hired her with a professional skipper, mate and cook. Eight people who'd never sailed before were kept cooped up in her with their daily lives under constant camera scrutiny. Each week the nation voted for one of them to walk the plank. Then suddenly the boat was wrecked on Tory on a clear day with no one at the helm. Everyone on board was saved. There was talk of litigation and then the case became *sub judice* and faded from the papers.

'It was all very weird but...' she giggled. 'We salvaged these bits from it!'

A shiver ran down my spine. One false move on my part, one miscalculation with *Ceana* in these waters and my thermos, spoons, forks and the odd joint from Fleming would end up on a Tory table as treasure trove.

That night the storm came. Safe in my seven million-euro harbour, I was nevertheless rocked relentlessly while the fenders scrunched and scraped and shrill notes sounded from some railings which had turned into pan pipes. Early, before I was properly awake, I thought I heard someone walking on my deck. I was too sleepy to care but when I eventually surfaced and checked my warps, I found someone had retied and tightened them. I thought of the family camping and wondered how they had fared, unaware that the King had interrupted his painting that night to check on them. When he found their tent had collapsed, he took them into his house.

Perhaps, I reflected, it was time for the Conservatives to re-brand themselves as the New Tories?

News, 20th August

Item 1: A potato blight warning was issued. Weather conditions over the previous month had raised the likelihood of an epidemic breaking out in Ireland to 'high'.

Item 2: A four-week-old Nigerian boy had died from loss of blood following a kitchen table attempt at circumcision in a Waterford home. A man who had campaigned for two years for proper hospital facilities to be made available for this operation was interviewed. He said this was a far from isolated incident. Because the practice was not common in Ireland and an eight-month waiting list for the operation was normal, immigrants for whom circumcision was a traditional necessity were forced to extreme measures. 'It's tragic and shameful', he added. 'Ireland has got to wake up to its responsibility towards its minority cultures.'

Potted History No 5

If the English ever found a solution to the Irish problem, the Irish would change the problem.

Sir Winston Churchill

Anyone who thinks they understand Northern Ireland has missed the point.   Anonymous.

The majority of the population of Northern Ireland - Protestant Unionists - had reluctantly accepted Home Rule when they realised that Southern Ireland could no longer be prevented from forming its own state. The Northern Ireland Parliament opened in June 1921 and the Irish Free State was established in December the same year. Just as civil war immediately broke out in the south, anarchy threatened to undermine the north. One-third of Northern Ireland's population was Catholic and bitterly hostile to the division of the country into separate entities. As they recognised neither the process that created this division nor the parliament that now governed it they felt bereft of any political voice and saw disruption and violence as their only effective means of protest.

Herein lay the crux of the problem: the Protestants controlled the government, manipulated the electoral boundaries to ensure their voice predominated and were then able to claim the moral high ground of 'defending' themselves and democracy by representing law and order, which naturally preserved their privileged position. The Catholics, suffering prejudice in employment and civil rights, were cast as the villains. Little wonder they saw their situation as desperate and hopeless. In 1922, 232 people were killed, almost a thousand injured and damage to property amounted to three million pounds. In addition to the British army, which the province still relied on to restore order in a crisis - and always would in future - two new 'defence' forces were created: the armed police of the Royal Ulster Constabulary and a volunteer auxiliary force, the Ulster Special Constabulary.

The Thirties brought hardship to both sides, but particularly to the Catholics, as linen and shipbuilding slumped in the persistent depression that affected all other industries as well. Unemployment reached 28% in 1931 and remained around 20% until the Second

World War. Sectarian violence erupted and subsided intermittently.

The war years brought a surge in economic activity and new military bases were created to enable thousands of troops to train in the province. Migrant Catholic workers from the south were issued with special permits to fill employment vacancies but, in accordance with the ethic 'a unionist parliament must always be in power', they were denied permanent residency or the right to vote.

Following the war an economic boom occurred as incentives to attract new industries, such as Courtaulds and Michelin Tyres, paid dividends. Soon the general levels of health care, education and welfare benefits in the north raced ahead far in advance of those in the Republic. Yet the violence continued with a new campaign running from 1956 to 1962. The descent into turmoil which followed was not always inevitable: there was a widespread desire for peace and stability. It became inevitable largely because one significant group was opposed to any form of conciliation. That group consisted of extreme right-wing unionists led by the Reverend Ian Paisley, an eloquent firebrand with a voice as incisive as a chainsaw.

By 1969 tensions had reached a new peak. Demonstrations by the recently-formed (Catholic) Civil Rights Association were consistently suppressed by the police and harassed by unionists. The escalating violence could not ultimately be contained by the Northern Ireland security forces and the government requested help from the British army. Westminster consented but on condition that major reforms would be implemented and these – including the redrawing of electoral boundaries, the disbanding of the exclusively Protestant special constabulary, and measures to eliminate religious discrimination in housing allocation and employment – fulfilled almost all the Civil Rights Association's demands.

Had the reforms been put into effect speedily a foundation for integrating this fragmented society might have been created, but it took time - four years. Too long for too many frustrated ambitions. A new Catholic political party was formed, the Social Democratic and Labour Party (SDLP), whose aims included a united Ireland but, unlike Sinn Féin, it rejected violence and sought to achieve its goal by consent and by working within Northern Ireland's political system. Had it been established in times of greater optimism then it might have won major support among Catholics but the impending breakdown of what little trust existed in the province was the wrong ambience for a pacifist party.

At first the British army was welcomed by both sides, each believing it would protect their interests, but as Catholic-Protestant confrontations continued and the army, barely able to cope, tended towards the heavy-handed suppression of what it perceived to be the direct cause of the unrest, the civil rights protestors, this image of impartiality disappeared. Once again, the same old cycle repeated itself: the Catholics, campaigning primarily for equality (though, ultimately, for the dissolution of Northern Ireland) were targeted as the anarchic, trouble-making villains, while the unionists inflamed trouble and then retreated into the sanctuary of privilege, power and moral right.

The early 1970s marked the darkest period in the history of 'The Troubles'. The IRA began an offensive of violence, resulting in the murder of soldiers, policemen and Protestants, and an unprecedented bombing campaign. The British government suspended the Northern Ireland Government, as it was to do repeatedly in later years each time the political system broke down, and introduced direct rule from Westminster. It also introduced internment, the imprisonment without trial of suspected IRA members. Over 300 men were arrested, many later found to be innocent. The scale of these arrests, the fact that internment applied only to suspected Catholic militants, and reports of abuses within the prisons, all helped to foment support for the IRA and exacerbate Catholic hostility. In 'retaliation' two new Protestant private armies emerged, the Ulster Defence Association and the Ulster Volunteer Force, adding more fuel to the fire. Two incidents from this era are still recalled with horror and hatred: the 'Bloody Sunday' killing of thirteen unarmed Catholic protestors in Derry (Londonderry) by the British army (30 January 1972) and the 'Bloody Friday' bombs planted by the IRA in Belfast which killed nine and injured 130 bystanders (21 July 1972).

Although internment was abandoned in 1976, Northern Ireland's jails continued to hold those convicted of 'terrorist' offences, still predominantly Catholics. In 1981 ten of these went on hunger strike in an attempt to be recognised as political prisoners. They all died. Most notable among them was Bobby Sands whose nomination as a candidate Member of Parliament was disqualified. This didn't prevent supporters from voting for him and his deathbed 'victory' in the elections brought a new wave of support.

In subsequent decades the essential differences have remained. Sporadic and prolonged campaigns of violence have occurred but never with the intensity of those terrible years in the seventies. A peace movement rose and foundered. Reconciliation centres were formed and continue to chip away at the towering blocks of prejudice. Truces came and went. Political compromises floated on hope and almost reached fruition but always sank. Despite Sinn Féin and the SDLP proving to be hard bargainers, both were ultimately prepared to make concessions to progress a political solution, but the unionists again and again remained intransigent. Despite the common aspiration, at the time of my journey, the unionists were far from united in determining how best to achieve it. Their political factions are many and varied and their internal disagreements add further obstructions to any process of reconciliation. Of their parties the one most determined to resist any concessions to Catholic power-sharing, and the most popular, continues to be the Reverend Ian Paisley's Democratic Unionist Party.

Meanwhile Northern Ireland's economy has been deteriorating. Unemployment has, naturally, affected most markedly those who previously had jobs, the majority Protestants. The Catholic population has experienced a greatly increased standard of social services and has increased from 35% of the province's population in 1961 to 47% in 2002. Four per cent of the population give their religion as 'other' and 49% as Protestant. A kind of parity is emerging.

Yet there are other complications. Over the decades of raising funds to support the violence, a culture of crime has taken root in both societies. Gun-running, drug-dealing, grant scams, fraud, robberies, extortion and protection rackets are now endemic. Many people have become rich on fear and intimidation. They do not want to see peace kill the market. Northern Ireland's institutions remain divided: schools are still segregated by religion, Protestant and Catholic housing enclaves are still preserved, and cherished. Such anachronisms strike the outsider as pathetic trophies and perhaps, just perhaps, a nuance of shame is becoming detectable among those who value them. It seems the desperate past has almost exhausted the nation. The old prejudices and ambitions remain but no one knows what to do about them any more. Each side argues its case and denounces the other, but increasingly it seems all vapid posture, a futile game beset by hopelessness.

If a solution comes, time will bring it. One day the Catholics will outnumber the Protestants and then, through the democratic process, the lifebelt guarantee to which the unionists have always clung – that Northern Ireland will remain in the UK as long as a majority of inhabitants desire it – will no longer support them.

Malin

After a U-boat slipped through the defences at Scapa Flow, Orkney, in October 1939 and shattered naval confidence by sinking the *Royal Oak,* the entire British Grand Fleet was evacuated and moved to Lough Swilly and its neighbour, Lough Foyle. At their peak these two loughs sheltered 149 US ships and sixty Royal Naval vessels. Like me, those in Swilly would have anchored off Portsalon. They must have hated it too. Portsalon in 1939 would have excited only a few locals and a horde of herbivores. Not much action for a thousand odd men in a vista of grass, a quay fit for a dozen rowing boats, a single pub and a mile of glowing sand. But Lyness, where they'd come from, was scarcely Clubsville. I would happily have swapped Portsalon 2003 for Portsalon 1939.

Two hundred holiday homes had driven out the cows. The buildings appeared to have moved in overnight, turned a couple of circles to flatten a patch and settled down in the fields. Sporadic architectural flourishes attempted to disguise their boxiness but only made them look smug. You could imagine the cracks behind the trellises, the conservatories sinking, the crazy paving going crazier. Each was a clone of the next with obligatory kit lists of barbecues, B&Q Derry garden furniture, playboats and discarded bikes. A golf course had been built and was offering bargain membership rates. Although this was the Republic, the cars bore Northern Ireland's registration plates.

I cut loose from Portsalon the next morning, bent on rounding Malin Head. It was another of my personal *bête noirs.* 'In no part of the world do such sudden and extraordinary changes in the weather take place', warned an old Irish Cruising Club Pilot. Not only did weather hang about there looking for trouble but a magnetic anomaly sent compasses haywire. The tidal streams were 'complex and have not been investigated in detail', and the direction of lateral buoyage changed at Malin Head for good measure. This meant that the arrows marked on charts to show on which side of passage-marker buoys a vessel should pass met each other head on at Malin. All in all it sounded a nasty piece of work.

Within Swilly's calmness existed a world of textures. Here a submerged rock with wrinkles rippling out like contours on a map, there a surface teaselled into spikes and beyond, ridges sustained by a current playing whirligigs along its edges. Further out the swell grew and carelessly tossed guillemots. A light north-westerly drove me steadily past the homespun browns and khakis of Donegal's hills. Every so often a slash of white sand seared the coastline. To my left lay Inishtrahull, a lonely lump of Lewisian gneiss and schist, the oldest rock in all Ireland, whose population of thirteen families was evacuated in 1928. It was hard to imagine how they could have subsisted on such a small platform in the Atlantic. In the days of sail a ship might be held up at this juncture between sea and ocean waiting for a favourable tide. The islanders would barter fish and poteen for salted horse, rope and the sail cloth in which, it was said, their babies were swaddled. Wallace Clark recorded an even stranger trade. Ships bound for the New World would offload stowaways on Inishtrahull in the knowledge that the islanders would receive them for a fee. When steam power replaced wind the trade was mutton for coal but Inishtrahull's currency was rapidly becoming worthless. By 1928 the people relied on passing ships for charity, and there were precious few that stopped to offer it.

My bow closed on Malin's nose, a Roman bulge with a ruined tower on its tip and a rough tumble from its base to the sea. The tide pushed against me and I found myself the sole eastbound vehicle in a contraflow of jellyfish. I hugged the coast in the clean water my chart assured me was there, waiting suspiciously for an unpleasant surprise. I spotted it two hundred yards away. A patch of water that had looked innocent up to that moment suddenly turned into a crosshatching of standing waves. Grey-topped like the rest of the sea their deep divides had remained invisible but now they lay before me as chasms in parallel. Inexplicably the tide had reversed and the jellyfish were now being carried into this trap with me.

There was no preamble. Hitting the first trough was like falling off a step. My stern was upended and I was pitched into my instrument panel as *Ceana* found the sea whipped from under her. She thrust her bow deep into the next wave and slowly, painfully slowly, rose above it in an indignity of surf. A din came from the cabin as its contents rearranged themselves. Over the next twenty minutes, as we reared and plunged through the havoc, it sounded as if the entire contents of my kitchen, pans, plates, cutlery, jars, bottles, were frog-hopping from end to end. I clung to the tiller, my knuckles white, my expression one I'd not care to see in a photograph. Then it ended as cleanly as it had begun. A final step down to flat water. At the same moment the tide turned half a knot against me.

By this time I was entering Garvan Sound where I would have to execute a jinking manoeuvre between reefs. I looked at the jellyfish and found we were on the same journey once more, doing 6.2

knots, an alarming pace given the hazards ahead. Even worse was the downward spiral of figures on the depth sounder. The seabed twenty-two metres down was thrusting up to meet me at a metre a second as *Ceana* was sucked towards the narrows with the rest of the Atlantic following. I could count the limpets on Rossnaburton as it raced past and held my breath for the trailing arabesque of eddies which I severed with the tiller hard to starboard. We were back in deep water. Malin and its dyspeptic tides were behind me. This was a calm day. I didn't like to think what it would be like with 'weather' about.

Suddenly I felt drained. It felt like I'd been sailing forever. I'd forgotten what a breakfast without tide tables and scribbled waypoints was like. The way ahead was always an unknown of formidable headlands, and Ireland endless. But now I had rounded the last unknown. I could see Islay and the Paps of Jura pale and distant on my left. Portrush was discernible as a speck ahead. The Republic was ending on my right. Inishowen Head was its swansong in heather, bracken and rocks. A sparsely inhabited moorland which was once an oasis of illicit distilling. Barley was easily smuggled in from Scotland. Before the 1810 purge on this trade the Inspector General of Excise believed that of Ireland's estimated 3000 unregistered distilleries, at least 1300 of them were to be found in Inishowen.

The Republic bowed out in a flourish of green and there was no code in the sands to the east of Lough Foyle to announce that Northern Ireland had taken over. Just a buoy equipped with a flute that sounded horribly like a fife.

The City

The name is a pitfall. Whatever you use will upset someone, brand you with your sympathies or sound clumsily pedantic. It is Derry (Catholic, nationalist), Londonderry (Protestant, unionist), 'DerrystrokeLondonderry' (correct radio-speak), Stroke City (joke) or The City (bland but safe).

I took to downtown The City at once. It was my kind of place, a hill encircled by medieval walls. I like old stones. I like their fanciful attributes of permanence and accumulated wisdom and I feel steadied by what I read as their mockery of our self-obsessed routines. Despite the fact that by 1975 three-quarters of the buildings inside the ancient defences had been destroyed by The Troubles, most had been rebuilt in the original materials. The rearranged Derry still looked old and a little sleepy. Its streets lay atilt and twisted into the intrigue of a maze. Narrow lanes of darkness opened into parades of light. Everywhere you ran into the medieval wall and a sense of the unfamiliar being contained and knowable. Peaceful nooks lurked beyond the busyness of markets and thoroughfares.

Maybe they were no more frequent than in other places but I thought I noticed more family-run shops, more women with wicker shopping bags, more oaks throwing up umbrellas of leaves. The place smelt European, of open-air coffee alternating with the latrine mud of the river Foyle. To walk about seemed like Malin Head all over again, a voyage in miniature through straits of activity that rocked me in conflicting currents before depositing me in backwaters where I was left alone wallowing in the simplicity of breathing and reflection. Best of all was the circumnavigation of the city walls which looked down on the living mural of history outside: the Protestant ghetto of The Fountain and the Catholic stronghold of Bogside, both of which had coloured their streets as flagrantly as would a tantrum child with few crayons.

In the tenth century the original settlement was renamed Doire Colmcille (St Columba's Oak Grove) but this became shortened and anglicised to Derry. In 1609 James 1 (VI of Scotland) decided to lay out a new settlement within a defensive wall as the colony was far from subdued. The estimated cost was £6000 but within three years this had risen to £20,000, a sum the crown was unable to afford. So he forced the London Guilds to buy shares in the venture and, as a sop to honour them, Derry's name was changed. Londonderry thus became the first planned city in the British Isles and one of the earliest Private Finance Initiatives.

The Guilds were also obliged to supply the colony with craftsmen and apprentices. The latter were mainly orphans who, it was hoped, would have little incentive to forsake their new home. When James II & VII began his attempt to regain the British throne from William of Orange by invading Ireland, his forces surrounded Derry in 1688. The city's elders were negotiating a surrender when thirteen apprentices mischievously shut the city gate in the face of the delegates, shouting 'No Surrender'. The siege that followed lasted 105 days. 8,000 of the city's population of 30,000 died of starvation. A year later James was routed at the Battle of the Boyne and driven into exile.

I left my boat at Moville on the republican bank of Lough Foyle. At the crossover into Northern Ireland there was no sign of a border, just a change in the status of petrol stations. The North was unable to compete with Éire's cheap prices so all pumps within an easy drive of the land of the euro had been converted to shops selling bulk wine, antiques, groceries or drive-thru meals. Suddenly a rash of flags appeared, urban fences multiplied again around public buildings. I hitched a lift with a laundry van driven by a middle-aged John who yodelled his vowels.

'Yoille foyend we Oirish are a very amenable foik', he announced as we passed some building buried in barbed wire, 'except amongst oireselves.'

His daughter was in a 'mixed marriage', he explained. She was Protestant, her husband Catholic. 'To nointy-oight per cent of the population this means nothing, nothing at oil. In fact, if onything moy sympathies lie with the Catholics. Up till nointeen seventy-tree – now think on that, just thorty years ago – you had to be a houseowner to have the vote. And if you had moire than one house you got moire than one vote. And few Catholics had a house at the toime. You moight get six families in one house and they got one vote for the house. And there was a Protestant businessman who had thorty-four houses, and he got thorty-four votes. That's how we Protestants kept the power, and it was wrong.'

From the city walls (above Butcher Street) I looked down on Rossville Street where the Bloody Sunday massacre took place.I could see the black granite memorial with its perpetual sparkle of flashing cameras. Beyond lay the modern blocks of flats of the redeveloped Bogside with murals on their gables, and the lone wall of a building shouting the words 'YOU ARE NOW ENTERING FREE

DERRY' to mark a boundary of the old community that the army eventually agreed not to cross. Yet it did not seem the active segregation and division that was Belfast's, more that of a dozy town with bad taste in art.

I had hoped to put The Troubles behind me but they wouldn't let me go. There were too many reminders of things I didn't understand and they held the key to knowing the city. I needed to understand Orangism. I decided to go to the office of William Hay, the incumbent Member of Parliament of Ian Paisley's Democratic Unionist Party. Somewhat lost I walked along Bishop Street Within until it passed through a gate in the old wall and became Bishop Street Without. I crossed the Craigavon Bridge into the Protestant suburb of Waterside whose streets clearly labelled their allegiance: Duke, King, Alfred, York, Spencer, Moore. I expected to have to pass through an elaborate security system but William Hay answered his door to my knock. His office was the lower floor of a house. Bundles of paper lay scattered over a stained grey carpet. He was harassed. His phone went constantly. During an interruption I picked up a leaflet on 'Surviving the Troubles – Coping with Trauma'.

'Oim not the person to advise you. Wait a moment.' He disappeared and I could hear his voice on the phone in the adjacent room. When he returned he handed me a piece of paper. 'Go and see Willie Kirk. Here's his address. If he's not there, call his mobile.'

Willie Kirk lived in George Street, The Fountain. In a Catholic precinct it was a Williamite enclave where sectarianism was palpably alive and ready to kick. 'LONDONDERRY WEST BANK', proclaimed a street slogan, 'LOYALISTS STILL UNDER SIEGE – NO SURRENDER'. Willie was having a new carpet laid and was out. I left a message on his mobile and he returned my call when I was in the heart of Bogside. Arranging to meet a past Master of the Orange Order within hearing of the enemy was unfortunate timing. I whispered. This made him suspicious. I raised my voice slightly. He agreed to meet me and chose the place. On a bench under a tree opposite the Apprentice Boys Memorial Hall. It all sounded fraught with duplicity.

We met as the clock on the Guildhall, whose pendulum, as a gesture of one-upmanship, was engineered to be a quarter of an inch longer than Big Ben's, struck one. I recognised Willie Kirk from the previous day.

'You were on the walking tour of the Wall, weren't you?'

He nodded.

I'd noticed the flecks of paint on his shoes and the way he'd hung around the outer edge of the group, an obvious outsider showing none of the trappings of a tourist or any interest in the subjects of the discourse. 'Why would someone who knows the city do that?'

He smiled. 'I like to make sure visitors are getting the right story. The guide got a few dates wrong and the bias was pro-Catholic. Some of the Bloody Sunday protestors *were* armed.'

His shoes bore the same silver-blue spatters. Perhaps he resprayed cars in his spare time, I thought. He was just beyond retirement age, a small roundish man in black Terylene trousers, yellow shirt and a patterned cardigan with a zip. Brilliantine glistened on a smear of hair above a broad forehead. His eyebrows had grown out of control and below them dark eyes gave an impression of predatory scrutiny.

'You wanted to know about the Orange Order', he offered. The history was complex, he explained, but he would try to keep it simple. He talked slowly, confidently, almost word-perfect as if this were an ordered talk he'd delivered many times before. 'It's had many names. For a long time it was the Loyal Orange Institution of Ireland. Then it became the Imperial Grand Orange Order. Up until 1969 the Grand Masters of Ireland were titled people, all the Right Honourable So-and-So. But a big change took place in that year and the first layman, so to speak, was elected Grand Master. The name was changed to the International Grand Orange Order but this was unpopular and so it was altered to what it is now, the Grand Orange Order of the World.'

'How many members do you have?'

'I've no idea. Membership is recorded on a local basis by each lodge, and there are some 1350 of them. We do not have centralised membership figures but, to give you an idea, it's estimated there are more coloured members than there are white.' He was gratified to see my puzzled expression. 'There are lodges in Ghana, Togo, South Africa...all over the world. Some years ago the Grand Master was black and French-speaking.'

'And women members?'

'They have a separate organisation.'

'So what's the purpose of the Order? Is it simply to commemorate the Battle of the Boyne and Protestantism's defeat of Catholicism?'

'No.' He grimaced and let out a long sigh. 'To understand you have to know our history. Orangism is a very convoluted thing from the past. In the early days what we now term collectively as 'Protestants' were not united. William's war brought together Reformed Presbyterians and Episcopalians, but his successor, Queen Anne, introduced penal laws against non-Episcopalians in 1704.' As he listed the discriminatory measures – the ban on Presbyterians holding civic, governmental or military posts, the closure of their churches and schools, official condemnation of their marriage ceremonies which resulted in all children being treated as illegitimate – I recognised the story. Subjects and objects kept changing throughout Ireland's history but the deeds were faithfully replicated and perpetrator and victim fed off each other in a conviction of divine retribution.

'Orangism stemmed from secret meetings to' – his voice intoned officialese – 'protect the social, physical and spiritual interests of *reformed* Protestants as monarchs changed. Various societies formed, such as the Britannic, but the first Orange Association met in Exeter in 1688. Here Protestants pledged support to William of Orange who had proved himself a staunch adherent to their faith. James II had already begun to persecute Protestants and to install only Catholics in official posts. In Ireland the Boyne Orange Society was founded and descendents of the siege started The Apprentice Boys of Derry Clubs.'

Copying the system used by the Masons, who styled themselves on the Templar Knights, the Boyne Orange Society adopted the Knights of Malta code, their degree structure and their purple and black colours. Their property was vested in the sovereign as a means of gaining immunity. Yet still their members suffered. In Antrim the better-off Scots and English were Episcopalians and they harassed the majority Presbyterians, who emigrated in masses from 1720 onwards.

'Persecution continued here right up until the American War of Independence when British troops were transferred to the colonies. The Boyne Orange Society formed the Irish Volunteer Militia as rival paramilitaries emerged. They were "right rough and brutal", nothing to be proud of, tit-for-tat murderers like we've had over the last thirty years. English and Scots Regiments were sent out to suppress us but this only strengthened our resolve and brought us new recruits. We changed our name to the Orange Order in 1795. Then we had to endure the 1855 Land Acts which turned rural Ireland from a landlord to a peasant-owned society. This finally united Protestants one and all for the Unionist cause.'

'Are the young joining?'

'Oh yes, we've a strong youth membership.'

'Why? What's the appeal?'

'Most join because it's a proud tradition and boys are brought up with it. Some join for religious or political reasons. Lodges differ on the focus of their interest so it might be a local project that attracts some to join. You have to realise that it's more than a club. Today the Orange Order has its own culture, its own community and its own social welfare systems. It provides medical insurance, death benefits, even its own credit unions. And Orangism is open to anyone. In the Apprentice Boys Memorial Hall we've dances open to all. We don't exclude anyone.'

'Even Catholics?'

'We don't exclude anyone', he repeated, then smiled. 'Not many choose to come, it must be said, but we don't stop them.'

It would take a brave heart to do that, I thought, imagining the polarisation in the dance hall and the probable gauntlet to be faced on leaving. I let the matter rest. He seemed content to confer on the Apprentice Boys the egalitarianism of the Scout movement. 'Are the Apprentice Boys affiliated to the Orange Order?'

'No, they're a separate organisation. Boys join at the age of thirteen and the clubs are solely to commemorate the original Apprentice Boys' bravery.'

'What about the marches? You can't claim they're just commemorative. They're provocative and antagonistic, and that's intentional.'

'You're wrong. You fail to appreciate the importance of Providence in our celebrations. The siege lasted a hundred and five days. Eight thousand died. This area around us was covered in their graves. Try to imagine how relieved the survivors were at their deliverance. They felt God had saved them so they were right. Thanksgiving was a vital part of medieval belief. Each guild had its own patron saint and on the saint's day members would form a procession through the streets with sacred relics. Our marches continue that custom. They're a thanksgiving for our welfare and deliverance. Our standards are the equivalent of the relics.'

I touched on Bloody Sunday and 'Free Derry'. He sneered at the 'other side's' supposed monopoly on victimisation and isolation. Why, he said, his community of The Fountain had suffered every bit as much isolation and violence. Worse, in fact. He controlled himself but under the surface venom swelled. The only conciliation was a throwaway word, a barely-noticeable regret adrift in a flow of recrimination, when he referred to the last three decades as 'madness'.

'Did you personally suffer a lot during the Troubles?'

He let out a rush of air, part laugh, part sigh. He was confronting the immensity of my naivety and I was broaching the inexpressible. 'I was an official in the Orange Order for thirty years during the worst of the violence. Latterly I was District Master of the Royal Arch Chapter. I was an obvious target. Let them kill me, I always thought. Five or six Catholics would have been taken out for my death. That's the way it was. There were attempts on my life, my father's and my brother-in-law's. Two of my cousins were shot. That's not easy to live with. It takes its toll.'

'Can you bring yourself to forgive these acts, or do they go too deep?'

'I can forgive them, but not at the cost of what we've struggled for.'

His lunch-break, from whatever he did, was over and he excused himself. I pondered on the sanitised explanation I'd just received. During the height of the Troubles in 1978, Dervla Murphy wrote in *A Place Apart*:

> The Orange tradition is an uncouth mixture of igno-
> rance, xenophobia, self-deception, suspicion, rabble-
> rousing, fear and aggression. Inevitably it produces a
> great deal of loutish behaviour, which its leaders seem
> unwilling or unable to correct. ...The Orange Order is
> utterly foreign to the British way of life in the 20th cen-
> tury – another Northern paradox, since the Orangeman
> is so deliriously proud of his Britishness.

For a long time I sat under the tree and watched life pass the Apprentice Boys' Hall. A diminutive gang of the 'other side' idled by in Celtic stripes. They were far short of their teens, skinny-legged and yet politically-sensitised; one gestured an erect finger at the hall in what appeared to be a subconscious ritual that went unnoticed by his friends.

And I thought of the famous exchange between the then Home Secretary, Jim Callaghan, on his first visit to Northern Ireland, and the Reverend Ian Paisley.

'Come now, Dr Paisley', Callaghan rebuked, 'we are all the children of God.'

'No, Home Secretary', Paisley replied, 'we are all the children of wrath.'

That evening was a repeat of Belfast. At six o'clock the shutters came down. The shops disappeared. The City became sheathed in steel daubed with graffiti. It fell silent with an eerie absence of people. I sat on a bench in Waterloo Place at a junction of four of the busiest streets in the old city, and counted nineteen people. They were walking quickly and with purpose as they would in a curfew. By day the place was charming, by night it withdrew into secrecy. The few cars about stopped briefly by doorways, gave a blast of the horn, collected a passenger and drove off. Sixty-five per cent of The City's population were under twenty-five. Where were they all, I wondered? Two of them, male, drunk, high or dangerously ebullient, fought in an alley. It was mock-serious and ended with one lying on the pavement for ten minutes while the other squatted over him, talking. Bouncers hovered at the entrance to nightclubs. They came from a single clone: white-shirted, black-trousered, pot-bellied, bald and smoking. They made me wonder whether there was some college somewhere from which they graduated with a common dress code and slit-eyed stares. A stretched limo drew up outside WICKED and eight yahoos got out. The one who paid the fare looked about fifteen. They stumbled towards the entrance where a particularly wicked baldy stopped them, but after a few words they were ushered inside. I tracked down some more Cityites in the Bound For Boston Bar where a band tuned up for an hour and then attached themselves to the drink counter for the duration of my patience, occasionally glancing at their instruments as if they might get going on their own. I felt out of synch with the place. Time seemed to stand still. So did the people. I couldn't understand how the streets were so empty and yet the bars full. In the end I gave up trying to fathom these urban depths and walked back to my guest house in a dilapidated Georgian area by Queen Street, all the time expecting to glimpse Willie Kirk following in the shadows.

Lough Foyle

My blessing had expired. Lough Foyle vandalised my boat. I returned after a two-day absence to find it had received an upper cut. The guardrail that ran round the bow was buckled. A crushed navigation light dangled from its wires. The stemhead, a jut of stainless-steel over which the anchor chain ran, had been thrust upwards with a force that ripped out screws and splintered the teak toerail. The perpetrator had not only cleared off without leaving any trace of his identity but had not bothered to rectify my now tenuous connection to the mooring buoy. With no hope of redress I nevertheless felt obliged to report the incident to the local authority. As my boat was on an official Visitor's Mooring close to the shore near Moville, I wrote to the local garda office.

Six weeks later I received a reply informing me that the incident was regrettable but it occurred in the territorial waters of Northern Ireland. I was advised to write to the police station in Limavady, County Derry. The Limavady police (in 'County Londonderry') advised me that by their understanding the responsibility lay with the Republic. For further clarification they suggested I contact the Harbour Master, Londonderry Port.

I phoned, not expecting a sympathetic reaction.

'I saw your yacht. I own *Firecracker* which was on the next mooring to yours. I don't know what happened but I'm ninety-nine per cent certain she was hit by a mussel boat. They start work at the end of August and always cause trouble. The half-deckers are the worst. They're run by a bunch of cowboys, farmers who don't know the sea and don't give a toss about anybody else.'

'Where are they based?'

'Moville, but they use Carrickarory pier which is where your boat was moored.' He sighed. 'It's complicated. Lough Foyle is an anomaly. There's never been a written agreement confirming territorial waters. The other sea lough shared in common, Carlingford Lough, is divided by a line up the middle. Lough Foyle's division has never been agreed. The UK used to claim up to the high water mark on the Republic's shore. Can you believe that! This meant that if you were walking below the line of dumped seaweed on the Donegal shore, as far as the UK was concerned you were in Northern Ireland! The Irish Republic claimed up to the halfway line dividing the lough. Over the last twenty years if you ask either authority, you don't get an answer. I'm astonished you got a letter from the Garda saying that the mooring was in Northern Ireland waters. Such an admission in writing is unheard of!'

'So what control over the water do you have?'

'We, as the Londonderry Port Authority, have the conservancy of the lough and we look after safety and shipping. All shipping dues are paid to us.'

'You mean the Republic doesn't try to get a share of the revenue?'

'No, because that would mean sharing the responsibility and administration. It's all chaotic. We used to own Carrickarory pier but we sold it not that long ago to Donegal County Council. Moville Harbour claims to have jurisdiction in a vaguely specified area round the harbour but the fact is that if there's any incident involving liability all that happens is they refer the parties to us. About twenty years ago a ship, the *Nelly N* I think it was, was blown up off the pier and there was a huge case as the insurers had to sort it out and the territorial waters issue came up. They had to come to some agreement and I think it was accepted that on this occasion the waters belonged to the Republic. But a later case went to the court in Dublin and the judge ruled that because the Londonderry Port Authority held the conservancy responsibility, the waters of Lough Foyle belonged to the UK and Northern Ireland. I don't think they'll sort out the territorial issue. There doesn't seem any incentive.'

I should have been splicing the mainbrace, if I could have found one. I should have been celebrating. I was nearing the completion of my three-month sea-circuit. Instead I felt more like the Germans must have done. Their entire fleet of U-boats surrendered here in 1945. Sixty-four of them were taken out to deep water and scuttled.

If I ever want to do a dastardly deed and get away with it, I'll go to that little rogue state of the British Isles that no one owns. I'll commit it west of centre in the no-man's-water of Lough Foyle.

Low Tide

M iles Smeeton[1] was staying at a friend's house by the sea. On a walk with his hostess along the shore one evening he was assailed by a foul odour.

'What an awful smell', he remarked. 'It must be low tide.'

It wasn't. It was almost high tide and the 'awful smell' turned out to be her perfume. Despite the faux-pas, Smeeton and the woman developed a long friendship. Thereafter bad smells and her perfume were jointly known as *l'eau tide*.

I was reminded of this on leaving the narrows at the entrance to Lough Foyle.

---

[1] Miles and Beryl Smeeton took to the sea in their fifties and became legendary circumnavigators. Their story is superbly told in *High Endeavours* by Miles Clark (son of Wallace and June).

Tying Up

The long frame of Portrush's harbour master loomed above me. He caught my rope.

'So you're back. I was wondering where you'd got to.'

He took in my floating world, the damaged bow, Fleming standing to attention at the stern, immaculately shipshape, and me at the centre of it all. He nodded thoughtfully. 'You need a shave.'

'I need a shave and a bath, and the boat's falling to pieces. Really, I just need to get home.'

I passed the Giant's Causeway below cliffs in a confectionery of colours and looked out for, but failed to see, the chimney of Bushmills Distillery, the oldest in the world. I met fishing boats I swore I'd seen before: *Luce Lady, Sea Harvest, Jagged Rose, Golden Dawn, Deliverance, Bountiful II, Mary Jane*...And in this dislocation of the strange and familiar, the raw and beautiful, the being amongst it all but never of it, suddenly I felt I understood this fractured land and people: their inspiration and dejection, nationalism and parochialism, ham-strung brilliance and deadening history, proud and imprisoning tradition, all their passion and unrequited love.

I took the east side of Rathlin, close to Bruce's Cave and peered into the darkness. A marching ripple carried me below cliffs now mostly devoid of birds. The season was over, the chicks had flown. A great skua idled by showing Adidas flashes on its wings. A phalanx of Manx shearwaters raced past in a formation so tight, and black and white, that it resembled a Max Escher illusion. Even in the empty sea I could hear the insistent mewing of a young guillemot though I never saw it or the mother who responded with a crabbity *Arggggh*. It seemed everything was on the move, or fractious to be off.

The tidal flow increased and drew me into its coils. I looked down into the hollow eyes of whirlpools as I was carried from one to the next. They no longer alarmed me. They could bump and jostle, spin and play but they were just inconveniences. I knew my boat now and her power. We passed through a helter-skelter chop of cross-currents and a badland of standing waves. My bow was fixed on a compass bearing of 030°, just to the left of the distant Mull of Kintyre, but the GPS gave my track as 100°. Once again I was going sideways but I'd done my calculations and knew that in a couple of hours a billion tons of the Irish Sea would reverse and compensate for the error. I was simply going with the flow.

'She's fair gathering her skirt and running now.'

I could imagine Wallace's voice as ten knots of wind filled *Ceana*'s sails. Over the next two days the land fell into a familiar pattern. I called into ports with a feeling of apprehension, fearing that my homeland would wither in comparison to the Emerald Isle. I was pleasantly surprised. Gigha was a paragon of tidiness, charm and welcome. There was an honesty box outside Achamore Gardens where a golden pheasant gazed down on me from the silky tangle of a Mexican pine. These, of course, were not everyday Western Scotland experiences but I grasped at trust and the exotic and held them as national icons. While we often travel to escape, we all like to believe there's no place like home when we return.

I was surprised how close the mountains were. In Ireland you see them from a distance; in Scotland you sail among them. But I missed the accents. The weather forecasts in Scottish or English seemed stark and bland, like tap water compared to something long steeped in a cask. I missed the music in those voices, their inbred delight. Radios Four and Scotland filled my cabin with a monotony of inferiority.

At 1545 off Jura a cyclone quivered over the sea. It metamorphosed into hundreds of kittiwakes and arctic terns dipping and snatching sprats which, I assumed, had been rounded up from below. When I was fifty yards away the surface surged. Minke whales appeared in a commotion of gaping mouths and thrashing flippers. Their explosive exhalations left a staleness in the air like perished rubber. With their mouths full and their momentum spent, they subsided into the depths, water gushing down the pale striations of their lower jaws. The scene was strangely theatrical, as if their slow disappearance was some mechanical ingenuity pulling props below the stage.

I was hounded through the Sound of Mull by Calmac ferries going at full bore, black and white bullies with red funnels bound for Coll and Tiree, Castlebay and Lochboisdale. Below clouds stacked in picturesque disorder, the odd rainbow and slanting slats of light, I made my way into Loch Sunart to find a quiet corner to drop anchor for my last night. Glendale Bay was a rocky haven fringed by pines but also paradise postponed by midges.

High above mountains came and went in the mist, alternately scowling and glowing in each appearance. The land appeared as inconsistent as the sea, as fickle a mixture of seduction and threat. But I was used to inconsistency now, used to living on and off the edge of comfort. Now that it was about to end I wanted its raw pleasures to endure. I would miss the dying rasp of waves on the shore, the companionable grumble and murmur of the current under the hull. I'd miss the elation of winning though an unknown passage and that exquisite moment as the anchor bites securely into a new resting place. I'd miss the cycles of excitement and relief. In time I'd probably even forget that a boat is not just a boat but a pernickety mechanism with a thousand things waiting to go wrong. That a mariner's prayer is for luck and a good-enough improvisation.

Tomás O'Crohan wrote in *The Islandman* that, as a young man in 1878, he had gone to Dingle with his fellow Blasket Islanders to sell pigs. Their festivities afterwards lasted two days and two nights. By the end he was anxious to get back to the jobs waiting for him at home and he tried to persuade his friends to leave. One old woman would have none of it.

'Yerra, wisha', says she, 'this is a day of our life, and we shan't always be in the way of a day like it.'

Boats take you out of the fast world and out of the yourself you've become in it. They slow you down to three, five knots. They force you to regulate your life in accordance with tide and weather. You cease to be omnipotent. You plan and plot but ultimately you must live by your wits and allow yourself to be blown by fate. You become a child of the universe again. This brings its own anxieties, its own frustrations, but there is also great power in it. Great insights are to be had. Boats bring days of your life and you won't always be in the way of days like them again.

All the same, it was a relief to get home.